CCIE Professional Develo
Advanced IP Network Design

Alvaro Retana, CCIE; Don Slice, CCIE; & Russ White, CCIE

Cisco Press

Cisco Press
201 West 103rd Street
Indianapolis, IN 46290 USA

CCIE Professional Development: Advanced IP Network Design

Alvaro Retana, Don Slice, & Russ White

Copyright© 2002 Cisco Press

Published by:
Cisco Press
201 West 103rd Street
Indianapolis, IN 46290 USA

Printed in the United States of America 3 4 5 6 7 8 9 0

Third Printing   July 2001

Library of Congress Cataloging-in-Publication Number: 99-61686

ISBN: 1-57870-097-3

Warning and Disclaimer

This book is designed to provide information about advanced IP network design. Every effort has been made to make this book as complete and as accurate as possible, but no warranty or fitness is implied.

The information is provided on an "as is" basis. The author, Cisco Press, and Cisco Systems, Inc., shall have neither liability nor responsibility to any person or entity with respect to any loss or damages arising from the information contained in this book or from the use of the discs or programs that may accompany it.

The opinions expressed in this book belong to the authors and are not necessarily those of Cisco Systems, Inc.

Trademark Acknowledgments

All terms mentioned in this book that are known to be trademarks or service marks have been appropriately capitalized. Cisco Press or Cisco Systems, Inc., cannot attest to the accuracy of this information. Use of a term in this book should not be regarded as affecting the validity of any trademark or service mark.

Feedback Information

At Cisco Press, our goal is to create in-depth technical books of the highest quality and value. Each book is crafted with care and precision, undergoing rigorous development that involves the unique expertise of members from the professional technical community.

Readers' feedback is a natural continuation of this process. If you have any comments regarding how we could improve the quality of this book, or otherwise alter it to better suit your needs, you can contact us through e-mail at feedback@ciscopress.com. Please make sure to include the book title and ISBN in your message.

We greatly appreciate your assistance.

Publisher	John Wait
Editor-in-Chief	John Kane
Cisco Systems Management	Michael Hakkert
	Tom Geitner
	William Warren
Managing Editor	Patrick Kanouse
Acquisitions Editor	Brett Bartow
Development Editor	Christopher Cleveland
Senior Editor	Dayna Isley
Copy Editor	Laura Loveall
Technical Editors	William V. Chernock III, CCIE
	Vijay Bollapragada, CCIE
Team Coordinator	Amy Lewis
Book Designer	Regina Rexrode
Cover Designer	Karen Ruggles
Production Team	Argosy
Proofreader	John Rahm
Indexer	Kevin Fulcher

CISCO SYSTEMS

Corporate Headquarters
Cisco Systems, Inc.
170 West Tasman Drive
San Josè, CA 95134-1706
USA
http://www.cisco.com
Tel: 408 526-4000
    800 553-NETS (6387)
Fax: 408 526-4100

European Headquarters
Cisco Systems Europe
11 Rue Camille Desmoulins
92782 Issy-les-Moulineaux
Cedex 9
France
http://www-
europe.cisco.com
Tel: 33 1 58 04 60 00
Fax: 33 1 58 04 61 00

Americas Headquarters
Cisco Systems, Inc.
170 West Tasman Drive
San Jose, CA 95134-1706
USA
http://www.cisco.com
Tel: 408 526-7660
Fax: 408 527-0883

Asia Pacific Headquarters
Cisco Systems Australia,
Pty., Ltd
Level 17, 99 Walker Street
North Sydney
NSW 2059 Australia
http://www.cisco.com
Tel: +61 2 8448 7100
Fax: +61 2 9957 4350

Cisco Systems has more than 200 offices in the following countries. Addresses, phone numbers, and fax numbers are listed on the Cisco Web site at www.cisco.com/go/offices

Argentina • Australia • Austria • Belgium • Brazil • Bulgaria • Canada • Chile • China • Colombia • Costa Rica • Croatia • Czech Republic • Denmark • Dubai, UAE • Finland • France • Germany • Greece • Hong Kong • Hungary • India • Indonesia • Ireland Israel • Italy • Japan • Korea • Luxembourg • Malaysia • Mexico • The Netherlands • New Zealand • Norway • Peru • Philippines Poland • Portugal • Puerto Rico • Romania • Russia • Saudi Arabia • Scotland • Singapore • Slovakia • Slovenia • South Africa • Spain Sweden • Switzerland • Taiwan • Thailand • Turkey • Ukraine • United Kingdom • United States • Venezuela • Vietnam • Zimbabwe

About the Authors

Our experience in the networking industry comes from both sides of the fence; we have managed networks, and we've taken calls from panicked engineers when the network melts. We have worked together on resolving issues in both large and small networks throughout the world, which range from minor annoyances to major meltdowns.

We've analyzed what went wrong after the meltdown, and we've helped redesign some large networks. All of us currently work for Cisco Systems in various capacities.

Alvaro Retana, CCIE #1609, is currently a Development Test Engineer in the Large Scale Switching and Routing Team, where he works first hand on advanced features in routing protocols. Formerly, Alvaro was a technical lead for both the Internet Service Provider Support Team and the Routing Protocols Team at the Technical Assistance Center in Research Triangle Park, North Carolina. He is an acknowledged expert in BGP and Internet architecture.

Don Slice, CCIE, is a Software Development Engineer with Cisco Systems, where he is responsible for writing new features and resolving software problems with Enhanced IGRP (EIGRP). Don has also provided Escalation support on network problems with EIGRP and other routing protocols to engineers in the Technical Assistance Centers and Network Supported Accounts teams worldwide for the past five years.

Russ White, CCIE #2635, is a Technical Lead on the Routing Protocols Deployment and Scalability Team, which works on improving the scalability of routing protocols, routing protocol design, and network design. Russ is the coauthor of several RFCs and other books, as well as a regular speaker at Networkers. Russ was formerly a senior engineer in the Routing Protocols Team in the Technical Assistance Center, and is well known within the TAC for his work with the Internetwork Operating System (IOS).

About the Technical Reviewers

William V. Chernock III, CCIE is a Senior Consultant specializing in Network Architecture and Design. During the past eight years, he has constructed large-scale strategic networks for the top ten companies within the Financial and Health Care Industries. William can be reached at wchernock@aol.com.

Vijay Bollapragada, CCIE is a Senior Engineer on the Internet Service Provider team with Cisco Systems. He works with Core Service Providers on large-scale network design and architectural issues. Vijay can be reached at vbollapr@cisco.com.

Dedications

This is for my best friend, my wife Dora. Thank you for always believing in me! I am because of you.

Alvaro Retana

To my wonderful wife, Pam, who has stuck by me through good times and bad, and who always provides me with a hug and a smile when I most need them. Thanks also to my beautiful daughters, Jessica, Amy, and Heather, for loving their Dad, faults and all. Thanks to my coworkers at Cisco, who have challenged me and kept me learning and growing. And finally, thanks to my Lord and Savior, Jesus Christ, who provides a light for my path and meaning to my days.

Don Slice

To my wife, Lori, who puts up with me, to my daughter Rebekah, and to my friends here at Cisco. Thanks also to God, who guides my life in His path.

Russ White

I would like to give special thanks to my wife, Pam, for her understanding and love, even when I'm stressed with deadlines and overworked. She masterfully keeps everything together while I'm busy trying to juggle all my commitments. I'd also like to thank my daughters, Jessica, Amy, and Heather, for being patient and for loving me even when I'm too busy trying to get things done to give them the attention that they deserve. And most of all, I'd like to thank God for His love and strength, sustaining me through every part of my life.

Don Slice

Acknowledgments

Thanks to the great folks at Cisco Press, who worked through this entire project with us and gave us a lot of guidance and help.

Contents at a Glance

Contents

Introduction

The inevitable law of networks seems to be the following: Anything that is small will grow large, anything that is large will grow into something huge, and anything that is huge will grow into a multinational juggernaut. The corollary to this law seems to be as follows: Once a network has become a multinational juggernaut, someone will come along and decide to switch from one routing protocol to another. They will add one more application, or a major core link will flap, and it will melt (during dinner, of course).

In *CCIE Professional Development: Advanced IP Network Design*, we intend to present the basic concepts necessary to build a scalable network. Because we work in the "it's broken, fix it (yesterday!)" side of the industry, these basics will be covered through case studies as well as theoretical discussion. This book covers good ways to design things, some bad ways to design things, and general design principles. When it seems appropriate, we'll even throw in some troubleshooting tips for good measure. You will find the foundation that is necessary for scaling your network into whatever size it needs to be (huge is preferred, of course).

What Is Covered

CCIE Professional Development: Advanced IP Network Design is targeted to networking professionals who already understand the basics of routing and routing protocols and want to move to the next step. A list of what's not covered in this book follows:

- **Anything other than Cisco routers**—You wouldn't expect Cisco Press to publish a book with sample configurations from some other vendor, would you?

- **Router configuration**—You won't learn how to configure a Cisco router in *CCIE Professional Development: Advanced IP Network Design*. The primary focus is on architecture and principles. We expect that everyone who reads this book will be able to find the configuration information that they need in the standard Cisco manuals.

- **Routing protocol operation**—The appendixes cover the basic operation of the protocols used in the case studies, but this isn't the primary focus of our work.

- **Routing protocol choice**—All advanced routing protocols have strengths and weaknesses. Our intent isn't to help you decide which one is the best, but we might help you decide which one is the best fit for your network. (Static routes have always been a favorite, though.)

- **RIP and IGRP**—These are older protocols that we don't think are well suited to large scale network design. They may be mentioned here, but there isn't any extensive treatment of them.

- **Router sizing, choosing the right router for a given traffic load, and so forth**—These are specific implementation details that are best left to another book. There are plenty of books on these topics that are readily available.

- **LAN or WAN media choice, circuit speeds, or other physical layer requirements**—While these are important to scalability, they are not related to IP network design directly and are covered in various other books on building networks from a Layer 1 and 2 perspective.

OSPF, IS-IS, EIGRP, and BGP are included because they are advanced protocols, each with various strengths and weaknesses that are widely deployed in large-scale networks today. We don't doubt that other protocols will be designed in the future.

Good design is focused on in this book because the foundations of good design remain the same regardless of the link speeds, physical technologies, switching technology, switching speed, or routing protocol used. You won't get network stability by installing shiny, new Layer 2 switches or shiny, new super-fast routers.

You won't get network stability by switching from one advanced routing protocol to another (unless your network design just doesn't work well with the one you are using). Network stability doesn't even come from making certain that no one touches any of the routers (although, sometimes it helps).

You will get long nights of good sleep by putting together a well-designed network that is built on solid principles proven with time and experience.

Motivation for the Book

The main reason that we wrote this book is because we couldn't find any other books we liked that covered these topics. We also wrote it because we believe that Layer 3 network design is one of the most important and least covered topics in the networking field. We hope you enjoy reading *CCIE Professional Development: Advanced IP Network Design* and will use it as a reference for years to come.

So, sit back in your favorite easy chair and peruse the pages. You can tell your boss that you're scaling the network!

PART I

Foundation for Stability: Hierarchical Networks

CHAPTER 1

Hierarchical Design Principles

Your boss walks into your cube, throws a purchase order on your desk, and says, "Here, it's signed. Purchasing says a thousand routers are going to take up a lot of space over there, so you need to have your people pick them up as soon as they come in. Now make it work." Is this a dream or a nightmare?

It certainly isn't real—real networks start with two routers and a link, not with a thousand router purchase order. But a network with even ten routers is so small that network design isn't an issue. Right? Wrong. It's never too early to begin planning how your network will look as it grows.

Where Do You Start?

Okay, you've decided you need to start thinking about network design. The best place to start when designing a network is at the bottom: the physical layer. For the most part, physical layer design is about bits and bytes, how to size a link properly, what type of media to use, and what signaling method to use to get the data onto and off of the wire.

These things are all important because you must have stable physical links to get traffic to pass over the network. Unstable physical links cause the changes that the routers in the network must adapt to. But the *topology*—the layout—of your network has a greater impact on its stability than whether ATM or Frame Relay is used for the wide-area connections.

A well-designed topology is the basis for all stable networks.

To understand why, consider the question: "Why do networks melt?" The simple answer is networks melt because the routing protocol never converges. Since all routing protocols produce routing loops while they converge, and no routing protocol can provide correct forwarding information while it's in a state of transition, it's important to converge as quickly as possible after any change in the network.

The amount of time it takes for a routing protocol to converge depends on two factors:

- The number of routers participating in convergence
- The amount of information they must process

The number of routers participating in convergence depends on the area through which the topology change must propagate. Summarization hides information from routers, and routers that don't know about a given destination don't have to recalculate their routing tables when the path to that destination changes or is no longer reachable.

The amount of information a router must process to find the best path to any destination is dependent on the number of paths available to any given destination. Summarization, coincidentally, also reduces the amount of information a router has to work with when the topology of the network changes.

So, summarization is the key to reducing the number of routers participating in convergence and the amount of data routers have to deal with when converging. Summarization, in turn, relies on an addressing scheme that is laid out well with good summarization points. Addressing schemes that are laid out well always rely on a good underlying topology.

It's difficult to assign addresses on a poorly constructed network in order for summarization to take place. While many people try to fix the problems generated by a poor topology and addressing scheme with more powerful routers, cool addressing scheme fixes, or bigger and better routing protocols, nothing can substitute for having a well thought out topology.

The Right Topology

So what's the right topology to use? It's always easier to tackle a problem if it is broken into smaller pieces, and large-scale networks are no exception. You can break a large network into smaller pieces that can be dealt with separately. Most successful large networks are designed hierarchically, or in *layers*. Layering creates separate problem domains, which focuses the design of each layer on a single goal or set of goals.

This concept is similar to the OSI model, which breaks the process of communication between computers into layers, each with different design goals and criteria. Layers must stick to their design goals as much as possible; trying to add too much functionality into one layer generally ends up producing a mess that is difficult to document and maintain.

There are generally three layers defined within a hierarchical network. As indicated in Figure 1-1, each layer has a specific design goal:

- The network *core* forwards traffic at very high speeds; the primary job of a device in the core of the network is to switch packets.

- The *distribution layer* summarizes routes and aggregates traffic.

- The *access layer* feeds traffic into the network, performs network entry control, and provides other edge services.

Figure 1-1   *Hierarchical Network Design*

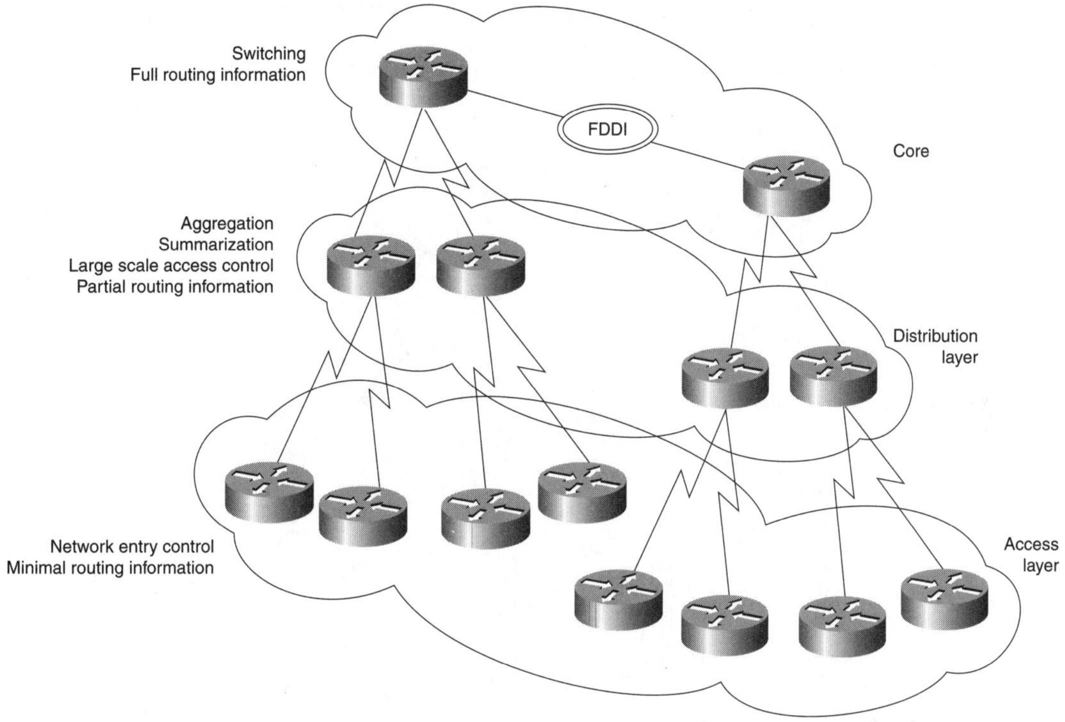

Now that you know the names of the layers, step back and look at how they relate to the fundamental design principles previously outlined. The following are two restated fundamental design principles. The next task is to see if they fit into the hierarchical model.

- The area affected by a topology change in the network should be bound so that it is as small as possible.

- Routers (and other network devices) should carry the minimum amount of information possible.

You can achieve both of these goals through summarization, and summarization is done at the distribution layer. So, you generally want to bound the convergence area at the distribution layer.

For example, a failing access layer link shouldn't affect the routing table in the core, and a failing link in the core should produce minimal impact on the routing tables of access layer routers.

In a hierarchical network, traffic is aggregated onto higher speed links moving from the access layer to the core, and it is split onto smaller links moving from the core toward the access layer as illustrated in Figure 1-2. Not only does this imply access layer routers can be smaller devices, it also implies they are required to spend less time switching packets. Therefore, they have more processing power, which can be used to implement network policies.

Figure 1-2   *Traffic Aggregation and Route Summarization at Layer Boundaries*

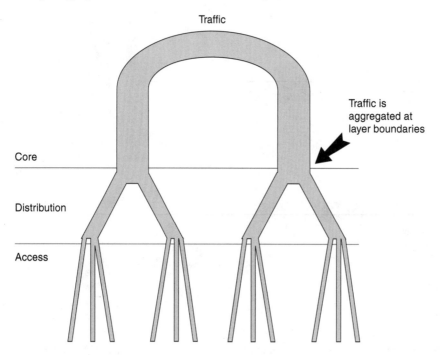

The one major weakness inherent in hierarchical network design is that it implies (or creates) single points of failure within the physical layer. The stronger the hierarchical model, the more likely you are to find places where a single device or a broken link can cause major havoc. Of course, if you don't like havoc, your network must have some measure of redundancy to compensate for this weakness. We'll cover this in Chapter 3, "Redundancy."

The Network Core

The core of the network has one goal: *switching packets*. Like engines running at warp speed, core devices should be fully fueled with dilithium crystals and running at peak performance; this is where the heavy iron of networking can be found. The following two basic strategies will help accomplish this goal:

- No network policy implementation should take place in the core of the network.
- Every device in the core should have full reachability to every destination in the network.

No Policy Implementation

Any form of policy implementation should be done outside the core; packet filtering and policy routing are two perfect examples. Even if the core devices can filter and policy-route packets at high rates of speed, the core is not the right place for these functions. The goal of the network core is to switch packets, and anything that takes processing power from core devices or increases packet switching latencies is seriously discouraged.

Beyond this, the complexity added to core router configurations should be avoided. It is one thing to make a mistake with some policy at the edge of the network and cause one group of users to lose connectivity, but to make a mistake while implementing a change in policy at the core can cause the entire network to fail.

Place network policy implementations on edge devices in the access layer or, in certain circumstances, on the border between the access layer and the distribution layer. Only in exceptional circumstances should you place these controls in the core or between the distribution layer and the core.

Case Study: Policy-Based Routing

Normally, routers forward traffic based only on the final destination address, but there are times when you want the router to make a forwarding decision based on the source address, the type of traffic, or some other criteria. These types of forwarding decisions, based on some criteria or policy the system administrator has configured, are called *policy-based routing*.

A router can be configured to make a forwarding decision based on several things, including

- Source address
- Source/destination address pair
- Destination address
- IP packet type (TCP, UDP, ICMP, and so on)
- Service type (Telnet, FTP, SMTP)
- Precedence bits in the IP header

Typically, configuring policy-based routing consists of the following three steps:

1 Build a filter to separate the traffic that needs a specific policy applied from the normal traffic.

2 Build a policy.

3 Implement the policy.

On a Cisco router, a policy is built using route maps and is implemented with interface commands.

For example, in the network illustrated in Figure 1-3, the system administrator has decided it would be best to send Telnet over the lower speed Frame Relay link and send the remaining traffic over the satellite link.

Figure 1-3   *Access Control Filters*

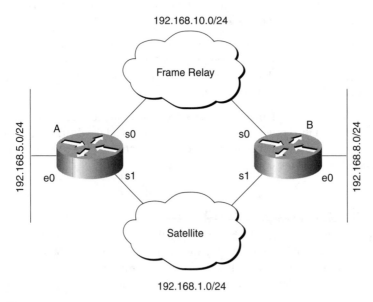

To apply this policy, the network administrator can apply the following configurations to both routers:

1 Build a filter to separate the traffic:

```
access-list 150 permit any eq telnet any
access-list 150 permit any any eq telnet
```

The first line in this **access-list** selects any TCP traffic destined to the Telnet port; the second one selects any TCP traffic with the Telnet port as its source.

2 Build a policy:

```
route-map telnetthroughframe permit 10
  match ip address 150
  set ip next-hop 192.168.10.x
```

These lines build a route map that matches any packets selected in the previous step (all packets sourced from or destined to the TCP Telnet port) and set the next hop for these packets to the IP address of the router on the other end of the Frame Relay link.

3 Apply the policy to the traffic:

```
interface ethernet 0
    ip policy route-map telnetthroughframe
```

4 Finally, tell the router that every packet received on the Ethernet 0 interface needs to have the policy built in the previous step applied to it.

Packets that are policy routed are process switched in all versions of IOS until 11.3. Process switching packets typically have a large negative impact on the router. Every packet that needs to be process switched must be scheduled for switching rather than processed through one of the optimized switching paths.

Full Reachability

Devices in the core should have enough routing information to intelligently switch a packet destined to any end device in the network; core routers should not use default routes to reach internal destinations. However, this doesn't mean a router in this layer should have a path to each individual subnet in every corner of the network. Summary routes can, and should, be used to reduce the size of the core routing table. Default routes should be used for reaching external destinations, such as hosts on the Internet.

The reason for the no default routes strategy is threefold:

- Facilitating core redundancy
- Reducing suboptimal routing
- Preventing routing loops

Traffic volume is at its greatest in the core; every switching decision counts. Suboptimal routing can be destabilizing in this type of an environment.

A perfect example of this strategy is the structure of the network access points (NAP) on the Internet. Devices that are connected to the NAPs aren't allowed to use default routes to reach any destination. Therefore, every attached device *must* carry a full Internet routing table. The full routing table, though, doesn't include every possible subnet; instead, aggregation is used heavily in the distribution layer (the routers that feed into the NAPs) to reduce the size of the Internet's routing table at the core.

Types of Cores

When networks are small, they tend to use *collapsed cores*, which means that a single router acts as the network core connecting with all other routers in the distribution layer. (If the network is small enough, the collapsed core router may connect directly to the access layer routers, and there may be no distribution layer.)

Collapsed cores are easy to manage (it's just one router, after all), but they don't scale well (it *is* just one router). They don't scale well because every packet that is carried through the network will cross the backplane of the central router; this will eventually overwhelm even the largest and fastest routers. Collapsed cores also result in a single point of failure almost too good for Murphy's Law to resist: If only one router in the entire network goes down, it will be this single core router.

Because a single router collapsed core cannot handle the needs of a large network, most large networks use a group of routers interconnected with a high speed local-area network (LAN) or a mesh of high speed WAN links to form a core network. Using a network as a core rather than a single router allows redundancy to be incorporated into the core design and to scale the core's capabilities by adding additional routers and links.

A well-designed core network can be just as easy to manage as a single router core (collapsed core). It also can provide more resiliency to various types of problems and can scale better than a single router core. Core network designs are covered fully in Chapter 3.

The Distribution Layer

The distribution layer has the following three primary goals:

- Topology change isolation
- Controlling the routing table size
- Traffic aggregation

Use the following two main strategies in the distribution layer to accomplish these goals:

- Route summarization
- Minimizing core to distribution layer connections

Most of the functions the distribution layer performs are dealt with in Chapter 2, "Addressing & Summarization"; Chapter 3, "Redundancy"; and Chapter 4, "Applying the Principles of Network Design"; many functions won't be covered in this chapter.

The distribution layer aggregates traffic. This is accomplished by funneling traffic from a large number of low speed links (connections to the access layer devices) onto a few high bandwidth links into the core. This strategy produces effective summarization points in the network and reduces the number of paths a core device must consider when making a switching decision. The importance of this will be discussed more in Chapter 3.

The Access Layer

The access layer has three goals:

- Feed traffic into the network
- Control access
- Perform other edge functions

Access layer devices interconnect the high speed LAN links to the wide area links carrying traffic into the distribution layer. Access layer devices are the visible part of the network; this is what your customers associate with "the network."

Feeding Traffic into the Network

It's important to make certain the traffic presented to the access layer router doesn't overflow the link to the distribution layer. While this is primarily an issue of link sizing, it can also be related to server/service placement and packet filtering. Traffic that isn't destined for some host outside of the local network shouldn't be forwarded by the access layer device.

Never use access layer devices as a through-point for traffic between two distribution layer routers—a situation you often see in highly redundant networks. Chapter 3 covers avoiding this situation and other issues concerning access layer redundancy.

Controlling Access

Since the access layer is where your customers actually plug into the network, it is also the perfect place for intruders to try to break into your network. Packet filtering should be applied so traffic that should not be passed upstream is blocked, including packets that do not originate on the locally attached network. This prevents various types of attacks that rely on falsified (or *spoofed*) source addresses from originating on one of these vulnerable segments. The access layer is also the place to configure packet filtering to protect the devices attached to the local segment from attacks sourced from outside (or even within) your network.

Access Layer Security

While most security is built on interconnections between your network and the outside world, particularly the Internet, packet level filters on access layer devices regulating which traffic is allowed to enter your network can enhance security tremendously.

For example, in the network in Figure 1-4, you need to apply filters on the access layer router to provide basic security.

Figure 1-4   *Basic Access Layer Security*

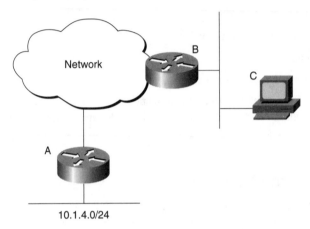

10.1.4.0/24

The basic filters that should be applied are

* No spoofing
* No broadcast sources
* No directed broadcast

No Spoofing
In Figure 1-4, only packets sourced from 10.1.4.0/24 should be permitted to pass through the router.

No Broadcast Sources
The broadcast address 255.255.255.255 and the segment broadcast address 10.1.4.255 are not acceptable source addresses and should be filtered out by the access device.

No Directed Broadcast
A *directed broadcast* is a packet that is destined to the broadcast address of a segment. Routers that aren't attached to the segment the broadcast is directed to will forward the packet as a unicast, while the router that is attached to the segment the broadcast is directed to will convert the directed broadcast into a normal broadcast to all hosts on the segment.

For example, in Figure 1-4, Router C could send a packet with a destination address of 10.1.4.255. The routers in the network cloud would forward the packet to Router A, which would replace the destination IP and physical layer addresses with the broadcast address

(255.255.255.255 for IP and FF.FF.FF.FF.FF for Ethernet) and transmit the packet onto the locally attached Ethernet.

Directed broadcasts are often used with network operating systems that use broadcasts for client-to-server communications. A directed broadcast can be generated using an *IP helper address* on the interface of the router to which the workstations are connected.

If you don't need directed broadcasts to reach servers or services on the local segment, use the interface level command **no ip directed broadcast** to prevent the router from converting directed broadcasts into local broadcasts and forwarding them. Configuring **no ip directed broadcast** on the Ethernet results in the router dropping packets destined to 10.1.4.255 from any source on the network.

One option to reduce the use of directed broadcasts is to use the actual IP address of the server when configuring IP helpers instead of the broadcast address of the server's segment. Even if you are using directed broadcasts to reach a device on the locally attached segment, you can still block directed broadcasts from unknown sources or sources outside your network.

Configuring these basic packet filters on your access layer devices will prevent a multitude of attacks that can be launched through and against your network.

Other Edge Services

Some services are best performed at the edge of the network before the packets are passed to any other router. These are called *edge services* and include services such as:

- **Tagging packets for Quality of Service (QoS) based forwarding**—If you are using voice-over-IP or video conferencing, you will probably want to tag the real time traffic with a high IP precedence flag so that they are forwarded through the network with less delay (assuming the routers are configured to treat such traffic preferentially).

- **Terminating tunnels**—Tunnels are typically used for carrying multicast traffic, protocols that aren't switched on the core, and secure traffic (virtual private links).

- **Traffic metering and accounting**—These services include NetFlow services in Cisco routers.

- **Policy-based routing**—Refer to "Case Study: Policy-Based Routing" earlier in this chapter.

Connections to Common Services

Common services consist of anything a large number of users on the network access on a regular basis, such as server farms, connections to external routing domains (partners or the

Internet, for example), and mainframes. The following are two typical methods of attaching these types of resources to your network:

- Attaching them directly to your network's core
- Attaching them through a DeMilitarized Zone (DMZ)

Where these services are connected depends on network topology issues (such as addressing and redundancy, which will be covered in Chapters 2 through 4 in more detail), traffic flow, and architecture issues. In the case of connections to external routing domains, it's almost always best to provide a buffer zone between the external domain and the network core. Other common services, such as mainframes and server farms, are often connected more directly to the core.

Figure 1-5 illustrates one possible set of connections to common services. All external routing domains in this network are attached to a single DMZ, and high-speed devices, which a large portion of the enterprise must access, are placed on a common high-speed segment off the core.

Figure 1-5   *Connections to Common Services*

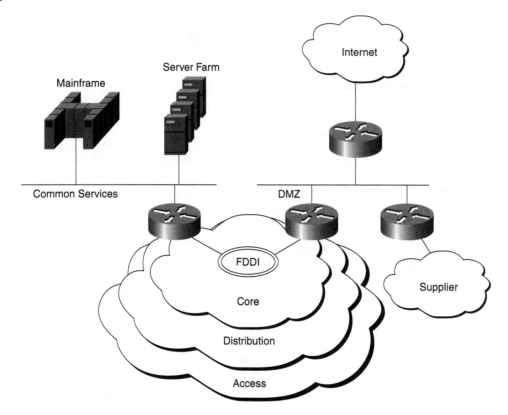

One very strong reason for providing a DMZ from the perspective of the physical layer is to buffer the traffic. A router can have problems with handling radically different traffic speeds on its interfaces—for example, a set of FDDI connections to the core feeding traffic across a T1 to the Internet. Other aspects of connecting to common services and external routing domains will be covered in Chapters 2 through 4.

Summary

Hierarchical routing is the most efficient basis for large scale network designs because it:

- Breaks one large problem into several smaller problems that can be solved separately
- Reduces the size of the area through which topology change information must be propagated
- Reduces the amount of information routers must store and process
- Provides natural points of route summarization and traffic aggregation

The three layers of a hierarchical network design are described in Table 1-1.

Table 1-1   *Summary of Goals and Strategies of Layers and Hierarchical Network Design*

Layers	Goals	Strategies
Core	Switching speed	*Full reachability*: No default routes to internal destinations and reduction of suboptimal routing
		No policy implementation: Access control, no policy routing, and reduction of processor and memory overhead
Distribution	Topology change isolation	*Route summarization*: Provides topology change isolation, hides detail from the network core, and hides detail from access layer devices
	Controlling the routing table size	*Minimizing core interconnections*: Reduces switching decision complexity and provides natural summarization and aggregation points
	Traffic aggregation	
Access	Feed traffic into the network	Preventing through traffic
		Packet level filtering
	Control access	Other edge services include flagging packets for QoS and tunnel termination

So when should you begin considering the hierarchy of your network? *Now.* It's important to impose hierarchy on a network in the beginning when it's small. The larger a network grows, the more difficult it is to change. Careful planning now can save many hours of correctional work later.

Case Study: Is Hierarchy Important in Switched Networks?

Switched networks are flat, so hierarchy doesn't matter, right? Well, look at Figure 1-6 and see if this is true or not.

Figure 1-6 *A Switched Network*

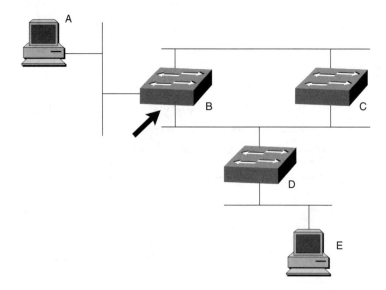

Assume that Switch C becomes the root bridge on this network. The two networks to which both Switches B and C are connected will be looped if both switches forward on both ports. Because the root bridge never blocks a port, it must be one of the two ports on Switch B.

If the port marked by the arrow on Switch B is blocking, the network may work fine, but the traffic from Workstation E to Workstation A will need to travel one extra switch hop to reach its destination.

Because Switch B is blocking on one port, the traffic must pass through Switch B, across the Ethernet to Switch C, and then to Switch A. If Switch B were to block the port connected to the other Ethernet between it and Switch C, this wouldn't be a problem.

You could go around manually configuring the port priorities on all the switches in the network to prevent this from occurring, but it's much easier to adjust the bridge so that a particular bridge is always elected as the root.

This way, you can be certain beforehand what path will be taken between any two links in the network. To prevent one link from becoming overwhelmed and to provide logical traffic flow through the network, you need to build hierarchy into the design of the switched network to provide good spanning-tree recalculation times and logical traffic flow.

It's important to remember that switched networks are flat only at Layer 3; they still require switches to choose which Layer 2 path to use through the network.

Review

1   Why is the topology of the network so important? Are the topology and the logical layout of a network the same thing?

2   Why are hierarchical networks built in "layers"?

3   Note the layer of the network in which each of these functions/services should be performed and why:

   — Summarize a set of destination networks so that other routers have less information to process.

   — Tag packets for quality of service processing.

   — Reduce overhead so that packets are switched as rapidly as possible.

   — Meter traffic.

   — Use a default route to reach internal destinations.

   — Control the traffic that is admitted into the network through packet level filtering.

   — Aggregate a number of smaller links into a single larger link.

   — Terminate a tunnel.

4   What two factors is speed of convergence reliant on?

5   What types of controls should you typically place on an access layer router to block attacks from within the network?

6   What are the positive and negative aspects of a single router collapsed core?

7   What aspects of policy-based routing are different than the routing a router normally performs?

8   Should you normally allow directed broadcasts to be transmitted onto a segment?

9   What determines the number of routers participating in convergence?

10   Should a failing destination network in the access layer cause the routers in the core to recompute their routing tables?

11   What is the primary goal of the network core? What are the strategies used to reach that goal?

12 Why is optimum routing so important in the core?

13 What are the primary goals of the distribution layer?

14 What strategies are used in the distribution layer to achieve its goals?

15 What are the primary goals of the access layer?

CHAPTER 2

Addressing & Summarization

Now that you've laid the groundwork to build your network, what's next? Deciding how to allocate addresses. This is simple, right? Just start with one and use them as needed? Not so fast! Allocating addresses is one of the thorniest issues in network design.

If you don't address your network right, you have no hope of scaling to truly large sizes. You might get some growth out of it, but you will hit a wall at some point. This chapter highlights some of the issues you should consider when deciding how to allocate addresses.

Allocating addresses is one of the thorniest issues in network design because:

- Address allocation is generally considered an administrative function, and the impact of addressing on network stability is generally never considered.

- After addresses are allocated, it's very difficult to change them because individual hosts must often be reconfigured.

In fact, *poor addressing contributes to almost all large-scale network failures*. Why? Because routing stability (and the stability of the routers) is directly tied to the number of routes propagated through the network and the amount of work that must be done each time the topology of the network changes. Both of these factors are impacted by summarization, and summarization is dependent on addressing (see Figure 2-1). See the section "IP Addressing and Summarization" later in this chapter for an explanation of how summarization works in IP.

Figure 2-1   *Network Stability Is Dependent on Topology, Addressing, and Summarization*

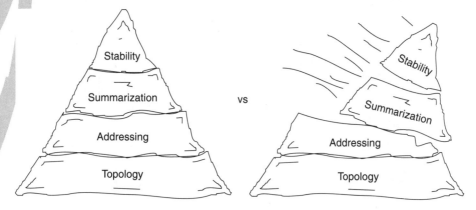

Addressing should, in reality, be one of the most carefully designed areas of the network. When deciding how to allocate addresses, keep two primary goals in mind:

- Controlling the size of the routing table

- Controlling the distance topology change information must travel (by controlling the work required when the topology changes)

The primary tool for accomplishing these goals is summarization. It is necessary to come back to summarization again because it is the fundamental tool used to achieve routing stability.

Summarization

Chapter 1, "Hierarchical Design Principles," stated that network stability is dependent, to a large degree, on the number of routers affected by any change. Summarization hides detailed topology information, bounding the area affected by changes in the network and reducing the number of routers involved in convergence.

In Figure 2-2, for example, if the link to either 10.1.4.0/24 or 10.1.7.0/24 were to fail, Router H would need to learn about these topology changes and participate in convergence (recalculate its routing table). How could you hide information from Router H so that it wouldn't be affected by changes in the 10.1.4.0/24, 10.1.5.0/24, 10.1.6.0/24, and 10.1.7.0/24 links?

Figure 2-2   *Hiding Topology Details from a Router*

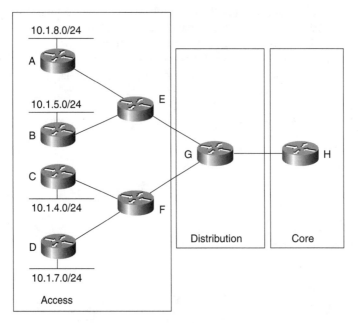

You could summarize 10.1.4.0/24, 10.1.5.0/24, 10.1.6.0/24, and 10.1.7.0/24 into one route, 10.1.4.0/22, at Router G and advertise this one summary route only to Router H. What would you accomplish by summarizing these routes on Router G?

Remove detailed knowledge of the subnets behind Router G from Router H's routing table. If any one of these individual links behind Router G changes state, Router H won't need to recalculate its routing table. Summarizing these four routes also reduces the number of routes with which Router H must work; smaller routing tables mean lower memory and processing requirements and faster convergence when a topology change affecting Router H does occur.

IP Addressing and Summarization

IP addresses consist of four parts, each one representing eight binary digits (*bits*), or an *octet*. Each octet can represent the numbers between 0 and 255, so there are 2^{32}, or 4,294,967,296 possible IP addresses.

To provide hierarchy, IP addresses are divided into two parts: the network and the host. The network portion represents the network the host is attached to; this literally represents a wire or physical segment. The host portion uniquely identifies each host on the network. The IP address is divided into these two parts by the mask (or the subnet mask). Each bit in the IP address, where the corresponding bit in the mask is set to one, is part of the network address. Each bit in the IP address, where the corresponding bit in the mask is set to zero, is part of the host address.

For example, Figure 2-3 shows 172.16.100.10 converted to binary format.

Figure 2-3   *IP Addressing in Binary Format*

172	16	100	10
1 0 1 0 1 1 0 0	0 0 0 1 0 0 0 0	0 1 1 0 0 1 0 0	0 0 0 0 1 0 1 0

Next, use a subnet mask of 255.255.240.0; the binary form of this subnet mask is shown in Figure 2-4.

Figure 2-4   *IP Subnet Mask in Binary Format*

255	255	240	0
1 1 1 1 1 1 1 1	1 1 1 1 1 1 1 1	1 1 1 1 0 0 0 0	0 0 0 0 0 0 0 0

By performing a logical AND over the subnet mask and the host address, you can see what network this host is on, as shown in Figure 2-5.

Figure 2-5   *Logical AND of Host Address and Mask*

	1	0	1	0	1	1	0	0	0	0	0	1	0	0	0	0	0	1	1	0	0	1	0	0	0	0	0	0	0	1	0	1	0
&	1	1	1	1	1	1	1	1	1	1	1	1	1	1	1	1	1	1	1	1	0	0	0	0	0	0	0	0	0	0	0	0
	1	0	1	0	1	1	0	0	0	0	0	1	0	0	0	0	0	1	1	0	0	0	0	0	0	0	0	0	0	0	0	0	0

172	16	92	0

The number of bits set in the mask is also called the *prefix length* and is represented by a /*xx* after the IP address. This host address could be written as either 172.16.100.10 with a mask of 255.255.240.0 or as 172.16.100.10/20. The network this host is on could be written 172.16.96.0 with a mask of 255.255.240.0 or as 172.16.96.0/20. Because the network mask can end on any bit, there is a confusing array of possible networks and hosts.

Summarization is based on the ability to end the network mask on any bit; it's the use of a single, short prefix advertisement to represent a number of longer prefix destination networks.

For example, assume you have the IP networks in Figure 2-6, all with a prefix length of 20 bits (a mask of 255.255.240.0).

Figure 2-6   *Networks That Can Be Summarized*

172	16	0	0

1	0	1	0	1	1	0	0	0	0	0	1	0	0	0	0	0	0	0	0	0	0	0	0	0	0	0	0	0	0	0	0
1	1	1	1	1	1	1	1	1	1	1	1	1	1	1	1	1	1	1	1	0	0	0	0	0	0	0	0	0	0	0	0

255	255	240	0

172	16	32	0

1	0	1	0	1	1	0	0	0	0	0	1	0	0	0	0	0	0	1	0	0	0	0	0	0	0	0	0	0	0	0	0
1	1	1	1	1	1	1	1	1	1	1	1	1	1	1	1	1	1	1	1	0	0	0	0	0	0	0	0	0	0	0	0

255	255	240	0

172	16	64	0

1	0	1	0	1	1	0	0	0	0	0	1	0	0	0	0	0	1	0	0	0	0	0	0	0	0	0	0	0	0	0	0
1	1	1	1	1	1	1	1	1	1	1	1	1	1	1	1	1	1	1	1	0	0	0	0	0	0	0	0	0	0	0	0

255	255	240	0

172	16	96	0

1	0	1	0	1	1	0	0	0	0	0	1	0	0	0	0	0	1	1	0	0	0	0	0	0	0	0	0	0	0	0	0
1	1	1	1	1	1	1	1	1	1	1	1	1	1	1	1	1	1	1	1	0	0	0	0	0	0	0	0	0	0	0	0

255	255	240	0

You can see that the only two bits that change are the third and fourth bits of the third octet. If you were to somehow make those two bits part of the host address portion rather than the network address portion of the IP address, you could represent these four networks with a single advertisement.

Summarization does just that by shortening the prefix length. In this case, you can shorten the prefix length by two bits to 18 bits total to produce a network of 172.16.0.0/18, which includes all four of these networks. The prefix length has been shortened in Figure 2-7 as an example.

Figure 2-7   *Summarized Network*

172	16	0	0
1 0 1 0 1 1 0 0	0 0 0 1 0 0 0 0	0 0 0 0 0 0 0 0	0 0 0 0 0 0 0 0
1 1 1 1 1 1 1 1	1 1 1 1 1 1 1 1	1 1 0 0 0 0 0 0	0 0 0 0 0 0 0 0
255	255	192	0

It's possible to summarize on any bit boundary, for example:

> 10.100.12.0/25 and 10.100.12.128/25 = 10.100.12.0/24
> 10.20.0.0/16 and 10.21.0.0/16 = 10.20.0.0/15
> 172.16.24.0/27 through 172.16.116.0/27 = 172.16.24.0/25
> 192.168.32.0/24 through 192.168.63.0/24 = 192.168.32.0/19

This last example is commonly called a classless interdomain routing (CIDR) block because it is a supernet of Class C addresses.

Where Should Summarization Take Place?

When deciding where to summarize, follow this rule of thumb: *Only provide full topology information where it's needed in the network.* In other words, hide any information that isn't necessary to make a good routing decision.

For example, routers in the core don't need to know about every single network in the access layer. Rather than advertising a lot of detailed information about individual destinations into the core, distribution layer routers should summarize each group of access layer destinations into a single shorter prefix route and advertise these summary routes into the core.

Likewise, the access layer routers don't need to know how to reach each and every specific destination in the network; an access layer router should have only enough information to forward its traffic to one of the few (most likely two) distribution routers it is attached to. Typically, an access layer router needs only one route (the default route), although dual-homed access devices may need special consideration to reduce or eliminate suboptimal routing. This topic will be covered more thoroughly in Chapter 4, "Applying the Principles of Network Design."

As you can see from these examples, the distribution layer is the most natural summarization point in a hierarchical network. When being advertised into the core, destinations in the access layer can be summarized by distribution routers, reducing the area through which any topology change must propagate to only the local distribution region. Summarization from the distribution layer toward access layer routers can dramatically reduce the amount of information these routers must deal with.

Look at Figure 2-8 for a more concrete example. Router A, which is in the distribution layer, is receiving advertisements for:

- 10.1.1.0/26
- 10.1.1.64.26
- 10.1.1.128/26
- 10.1.1.192/26

Router A is, in turn, summarizing these four routes into a single destination, 10.1.1.0/24, and advertising this into the core.

Figure 2-8   *Summarizing from the Distribution Layer into the Core*

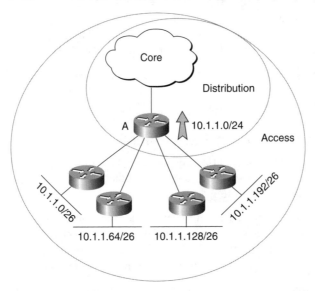

Because the four longer prefix networks 10.1.1.0/26, 10.1.1.64/26, 10.1.1.128/26, and 10.1.192/26 are hidden from the core routers, the core won't be affected if one of these networks fails, so none of the routers on the core will need to recalculate their routing tables. Hiding detailed topology information from the core has reduced the area through which the changes in the network must propagate.

Note that all the addresses in a range don't need to be used to summarize that range; they just can't be used elsewhere in the network. You could summarize 10.1.1.0/24, 10.1.2.0/24, and 10.1.3.0/24 into 10.1.0.0/16 as long as 10.1.4.0 through 10.1.255.255 aren't being used.

Figure 2-9 is an example of a distribution layer router summarizing the routing information being advertised to access layer devices. In Figure 2-8, the entire routing table on Router A has been summarized into one destination, 0.0.0.0/0, which is called the *default route*.

Because this default route is the only route advertised to the access layer routers, a destination that becomes unreachable in another part of the network won't cause these access layer routers to recompute their routing tables. In other words, they won't participate in convergence.

The downside to advertising the default route only to these routers is that suboptimal routing may result from doing so.

Figure 2-9   *Summarizing from the Distribution Layer into the Access Layer*

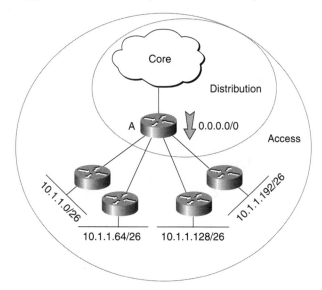

Strategies for Successful Addressing

You can allocate addresses in four ways:

- **First come, first serve**—Start with a large pool of addresses and hand them out as they are needed.
- **Politically**—Divide the available address space up so every organization within the organization has a set of addresses it can draw from.
- **Geographically**—Divide the available address space up so that each of the organization's locations has an office that has a set of addresses it will draw from.
- **Topologically**—This is based on the point of attachment to the network. (This may be geographically the same on some networks.)

First Come, First Serve Address Allocation

Suppose you are building a small packet switching network (one of the first) in the 1970s. You don't think this network will grow too much because it's restricted to only a few academic and government organizations, and it's experimental. (This prototype will be replaced by the real thing when you're done with your testing.)

No one really has any experience in building networks like this, so you assign IP addresses on a first come, first serve basis. You give each organization a block of addresses, which seems to cover their addressing needs. Thus, the first group to approach the network administrators for a block of addresses receives 10.0.0.0/8, the second receives 11.0.0.0/8, and so on.

This form of address allocation is a time-honored tradition in network design; first come, first serve is, in fact, the most common address assignment scheme used. The downside to this address allocation scheme becomes apparent only as the network becomes larger. Over time, a huge multinational network could grow to look like the Internet — a mess in terms of addressing. Next, look at why this isn't a very good address allocation scheme.

In Figure 2-10, the network administrators have assigned addresses as the departments have asked for them.

Figure 2-10   *First Come, First Serve Address Allocation*

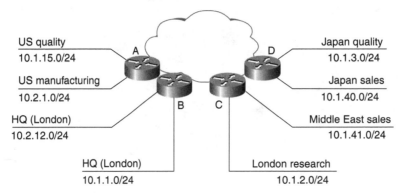

This small cross-section of their routers shows:

- Router A has two networks connected: 10.1.15.0/24 and 10.2.1.0/24
- Router B has two networks connected: 10.2.12.0/24 and 10.1.1.0/24
- Router C has two networks connected: 10.1.2.0/24 and 10.1.41.0/24
- Router D has two networks connected: 10.1.40.0/24 and 10.1.3.0/24

There isn't any easy way to summarize any of these network pairs into a single destination, and the more you see of the network, the harder it becomes. If a network addressed this way grows large enough, it will eventually have stability problems. At this point, at least eight routes will be advertised into the core.

Addressing by the Organizational Chart (Politically)

Now, start over with this network. Instead of assigning addresses as the various departments asked for them, the network administrators decided to put some structure into their addressing scheme; each department will have a pool of addresses to pull networks from:

- Headquarters: 10.1.0.0/16
- Research: 10.2.0.0/16
- Quality: 10.3.0.0/16
- Sales: 10.4.0.0/16
- Manufacturing: 10.5.0.0/16

With this addressing scheme in place, the network now looks like Figure 2-11.

Figure 2-11   *Addressing on the Organizational Chart*

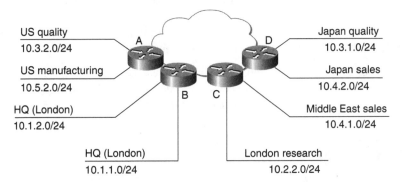

Now, there may be some opportunities for summarization. If 10.1.3.0/24 isn't assigned, it might be possible to summarize the two headquarters networks into one advertisement. It's not a big gain, but enough little gains like this can make a big difference in the stability of a network.

In general, though, this addressing scheme leaves you in the same situation as the first come, first serve addressing scheme—the network won't scale well. In Figure 2-11, there will still be at least seven or eight routes advertised into the core of the network.

Addressing Geographically

Once again, you can renumber this network; this time assign addresses based on the geographic location. The resulting network would look like Figure 2-12.

Note the address space has been divided geographically; Japan is assigned 10.2.0.0/16, the United States is assigned 10.4.0.0/16, and so on. While it's probable that some gains can be made using geographic distribution of addresses, there will still be a lot of routes that cannot be summarized.

Figure 2-12   *Addressing by Geographic Location*

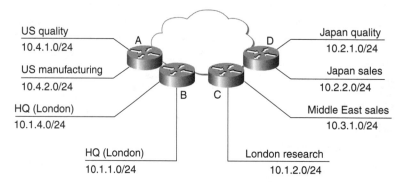

Just working with the networks illustrated here, you can summarize the two US networks, 10.4.1.0/24 and 10.4.2.0/24 into 10.4.0.0/16, so Router A can advertise a single route into the core. Likewise, you can summarize the two Japan routes, 10.2.1.0/24 and 10.2.2.0/24, into 10.2.0.0/16, and Router D can advertise a single route into the core.

London, however, presents a problem. London Research, 10.1.2.0/24, is attached to Router C, and the remainder of the London offices are attached to Router B. It isn't possible to summarize the 10.1.x.x addresses into the core because of this split.

Addressing by Topology

The most effective way of making certain that routes can be summarized is to assign addresses based on the router to which the network is attached or, rather, the topology of the network. Addressing this network based on the topology results in Figure 2-13.

Figure 2-13   *Topological Address Assignment*

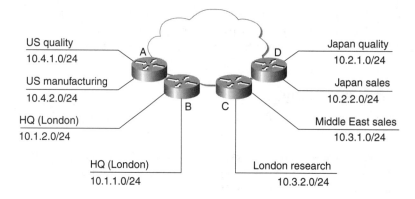

Summarization can now be configured easily on Router A, Router B, Router C, and Router D, reducing the number of routes advertised into the rest of the network to the minimum possible. This is easy to maintain in the long term because the configurations on the routers are simple and straightforward.

Topological addressing is the best assignment method for ensuring network stability.

Combining Addressing Schemes

One complaint about assigning addresses topologically is it's much more difficult to determine any context without some type of chart or database—for example, the department to which a particular network belongs. Combining topological addressing with some other addressing scheme, such as organizational addressing, can minimize this.

Because an IP address is made up of four octets, it's possible to use the left two octets for geographic numbering and the third for departments (or some other combination). For example, if you assign the following numbers to the following departments:

- Administration: 0-31
- Research: 32-63
- Sales: 64-95
- Manufacturing: 96-127

and the following attachment points to the following numbers:

- Router A: 4
- Router B: 1
- Router C: 3
- Router D: 2

some sample addresses would be:

- Administration off of Router A: 10.4.0.0/24 through 10.4.31.0/24
- Research off of Router A: 10.4.32.0/24 through 10.4.63.0/24
- Manufacturing off of Router C: 10.3.96.0/24 through 10.3.127.0/24

Combining addressing schemes will allow less summarization than assigning addresses strictly based on the connection point into the network, but it may be useful in some situations.

IPv6 Addressing

When you run out of addresses, what do you do? If you're the Internet, you *create* a new version of IP that has a larger address space! To the average end user of the Internet, the main difference between IPv4 (the one that is standard on the Internet right now) and IPv6 is just that—more address space. While an IPv4 address has 32 bits and is written in decimal octets (172.16.10.5/24), an IPv6 address has 128 bits and is written as eight 16-bit sections (FE81:2345:6789:ABCD:EF12:3456:789A:BCDE/96).

The /xx on the end still denotes the number of bits in the subnet (which can be rather long since there are now 128 bits in the address space). Because these addresses are so long, and it will take some time to convert from IPv4 to IPv6, there are some special conventions that can be used when writing them. For example, any single section that is all 0s may be replaced with a double colon.

>   FE80:0000:0000:0000:1111:2222:3333:4444

can be written as

>   FE80::1111:2222:3333:4444

Note that only one series of 0s may be replaced in this way because there is no way to determine how many 0s have been replaced otherwise. Also, the last 32 bits may be written as an IPv4 address:

>   FE80::172.16.10.4

Other differences in addressing are not readily apparent; for example, in IPv4, the class of an address is determined by the first few bits in the address:

>   0 Class A (0.0.0.0 through 126.255.255.255)
>   10 Class B (128.0.0.0 through 191.255.255.255)
>   110 Class C (192.0.0.0 through 223.255.255.255)
>   1110 Class D (multicast, 224.0.0.0 through 239.255.255.255)
>   1111 Class E (experimental, 240.0.0.0 through 255.255.255.255)

In IPv6, the first few bits of the address determine the *type* of IP address:

>   010—service provider allocated unicast addresses (4000::0 through
>   5FFF:FFFF:FFFF:FFFF:FFFF:FFFF:FFFF:FFFF)
>   100—geographically assigned unicast addresses (8000::0 through
>   9FFF:FFFF:FFFF:FFFF:FFFF:FFFF:FFFF:FFFF)
>   1111 1110 10—link local addresses (FE80::0 through
>   FEBF:FFFF:FFFF:FFFF:FFFF:FFFF:FFFF:FFFF)
>   1111 1110 11—site local addresses (FEC0::0 through
>   FEFF:FFFF:FFFF:FFFF:FFFF:FFFF:FFFF:FFFF)
>   1111 1111—multicast addresses (FF00::0 through all F's)

There are also some special addresses in IPv6:

>   0::0—unspecified
>   0::1.1.1.1 through 0::255.255.255.255—IPv4 addresses
>   0::0001—loopback

Note that there is no broadcast address defined any longer; the all hosts multicast is used instead. There are many other differences between IPv4 and IPv6—everything from packet formats to how a host determines its address. Several books and RFCs cover IPv6; you should consult them to learn more about these differences.

General Principles of Addressing

It's obvious when examining the network addressed with summarization and stability as goals that there would be some amount of wasted address space; this is a fact of life in hierarchical networks. For example, by the middle of the 1990s, with about 10 million connected hosts, the Internet was having problems finding enough addresses to go around even though there are about 4.2 billion possible addresses.

When you factor in connecting networks (links between routers with no hosts attached), wasted addresses, and reserved addresses, you see how address space could be quickly depleted. The key is to start off with a *very* large address space—much larger than you think you will ever need. In principle, addressing for summarization and growth is diametrically opposed to addressing to conserve address space.

Large address spaces also allow you to leave room for growth in your addressing. It's of little use to thoroughly plan the addressing in your network only to run out of addresses later and end up with a mess.

The problem with using a large address space is that public addresses are scarce, and they probably will be until IPv6 is implemented. (Hopefully, there will be a new edition of this book by then.) It's difficult to obtain a single block of registered addresses of almost any size, and the larger the address range you need, the more difficult it is to obtain.

One possible solution to this addressing dilemma is to use private address blocks in your network and then use *Network Address Translation* (NAT) to translate the private addresses when connecting to external destinations. The private IPv4 addresses defined by the IETF are

- **10.0.0.0 through 10.255.255.255**—a single Class A network
- **172.16.0.0 through 172.31.255.255**—16 Class B networks
- **192.168.0.0 through 192.168.255.255**—256 Class C networks

Using NAT does have problems: Some applications don't work well with it, and there is the added complexity of configuring NAT on the edges of the network.

Summary

The primary goals of addressing and summarization are controlling the size of the routing table and controlling the distance that topology change information must travel. The size of the routing table should be fairly constant throughout the network with the exception of remote devices that use a single default route to route all traffic. See Figure 2-14 for a graphical representation of this principle.

Figure 2-14 *Routing Table Size Should Remain Relatively Constant Throughout the Network*

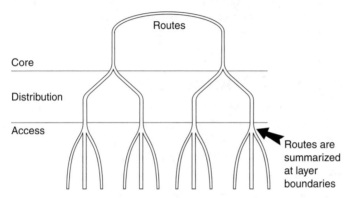

Addressing and summarization are critical to a stable network. Addressing must be carefully planned to allow for summarization points; summarization, in turn, hides information, promoting network stability. These principles are covered in Table 2-1 for future reference.

Table 2-1 *Summarization Points and Strategies*

Summarization Points	Strategies
Distribution layer to core	Summarize many access layer destinations into a few advertisements into the core.
	Hide detailed distribution layer and access layer topology information from the core.
Distribution layer to access layer	Summarize entire network topology down to a very small set of advertisements to access layer devices (default route if possible).
	Provide route to nearest distribution layer router with access to the core.
	Hide topology of core and distribution layer from access layer devices.

The general principles of addressing are

- Use a large address space if possible
- Leave room for future growth

There are four common ways of allocating the address space in a network: first come, first serve, politically, geographically, and topologically. These are covered in Table 2-2.

Table 2-2   *Summary of Addressing Schemes*

Addressing Scheme	Advantages and Disadvantages
First come, first serve	Doesn't require any planning.
	Almost always results in an impossible to manage network.
Politically	Requires minimal planning.
	Easy to resolve an address to a particular part of the organization.
	If the organization is subdivided geographically, this scheme works well; otherwise, it can produce a network that will not scale.
Geographically	Requires planning.
	Enables some degree of summarization.
Topologically	Requires planning.
	Enables summarization, drastically reduces routing table sizes in the core in large-scale networks.
	Scales well.
	Generally easy to configure and maintain.

Allocation schemes can sometimes be combined to provide a solution that is easy to manage and scale.

Case Study: Default Routes to Interfaces

From time to time, routers are configured with a default route pointing to an interface. In some situations, this is fine, but in others, this can be disastrous. The problems have to do with the link type, ARP, and proxy ARP, which is not well understood.

In Figure 2-15, Router A has a default route configured out interface Ethernet 0:

> ip route 0.0.0.0 0.0.0.0 Ethernet 0

Router B has a default route configured out interface serial 0:

> ip route 0.0.0.0 0.0.0.0 serial 0

The complaint is that Router A seems to have extremely high processor utilization and is providing sluggish performance at best. Examine the actions of Router B when ws2, which is configured to use Router B as its default gateway, sends a packet to the Internet. Seeing that the destination it seeks is not on the local segment, ws2 sends the packet to its default gateway; when B receives the packet, it examines its routing table to find a forwarding entry for the destination. Assuming it has no entry, it will forward the packet along its default route, which is pointing to its serial interface.

Figure 2-15   *Default Route to a Broadcast Interface*

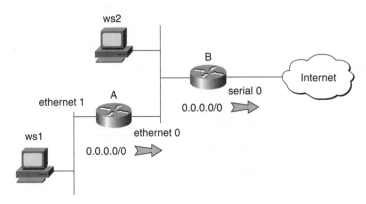

Given that the serial interface on Router B is attached to a point-to-point circuit, there is no place for Router B to forward the packet other than the other end of the circuit. Router B's decision is clear-cut: place the packet on the point-to-point circuit.

Now, consider what takes place when ws1 sends a packet that is destined to some host on the Internet. Noting the final destination is not on its local network, ws1 forwards the packet to its default gateway (in this case, Router A). When Router A receives the packet, it examines its forwarding table for a route to this destination and decides to use its default route, which points to its Ethernet 0 port.

The problem for Router A is this: Ethernet 0 is connected to a multi-access link, and Router A doesn't know which next hop to use to get to the destination in question (because the route points to the interface rather than a specific IP address). So, Router A will ARP the Ethernet segment. Essentially, Router A believes that everything for which it does not have a specific route is actually connected to its Ethernet 0 port.

Router B will receive the ARP request and examine its routing table to see if it knows how to reach this destination. Router B finds a default route in its table, which will do nicely, so it replies to Router A's ARP request. Router A installs an ARP cache entry for this destination IP address bound to Router B's Ethernet address. Router B's ARP reply is called a *proxy ARP* because Router B is essentially proxying for every destination on the Internet.

This works fine, except that Router A will attempt to hold every destination ws1 ever tries to reach in its ARP cache—and while it may succeed, it will pay a heavy price in memory usage and processor utilization. Router A will eventually begin aging out ARP cache entries simply to make room for new requests, and over time it will begin thrashing the ARP cache. This can cause very poor routing performance.

So if this is the problem, why would you ever want to point a static route to an interface? Go back and examine Router B to see why. In this case, the default route points to a point-to-point interface, which means there will not be any ARP cache entries against this interface. (There are no MAC-layer addresses on a point-to-point link.)

There is one advantage to Router B's configuration—speed. Suppose that Router B has a dial backup link to the Internet, which is activated through a floating static route. If serial 0 goes down, Router B will take the directly connected network out of its routing table immediately. The static route to the next hop, however, could take up to one second to remove from the routing table because Router B will need to go through the process of realizing that the recursive route to the next hop is down.

Using the static route pointing directly to the interface could decrease the amount of time the router will wait before bringing up a backup link (an ISDN link, for example).

Case Study: Network Address Translation

Network Address Translation (NAT) allows a network administrator to translate one set of IP addresses into another—for example, allowing a host with a private address to appear on the Internet with a registered address. NAT can also be used to load balance between servers, provide server redundancy, and connect companies that use the same address space.

The host in Figure 2-16, 10.1.4.1, wants to reach 109.10.1.4, which is a server on the Internet. However, its address, 10.1.4.1, is a private address and cannot be routed on the Internet. To resolve this addressing problem, Router A can translate the packets sourced from 10.1.4.1 so they appear to be sourced from a registered Internet address, 127.10.1.10.

Figure 2-16   *NAT Network*

The resulting source and destination addresses are shown in Figure 2-17.

Figure 2-17   *NAT Source and Destination Addresses*

	Before Translation		After Translation	
Direction	Source	Destination	Source	Destination
Host to Server	10.1.4.1	109.10.1.4	127.10.1.10	109.10.1.4
Server to Host	109.10.1.4	127.10.1.10	109.10.1.4	10.1.4.1

10.1.4.1 (the inside address) appears as 127.10.1.10 (the outside address) on the Internet after translation. On Cisco routers, 10.1.4.1 is called the *inside local address*, 127.10.1.10 is called the *inside global address*, and 109.10.1.4 is called the *outside global address*.

The configuration of the router running NAT (Router A) may look like this:

```
ip nat pool tothenet 127.10.1.10 127.10.1.10 prefix-length 24
ip nat inside source list 1 pool tothenet
!
interface Ethernet 0
 ip nat inside
!
interface Serial 0
 ip nat outside
!
access-list 1 permit 10.0.0.0 0.255.255.255
```

This one-to-one translation of inside local addresses to inside global addresses is useful, but it doesn't help much when you have a large number of hosts on the inside network and only a few addresses to use on the outside.

Because it's common to have a large number of inside addresses translated into a much smaller pool of outside addresses, most NAT implementations allow a finer granularity of address assignment called Port Address Translation (PAT), or *overloading*.

In PAT, for each session the inside host initiates, it's assigned a *port number* on the inside global (or translated) address. This allows about 32,000 simultaneous sessions from the inside to the outside using one inside global address. See Figure 2-18 for an example of PAT translated address.

Figure 2-18   *PAT Translations*

Direction	Before Translation		After Translation	
	Source	Destination	Source	Destination
Host to Server	10.1.4.1 port 5312	109.10.1 port 80	127.10.1.10 port 1254	109.10.1.4 port 80
Server to Host	109.10.1.4 port 80	127.10.1.10 port 1254	109.10.1.4 port 80	10.1.4.1 port 5312

Assuming that each inside host is likely to have 10 open sessions to outside hosts at any time, about 3,000 inside hosts could be represented by one outside address. The configuration on Router A (refer to Figure 2-16) may look like this:

```
ip nat pool tothenet 127.10.1.10 127.10.1.10 prefix-length 30
ip nat inside source list 1 pool tothenet overload
!
interface Ethernet 0
 ip nat inside
!
interface Serial 0
 ip nat outside
!
access-list 1 permit 10.0.0.0 0.255.255.255
```

Cisco routers don't assign the port on the inside global address randomly; the router assigns ports from a series of pools. The ranges are

1–511
512–1023
1024–4999
5000–65535

If the inside hosts used port 500 as its source port, for instance, the router will choose a port between 1 and 511 for the source port when it translates the address.

Review

1 Why is it difficult to change addresses after they've been assigned?

2 Why is address allocation so closely tied to network stability?

3 What are the goals you should keep in mind when allocating addresses?

4 What does it mean to say that summarization hides topology details?

5 How does hiding topology details improve stability?

6 Where should summarization take place?

7 What is the one case where access layer devices should be passed more than a default route? Why?

8 An IP address can be divided into two parts; what are they?

9 What is the prefix length of a network?

10 Find the longest prefix summary for these addresses.

 — Set A: 172.16.1.1/30, 172.16.1.5/30, 172.16.1.9/30, 172.16.1.14/30

 — Set B: 10.100.40.14/24, 10.100.34.56/24, 10.100.59.81/24

 — Set C: 172.18.10.10/23, 172.31.40.8/24, 172.24.8.1/22, 172.30.200.1/24

 — Set D: 192.168.8.10/27, 192.168.60.14/27, 192.168.74.90/27, 192.168.101.48/27

11 Explain the effects of pointing a default route to a broadcast network interface.

12 What does a pair of colons with no numbers in between signify in an IPv6 address? How many times can you use this symbol in an address?

13 Explain the difference between Network Address Translation (NAT) and Port Address Translation (PAT).

14 Address the network depicted in Figure 2-19 by

 — Organization

 — Geographical location

 — Topology

Figure 2-19 *Exercise Network*

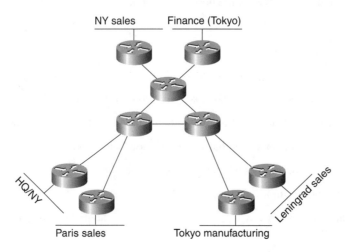

15 Which addressing scheme is the best? Is there any way to combine two different addressing schemes to provide administrative ease?

CHAPTER 3

Redundancy

A single point of failure is any device, interface on a device, or link that can isolate users from the services they depend on if it fails. Networks that follow a strong, hierarchical model tend to have many single points of failure because of the emphasis on summarization points and clean points of entry between the network layers. For example, in a strict hierarchical network, such as the one depicted in Figure 3-1, every device and every link is a single point of failure.

Figure 3-1   *Every Device and Link in This Network Is a Single Point of Failure*

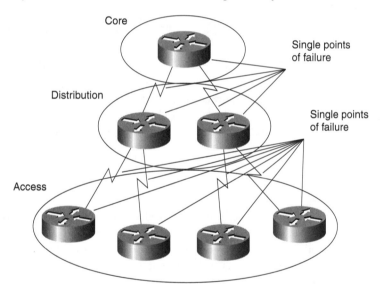

However, this network will be safe if it's protected by dial backup. Redundancy can save the day.

Redundancy provides alternate paths around these failure points, providing some measure of safety against loss of service. Be careful, though: Redundancy, if not designed and implemented properly, can cause more trouble than it is worth. Each redundant link and each redundant connection point in a network weakens the hierarchy and reduces stability.

How do you implement redundant designs without destroying your network's stability? First, start with some issues, strategies, and design goals and then examine redundant designs in each layer of the hierarchical model.

Issues and Strategies of Redundancy

Keep the following two goals in mind when adding redundancy to a hierarchical design:

- Redundant paths should be used only when the normal path is broken, unless the paths are carefully engineered for load balancing. Although a network can use redundant links for load sharing as well as redundancy, this should be the *exception* rather than the rule. Load sharing must be carefully engineered to anticipate and prevent network instability when failures occur.

- Traffic shouldn't pass through devices or links that aren't designed to handle through traffic. Preventing backup paths from being used for normal traffic flow normally involves hiding them as long as the main (or normal) path is available. Floating static routes (see "Case Study: What's the Best Route?" later in this chapter), dial-on-demand circuits, and metric adjustments are good ways to hide a backup path until it's needed.

Core Redundancy

Core redundancy design is generally simplified because all devices should have complete routing information (full reachability). The only exception to this general rule should be the default route used to reach external routing domains (such as the Internet or a corporate partner).

Because all devices have full routing information, there is little chance of a routing loop forming within the core itself under normal circumstances. (Note that running multiple interior routing protocols within the core is *not* considered a normal circumstance.) It *is* possible to forward packets along a suboptimal route, but loops with full routing information aren't very likely.

Redundant Core Design

Numerous designs provide redundancy in the core. If your entire core network is in one building, it's generally easy to connect each router to two high speed LANs, such as high speed Ethernet or a fiber ring, which Figure 3-2 illustrates. Note that this type of design logically appears as a full mesh topology (described later in this chapter) and can exhibit many of the same scaling issues.

If your core routers aren't all in one building (or on one campus), your options become more limited (and more expensive, of course). With larger scale core networks, three competing goals must be balanced for good design:

- Reducing hop count
- Reducing available paths
- Increasing the number of failures the core can withstand

The following sections depict some designs that illustrate these principles.

Figure 3-2   *Redundant High Speed LANs Interconnecting Core Routers*

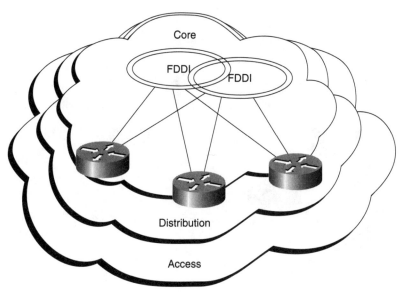

Ring Core Design

Ring core designs, such as the one pictured in Figure 3-3, are relatively common; they are easy to design and maintain (for the most part). Note that this ring core is the type formed using multiple point-to-point links to interconnect multiple routers. There are some designs that rely on a ring at the lower (physical) layer. (To the routers, they appear to be a single high-speed broadcast network—see the following "Redundant Fiber Ring Technologies" section.)

Following are the properties of the ring core design shown in Figure 3-3:

- There are two paths to any given destination from every core device.
- A packet crosses a maximum of four hops with the entire core intact.
- Losing a single link increases the maximum number of hops through the core to six.
- Losing any two links isolates at least one piece of the network.

Ring core designs do well with reducing the number of available paths while still providing redundancy, but they fail miserably at the other goals.

The number of possible routes through the network is low during normal operation, but the number of hops a packet may have to cross with a single link down is unreasonable. A two-hop path to reach a server could become a six-hop path if a single link fails. A big jump like this can cause session timeouts and other problems.

Figure 3-3 *A Ring Core*

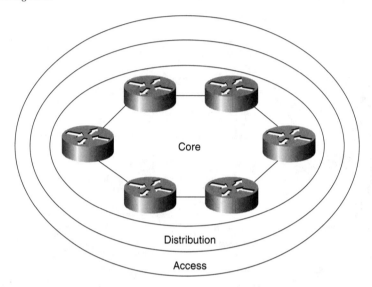

There's not a lot of redundancy afforded with a ring design; losing any two links on the core will isolate some piece of the network. There are ways of circumventing this, but they involve backups of backups, or other types of kludges, which will end up being difficult to maintain and scale in the long term. It's better to design it right the first time.

Redundant Fiber Ring Technologies

While ring cores typically tend to have many disadvantages, some ring technologies have redundancy designed in. One of these technologies is Synchronous Optical Network (SONET), also known as Synchronous Digital Hierarchy (SDH). This technology was standardized by the CCITT as G.707, G.708, and G.709.

SONET networks consist of a pair of fiber optic links between each node on the ring. The first fiber is normally used to pass data at speeds of up to OC-48 (2488.32 Mbps). The second fiber is used as a redundant path. If the first fiber is cut or becomes otherwise unusable, traffic is automatically shifted to the second fiber.

FDDI is another technology that provides this sort of redundancy with two rings on which the data rotates in opposite directions (two counter rotating rings). If the fiber fails at any point between two dual attached nodes (devices that are attached to both rings), the ring will wrap, healing the break.

These technologies provide the redundancy at Layer 2 in the OSI model, resolving many of the issues with providing redundancy at the network layer. This type of technology could be emulated with normal point-to-point technologies by installing two links between each device in the core ring and only advertising the backup path when the primary path becomes unusable.

These methods do not, however, provide redundancy for the devices on the core; they only provide redundancy for the links between the devices. Redundancy for device failures almost always requires a network layer solution or Layer 2 switching.

Full Mesh Core Design

Full mesh designs, where every core router has a connection to every other core router, provide the most redundancy possible. The design in Figure 3-4 provides the following:

- A large number of alternate paths to any destination.
- A two hop path to any destination under normal use.
- A four hop maximum path in the worst case scenario (multiple links down with full connectivity).
- Exceptional redundancy; because every router has a link to every other router, this network would have to lose at least three links before any destination became unreachable.

Figure 3-4   *A Full Mesh Core*

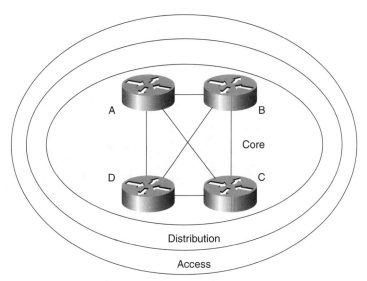

Full mesh designs do well in the hop count and maximum redundancy areas. Unfortunately, full mesh designs can provide too much redundancy in larger networks, forcing a core router to choose between a large number of paths to any destination, which increases convergence times.

In Figure 3-4, Router A has five paths to Router C:

- Router A to Router C
- Router A to Router B to Router C
- Router A to Router D to Router C
- Router A to Router B to Router D to Router C
- Router A to Router D to Router B to Router C

Adding another router to the network in Figure 3-4 would increase the number of paths between Router A and Router C to nine; the addition of a sixth router would increase the number of paths to fourteen. In general, full mesh networks with n nodes will have $(n(n-1))/2$ links (which is almost exponential). By the time you install eight or nine nodes on this full mesh core, there could be too many paths to consider, as you can see from Figure 3-5.

Figure 3-5   *Routers Versus Paths in a Full Mesh*

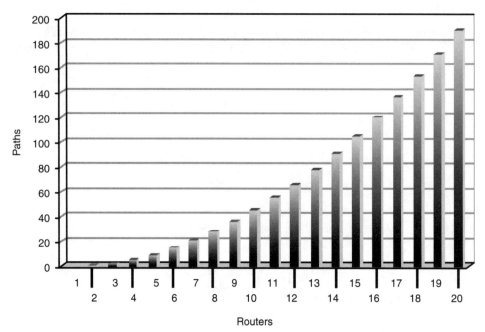

Full mesh networks can be expensive because of the number of links required. These networks also need a lot of configuration management because there are many places to make mistakes when implementing a change. It's difficult to engineer traffic on a full mesh network; the path that traffic normally takes can be confusing, making it difficult to decide how to size physical links (see "Case Study: What's the Best Route?" at the end of this chapter for further information).

Partial Mesh Core Design

Partial mesh cores tend to be a good compromise in hop count, redundancy, and the number of paths through the network. In Figure 3-6, there are four paths between any two points on the network, for example, between Router A and Router F:

- Router A to Router D to Router F
- Router A to Router C to Router F
- Router A to Router D to Router E to Router C to Router F
- Router A to Router C to Router B to Router D to Router F

Figure 3-6   *Partial Mesh Core*

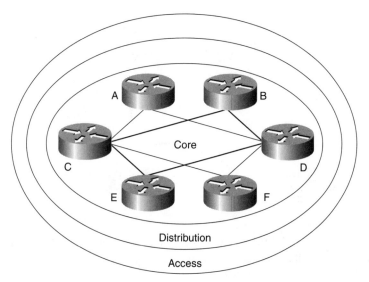

There is a clear difference in the lengths of the four paths available, which means only the two equal length paths will be used at any time for normal traffic flow. No more than three hops will be required to traverse the network during normal operation; if any single link fails, the maximum number of hops to traverse the network will increase to four. These low hop counts tend to stay low as a partial mesh core grows.

The redundancy provided by a partial mesh design is good, as well: The network in Figure 3-6 provides full connectivity with three links down as long as no single router loses both of its connections to the mesh.

The major drawback for partial mesh cores is that some routing protocols don't handle multipoint partial mesh designs well, so it's much better to stick with point-to-point links of some type in the core (such as point-to-point subinterfaces for ATM or Frame Relay).

Routing Protocols and Partial Mesh Technologies

Each router in Figure 3-7 only has one physical interface, which connects to the Frame Relay network. The Frame Relay interface on Router A has two permanent virtual circuits (PVCs) configured through one interface: one to Router B, and the other to Router C. Routers B and C each connect to one PVC. Each router sees this Frame Relay cloud as a logical subnet. Frame Relay, ATM, and Primary Rate ISDN interfaces typically provide this type of connectivity, called *point-to-multipoint* or *nonbroadcast multi-access (NBMA)*.

Figure 3-7   *Routing Protocols in a Partial Mesh Topology*

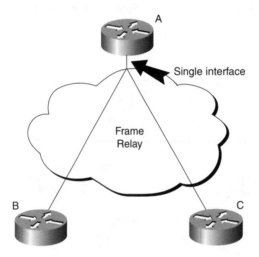

By default, OSPF treats NBMA networks as if they were *broadcast* links, which means a designated router will be elected. (See Appendix A, "OSPF Fundamentals," for more information on designated routers.)

This isn't really a broadcast network, though. Because Router A has direct connections to both Router B and Router C, Router A will receive any broadcasts Router B or Router C send. Router B, however, won't receive any broadcasts Router C transmits because there is no link between them; likewise, Router C won't receive any broadcasts transmitted by Router B.

For OSPF, this means only Router A will receive Router B's and Router C's Hellos; Router B won't receive Router C's Hellos, and Router C won't receive Router B's Hellos. Router A, Router B, and Router C will all have different views of the designated router election process. Router A might think that Router B is the designated router, but Router C wouldn't know this because it doesn't receive Router B's hello packets.

Then how do you handle NBMA networks in an OSPF environment? There are three ways, each with advantages and disadvantages.

You can configure the OSPF router priorities so that only Router A can become the designated router. This is an easy solution, which allows all the addresses on this one multipoint circuit to be in the same IP subnet. The disadvantage is that one misconfigured remote router can bring this entire link down.

It's also possible, on Cisco routers, to configure logical subinterfaces and treat each PVC as a point-to-point link. Using point-to-point subinterfaces is very clean, allowing different costs to be associates with each PVC, different output queues, and better tracking of the interface status against the PVC status. The disadvantage of using point-to-point subinterfaces is each point-to-point subinterface must be in its own IP subnet, which means using a fair amount of address space just for these point-to-point serial links.

The final way to handle NBMA networks in an OSPF environment is to have each router configured with an OSPF network type of point-to-multipoint. The advantages of a point-to-multipoint configuration are it's easy to configure, and it allows all the links in the multipoint network to share the same IP subnet. The disadvantage is that a host route will be created for each neighbor the hub or core router has, which could add a *lot* of routes to your routing tables.

What's the best solution for OSPF? It depends. The network designer should carefully consider each option and decide which one fits into the network at large. Different solutions will most likely be appropriate for different situations.

In the case of IS-IS, NBMA clouds like this won't work at all. The only solution is to use point-to-point subinterfaces. That's a simple decision!

Because EIGRP is an advanced distance vector protocol, it will work well on NBMA networks; there are no special configurations required for either point-to-multipoint or point-to-point subinterfaces. Point-to-point subinterfaces allow more control over the metric used between the hub or core router and each endpoint router. Therefore, it might be better in some situations.

Distribution Redundancy

Now that some core designs have been covered, the redundant designs for the distribution layer will be discussed. The distribution layer is covered more thoroughly in Chapter 4, "Applying the Principles of Network Design." Additional issues with redundancy and addressing are discussed in that chapter.

The two most common methods for providing redundancy at the distribution layer are dual homing and backup links to other distribution layer routers. The main consideration when designing redundancy in the distribution layer is unexpected traffic patterns.

Dual Homing to the Core

In Figure 3-8, Router A has two connections to the core through separate routers. While this provides very good redundancy—the loss of a single core router or a single link won't make any destinations behind Router A unreachable—it can also create some problems.

Figure 3-8   *Dual Homing in the Distribution Layer*

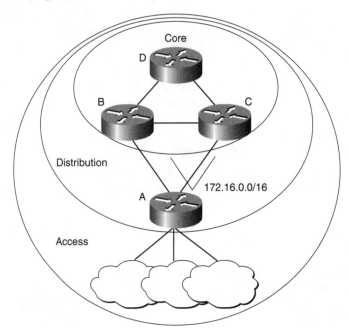

If Router A were connected only to one core router, Router D would have two paths to 172.16.0.0/16:

- Router D to Router B to Router A
- Router D to Router C to Router B to Router A

With Router A dual-homed to the core, Router D has four paths to this destination:

- Router D to Router C to Router A
- Router D to Router B to Router A
- Router D to Router C to Router B to Router A
- Router D to Router B to Router C to Router A

Dual homing Router A to the core effectively doubles the number of paths available to 172.16.0.0/16 in the core. This doubling of possible routes for every dual-homed distribution layer router slows network convergence.

It's sometimes possible to force the metric or cost of one of the two paths to be worse so that traffic will normally flow over only one link. The number of paths is still doubled, so this isn't a very effective solution for advanced routing protocols. A better solution would be to only advertise 172.16.0.0/16 over one link unless that link becomes unusable. Conditional advertisement and floating static routes can be used to only advertise a route when necessary.

Dual homing also presents one other problem: If the link between Router B and Router C goes down, Router A could be effectively drawn into a core role, passing transit traffic between Router B and Router C. This may be a valid design if it's anticipated and planned for, but it's generally not. The easiest way to prevent this from occurring is to configure Router D so it doesn't advertise routes learned from Router C back to Router B, and so it doesn't advertise routes learned from Router D back to Router C.

Redundant Links to Other Distribution Layer Devices

Installing links between distribution layer routers to provide redundancy has the following drawbacks (see Figure 3-9):

- **Doubling the core's routing table size**—As was discussed when looking at dual homing distribution layer devices to the core, adding the link between Router A and Router B in Figure 3-9 doubles the size of the core routing table because Router D now has paths through both Router A and Router C to the 172.16.0.0/16 network.

- **Possible use of the redundant path for traffic transiting the core**—If the link between Router D and Router C fails in Figure 3-9, it's possible that Router D could begin forwarding traffic to Router A, which is destined someplace beyond Router C, rather than forwarding the traffic to Router E. Router A and Router B can be effectively drawn into a core routing role.

- **Preferring the redundant link to the core path**—Distribution layer routers may end up preferring the redundant path through the distribution layer, rather than the path through the core. In Figure 3-9, it's possible that Router B would prefer the redundant link to the path through the core to reach the 172.16.0.0/16 network.

- **Routing information leaks**—Routing information will leak between the distribution layer branches because the routers in one branch will need to be able to advertise the destinations in another branch as reachable through the redundant link. In Figure 3-9, this can result in instabilities occurring beyond Router A and spreading through all the distribution layer branches, rather than being contained. It can also slow convergence time because routing tables in the distribution layer routers become larger.

Figure 3-9   *Redundant Links between Distribution Layer Devices*

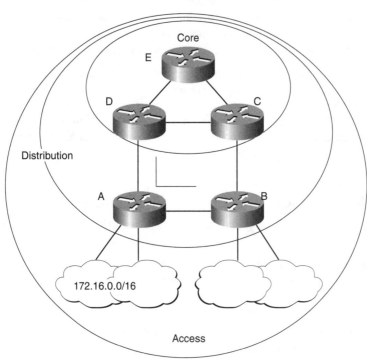

Access Redundancy

The access layer presents many of the same challenges and issues as the distribution layer, and it also shares some of the same strategies for resolving these drawbacks. Dual homing access layer devices are the most common way of providing redundancy to remote locations, but it's also possible to interconnect access layer devices to provide redundancy.

In Figure 3-10, Router G and Router H are access layer routers that are dual-homed with the backup circuit connected to different branches of the distribution layer. If these redundant links are actually constantly up and carrying traffic, the number of paths between 10.2.1.0/24 and 10.1.1.0/24 is excessive:

- Router H to Router F to Router B to Router A to Router C to Router G
- Router H to Router F to Router B to Router E to Router G
- Router H to Router D to Router A to Router B to Router E to Router G
- Router H to Router D to Router A to Router C to Router G

Figure 3-10   *Access Layer Redundancy—Dual Homing through Different Distribution Branches*

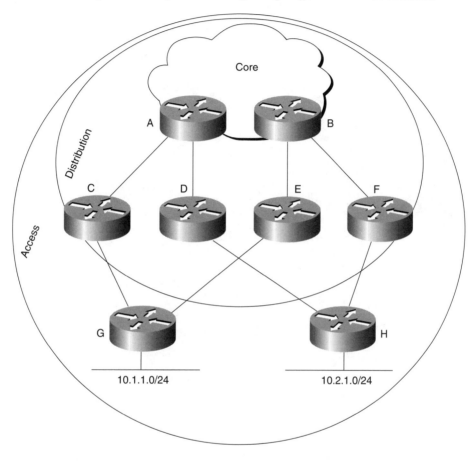

With each addition of a dual-homed access layer router, things get worse. This plethora of paths causes major problems in the core; the size of the routing table in the core will mushroom. This is the general rule: If the redundant link crosses the boundary of a distribution layer branch, it should not be advertised as a normal path.

Another option to provide access layer redundancy (and another illustration of the general rule above) is to provide links between the access layer routers themselves. In Figure 3-11, this saves one link, and it also reduces the number of paths between 10.1.1.0/24 and 10.2.1.0/24 down to two. If access layer redundancy is provided using links between access devices, it's important to provide enough bandwidth to handle the traffic from both remote sites toward the core.

Figure 3-11 *Redundancy through Interconnected Access Layer Devices*

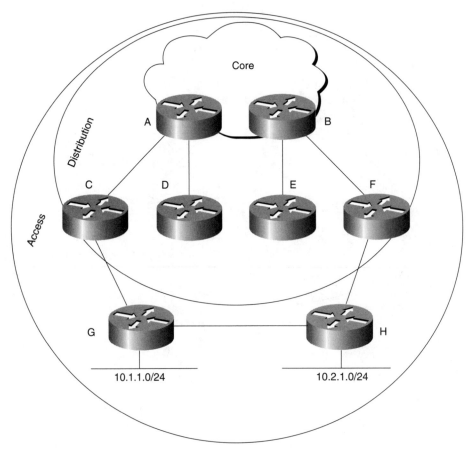

Either of these solutions would work well as long as the redundant route is not advertised until needed, so traffic won't normally flow across the redundant link. Dial-on-demand circuits work well for these types of applications.

It is possible to design load sharing and redundancy within the access layer, as Figure 3-12 illustrates. In this case, both links to Router G are connected to routers within the same distribution layer branch, as are both links to Router H.

Figure 3-12   *Access Layer Redundancy through the Same Distribution Layer Branch*

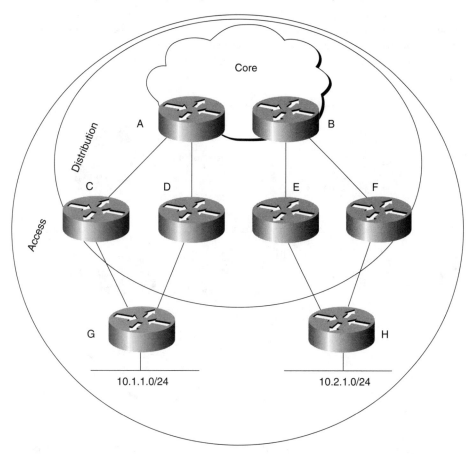

It's still possible for packets traveling from Router C to Router D to pass through Router G, but this can be remedied with route filtering. Router G and Router H should only advertise the networks below them in the hierarchy. In Figure 3-12, this is 10.1.1.0/24 for Router G and 10.2.1.0/24 for Router H. If correct filtering is installed in Router G, Router C will not learn any paths through Router D by way of Router G.

One way to get around all of the problems associated with dual homing is to use dial backup. There are two sections at the end of this chapter, "Case Study: Dial Backup with a Single Router" and "Case Study: Dial Backup with Two Routers," that cover these options.

Connections to Common Services

As was briefly mentioned in Chapter 1, "Hierarchical Design Principles," common use resources, such as server farms and connections to the Internet, can be connected directly to the core of the network or through a DMZ. If these common services are attached directly to the core, the most visible single point of failure will be the network these common services are attached to. Side A of Figure 3-13 illustrates this single point of failure.

Figure 3-13 *Redundancy to Common Shared Resource, Such as a Server Farm*

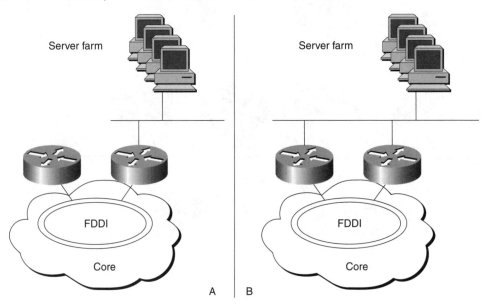

In the network illustrated by Side B of Figure 3-13, the server farm has been connected to two core routers, so the failure of a single router will not affect the reachability of the server farm.

In a similar way, Figure 3-14 illustrates multiple connections to an external routing domain for redundancy. In this case, the links to the external routing domain are directly attached to the core.

Providing redundancy for links through a DMZ is more complicated because there are two points of failure that need to be considered: the link between the core and the DMZ, and the link between the DMZ and the external domain. Figure 3-15 illustrates an external routing domain attached through a redundant DMZ.

Figure 3-14   *Redundancy to an External Domain*

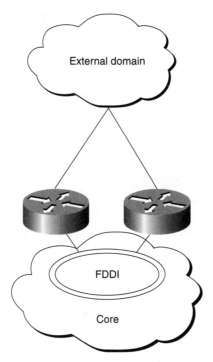

Listed below are some issues with having redundant links to external routing domains:

- Any routes the external routing domain is injecting into your network will be injected twice—once through each connection.

- Care must be taken so the core of your network doesn't become a transit network for traffic between two destinations in the external domain. This is particularly true for connections to the Internet.

- If multiple DMZs are used with separate firewall devices, either the firewall devices must coordinate their activities or some effort must be made to prevent a session, which initially uses the path through one firewall, from switching to the path through the other firewall in the middle of the session.

Figure 3-15 *Redundant DMZs*

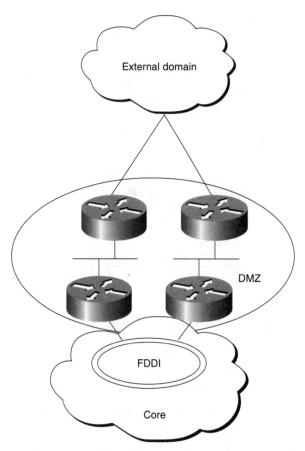

Summary

Strong hierarchical design tends to create a lot of places in a network where a single link or device failing can cause portions of the network to become unreachable; these are single points of failure. Redundancy provides backups and alternates to these single points of failure, but too much redundancy can be worse than no redundancy at all. Table 3-1 highlights important concepts about redundancy at the various layers.

Table 3-1   *Summary of Issues and Strategies at Various Layers in a Network*

Layer	Method	Issues & Strategies
Core	Ring	Hop count too large with single link loss.
		Only tolerates one broken device or link.
	Full mesh	Routing table too large.
	Partial mesh	Good compromise between hop count, redundancy, and routing table size.
		Be careful with routing protocols that may not handle partial mesh well.
Distribution	Dual-homed to core	Be careful with core routing table size.
		Make certain that route leakage between the branches of the distribution layer doesn't occur.
Access	Dual-homed to same distribution layer branch	Restricts destinations advertised to prevent transit traffic through the access layer router.
	Alternate path to another access layer device	Don't use the redundant link for normal traffic flow.
		Restricts destinations advertised to prevent transit traffic through the access layer router.
	Dual-homed to different distribution layer branches	Don't use the redundant link for normal traffic flow.
		Restricts destinations advertised to prevent transit traffic through the access layer router.

Case Study: What's the Best Route?

Floating static routes have been discussed quite a bit in this chapter, so it might help to understand how they work. The key to understanding floating static routes is in understanding how a Cisco router chooses which route to place in its forwarding table (which route to use). If a Cisco router has the following five paths available to 10.1.1.1, which would it use:

- 10.1.1.0/24, metric 44560, EIGRP, administrative distance 90
- 10.1.1.0/24, metric 56540, EIGRP, administrative distance 90
- 10.1.1.0/24, metric 2, RIP, administrative distance 120
- 10.0.0.0/8, metric 12500, EIGRP, administrative distance 90
- 10.0.0.0/8, metric 1, static, administrative distance 200

A router first looks at the prefix length of the paths and chooses the one with the longest prefix (the most bits set, or the most 1s). Because the three routes to 10.1.1.0/24 have a longer prefix length than 10.0.0.0/8, the 10.1.1.0/24 routes are preferred.

But which of the three 10.1.1.0/24 routes should the router use? Two of these routes are learned through EIGRP, and the third through RIP. Because RIP uses hop count as it's metric, and EIGRP uses a metric based on bandwidth and delay, the metrics can't be compared between protocols.

Because the router has no way to directly compare the various metrics and costs each protocol uses internally, it uses an external measure of the reliability of a protocol—the *administrative distance*. Lower administrative distances are preferred.

In this case, the path with an administrative distance of 120 is removed from the running, leaving the two paths with an administrative distance of 90. The router chooses between these two paths by looking at the internal metric of the protocol according to the rules of that protocol (in this case EIGRP) and choosing the one with the better metric. In this case, the first route is preferred.

Because the administrative distance is so important in making routing decisions, it will be covered in a bit more detail. How is the administrative distance determined? Each routing protocol has a default administrative distance:

- connected: 0
- static: 1
- EIGRP Summary: 5
- BGP External: 20
- EIGRP Internal: 90
- IGRP: 100
- OSPF: 110
- IS-IS: 115
- RIP: 120
- EGP: 140
- EIGRP External: 170
- BGP Internal: 200
- Unknown: 255

The administrative distance for connected routes cannot be changed, but it can be changed for other protocols. Each of the routing protocol's administrative distances can be changed using the **distance** command in router configuration mode. The administrative distance for each static route can be set using an option in the **ip route** command:

```
ip route 10.1.1.0 255.255.255.0 x.x.x.x 200
```

The ability to change the administrative distance of a static route this way has led to the concept of a *floating static route*, which is a static route with a high administrative distance, typically 200 or above.

These floating statics are useful for backing up primary routes or conditionally advertising a route.

Case Study: Redundancy at Layer 2 Using Switches

It's often possible to build redundancy into a network at the data link layer rather than the network layer. One example of this is the FDDI ring, which has two physical paths between each station on the ring. Another possibility is to use switches running the Spanning-Tree Algorithm to choose between redundant paths.

For example, in the network in Figure 3-16 there are actually eight paths from Router G to the FDDI ring, but Router G would see only two of them. Spanning tree running between Switches C and D would block some ports to eliminate any loops.

Figure 3-16   *Redundancy at Layer 2*

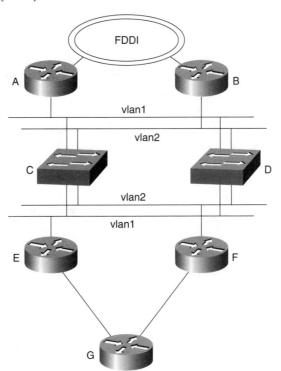

Following is an example of one pair of paths through the network. There are two possible paths between Router A and Router E: Router A to Switch C to Router E and Router A to Switch D to Router E, crossing VLAN 1.

If both switches were to forward traffic on all ports, there would be a bridging loop between these links: From Switch C's port on VLAN 1 to Switch D's port on VLAN 1 to Switch D's port on VLAN 1 and finally to Switch C's port on VLAN 1. After running spanning-tree calculations, one of the two switches would block traffic on one of these four ports to break the loop, leaving only one path between Router A and Router E.

Assume that the port which blocks is Switch D's port onto VLAN 1. If Switch D fails, Switch C would recalculate spanning tree and begin forwarding traffic across VLAN 1. The routers wouldn't even know that a network failure had occurred.

If Router E were to fail, Router G would begin using the alternate routed path through Router F to reach the FDDI ring. No single link or equipment failure would cause an outage on this network.

While this example shows LANs (specifically Ethernet VLANs) being used as intermediate links, it's also possible to use switches to provide redundancy over wide area links, such as Frame Relay or ATM.

When using switched virtual circuits rather than permanent virtual circuits (or in combination with permanent virtual circuits), it's possible to have a mesh of redundant connections between switches that are completely transparent to the routers on the edges of the network cloud. Physical layer redundancy is often easier to implement and can provide faster recovery than providing redundancy at the network layer. It can also be less complicated to maintain and manage.

Physical layer redundancy doesn't provide fallbacks for failure in the routers at the edge, however. Because routers are Layer 3 devices, router redundancy must be provided for at Layer 3 with a routing protocol (or something along the lines of floating static routes).

Case Study: Dial Backup with a Single Router

While BGP is capable of conditional advertisement, most other routing protocols aren't. You need to find a way to advertise backup links only under certain conditions, particularly if they are dial-on-demand, such as ISDN.

Figure 3-17 depicts a common scenario; Router B has a point-to-point link through Serial 0 to Router A, and a dial-on-demand backup link through BRI 0 to Router C. The routing protocol is EIGRP, and Router B is only receiving 0.0.0.0/0 advertised from Router A (the default route). The network administrator doesn't want the ISDN link up unless the serial link fails.

Figure 3-17   *ISDN Dial-on-Demand*

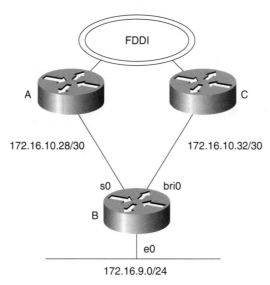

There are two possibilities for bringing the ISDN dial-on-demand link up when the serial interface fails:

1 Configuring the ISDN link as a *backup interface*. Configuring an interface as a backup, as the name implies, instructs the router to bring a dial interface up in response to another interface's line state changing to down.

2 Using a combination of floating static routes and a dynamic routing protocol to redirect traffic over the ISDN link.

It's relatively simple to configure the ISDN interface as a backup interface for Serial 0 in Figure 3-17. On Router B:

```
isdn switch-type basic-ni1
!
interface BRI0
 ip address 172.16.10.33 255.255.255.252
 encapsulation ppp
 no ip route-cache
 no ip mroute-cache
 bandwidth 128
 dialer idle-timeout 600
 dialer map ip 172.16.10.34 name C 5551212
 dialer-group 1
 isdn spid1 91955588880100
 isdn spid2 91955588880100
 no fair-queue
 no cdp enable
 ppp authentication chap
 ppp multilink
!
interface Serial 0
 ip address 172.16.10.29 255.255.255.252
 encapsulation frame-relay
 backup interface bri 0
 backup delay 10 120
!
router eigrp 1
network 172.16.0.0
!
ip classless
access-list 101 deny eigrp any any
access-list 101 permit ip any any
dialer-list 1 protocol ip list 101
```

Configuring the ISDN link as a backup interface relies on the serial interface actually going down to trigger the switch from the serial link. Unfortunately, the condition of the interface doesn't necessarily reflect the condition of Layer 3 connectivity, particularly for Frame Relay networks.

When the physical layer can't be used to indicate IP connectivity across a link, it's better to use routing to bring the backup link into operation—a job for floating static routes. The configuration follows:

```
isdn switch-type basic-ni1
!
interface BRI0
 ip address 172.16.10.33 255.255.255.252
 encapsulation ppp
 no ip route-cache
 no ip mroute-cache
 bandwidth 128
 dialer idle-timeout 600
 dialer map ip 172.16.10.34 name C 5551212
 dialer-group 1
 isdn spid1 91955588880100
 isdn spid2 91955588880100
 no fair-queue
 no cdp enable
 ppp authentication chap
 ppp multilink
!
interface Serial 0
 ip address 172.16.10.29 255.255.255.252
 encapsulation frame-relay
!
ip route 0.0.0.0 0.0.0.0 172.16.10.34 200
access-list 101 deny eigrp any any
access-list 101 permit ip any any
dialer-list 1 protocol ip list 101
```

The number at the end of the IP route command indicates an administrative distance. Because Router C would normally have a 0.0.0.0/0 route from Router A through EIGRP, this static route will not normally be used (placed in the routing table). If Router A were lost as an EIGRP neighbor, though, Router C would begin using this static, which points out through the ISDN link.

Once interesting traffic begins to be forwarded out of interface BRI 0 (as defined by **dialer-list 1**), the router will begin the ISDN link up. Once the serial link is restored, the 0.0.0.0/0 route learned through EIGRP from Router A should once again be installed in the routing table, and all traffic should be forwarded through the serial interface.

Because EIGRP is not considered interesting traffic, the router will eventually bring the ISDN link down.

Note that in both of these configurations, IP route-cache is disabled on the ISDN interface. It's important that the router not cache any destinations as reachable through the ISDN interface because it will continue sending traffic for those destinations through the ISDN interface, regardless of the state of the serial interface, until the route cache entry times out.

Case Study: Dial Backup with Two Routers

Dial backup using a single router at the remote site still leaves a single point of failure—the router at the remote site. The obvious solution is to install two routers at the remote site, as illustrated in Figure 3-18.

Figure 3-18   *Dial Backup with Two Routers*

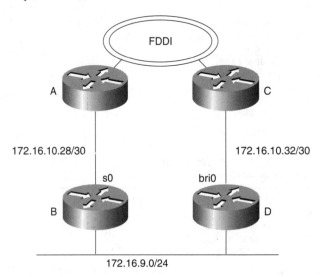

There are two problems with this solution; the first is that hosts on the 172.16.9.0/24 network must set their default gateways to either Router B's or Router D's Ethernet IP address to reach the rest of the network. No matter which one is used, if that router fails completely, all connectivity to this segment will effectively be lost.

The second is Router B must be able to signal Router D that its serial link to Router A has failed.

The first problem can be resolved using Hot Standby Router Protocol (HSRP). HSRP allows Router B and Router D to share a virtual IP address between them with only the active HSRP router accepting (and forwarding) traffic destined to that IP address. Following is an example of how this would work.

On Router B, the configuration is as follows:

```
interface e0
 ip address 172.16.9.2 255.255.255.0
 standby ip 172.16.9.1
 standby priority 10
 standby preempt
```

On Router D, the configuration is as follows:

```
interface e0
 ip address 172.16.9.3 255.255.255.0
 standby ip 172.16.9.1
 standby priority 20
 standby preempt
```

Router B and Router D are both configured to act as standby routers for 172.16.9.1. They will also create a virtual physical layer address between them, and the active router will forward or process traffic transmitted to that physical layer address.

Because Router B needs to be the active route in normal operation, **standby priority** and **standby preempt** have been configured. The hosts on the 172.16.9.0/24 segment will be configured to use 172.16.9.1 as their default gateway.

When a host on the 172.16.9.0/24 network attempts to transmit a packet to a destination that is off the local segment, it will ARP for its default gateway's physical address, and the HSRP active router will answer with the virtual address. The host will then send all off-segment traffic to the virtual address.

If Router B fails, Router D will take over as the active HSRP router and will begin forwarding traffic across the ISDN link. This resolves the first problem—how to configure the host's default gateway—but doesn't resolve the second problem.

How would Router B notify Router D that its serial link has failed? The simplest way is to configure HSRP to track the state of the serial interface on Router B; if the serial interface fails, Router D should take over.

On Router B, the configuration is as follows:

```
interface e0
 ip address 172.16.9.2 255.255.255.0
 standby ip 172.16.9.1
 standby priority 10
 standby preempt
 standby track serial 0 20
```

When Router B's serial interface fails, it will increase its standby priority to 30, and Router D will take over as the HSRP active router. Note this solution still relies on the physical layer failing on Router B's Serial 0; on some types of links, it is possible to lose IP connectivity while physical layer connectivity still appears to be good.

To track IP connectivity, use a routing protocol. Assuming a single default route (0.0.0.0/0) is the only route Router B is learning from Router A, Router B's configuration could be:

```
interface e0
 ip address 172.16.9.2 255.255.255.0
 standby ip 172.16.9.1
 standby priority 10
 standby preempt
 standby track serial 0 20
!
router ospf 1
 network 172.16.0.0 0.0.255.255 area 0
!
ip classless
ip route 0.0.0.0 0.0.0.0 172.16.9.3 200
```

Note that Router B is still tracking the state of its serial interface and will resign the HSRP active role if its serial interface fails. The addition of the floating static route means Router B will forward packets to Router D if it loses its OSPF neighbor across Serial 0 as well.

On Router D, you could have:

```
interface e0
 ip address 172.16.9.3 255.255.255.0
 standby ip 172.16.9.1
 standby priority 20
!
interface BRI0
 ip address 172.16.10.33 255.255.255.252
 encapsulation ppp
 no ip route-cache
 no ip mroute-cache
 bandwidth 128
 dialer idle-timeout 600
 dialer map ip 172.16.10.34 name C 5551212
 dialer-group 1
 isdn spid1 91955588880100
 isdn spid2 91955588880100
 no fair-queue
 no cdp enable
 ppp authentication chap
 ppp multilink
!
router ospf 1
 network 172.16.0.0 0.0.255.255 area 0
!
ip classless
ip route 0.0.0.0 0.0.0.0 172.16.10.34 200
access-list 101 deny ospf any any
access-list 101 permit ip any any
dialer-list 1 protocol ip list 101
```

Normally, Router D would learn a default route through Router B from OSPF, so the floating static to 0.0.0.0/0 through 172.16.10.34 won't be used. If Router B loses its neighbor relationship with Router A, then Router D would stop learning this default route through OSPF. It would then install this default route and start forwarding traffic through the ISDN link.

So, any possible failure condition is accounted for using both the floating static and HSRP. If the serial link between Router A and Router B fails entirely (or Router B fails entirely), Router D will take over as the HSRP active router and begin forwarding traffic through the backup ISDN link.

If the OSPF neighbor relationship between Router A and Router B fails for any other reason, Router B still acts as the HSRP active router, but it forwards all traffic to Router D. Router D forwards all traffic through its BRI interface to Router C.

Review

1   Why is it important to consider link capacities when designing redundancy?

2   Why is designing redundancy in the core easier than at other layers?

3   If all the core routers are in one building, what is a natural way to provide redundancy?

4   How many links on a ring core can fail before at least one section of the core is isolated?

5   Do ring designs provide consistent hop count through the core network when a link fails?

6   What ring technologies provide redundancy at Layer 2?

7   Do redundant ring technologies provide redundancy against failed devices?

8   Given a full mesh core with 25 routers, how many paths would there be through the network?

9   What method does a Cisco router use to differentiate between routes from two different routing protocols?

10   What is the first, and most important factor, used in deciding which route to use for a particular destination?

11   What mechanism in OSPF needs to be considered when it is being configured on a partial mesh network?

12   What are the possible techniques you can use in OSPF partial mesh network designs to get around this problem?

13   When dual homing a distribution layer or access layer router, what major problem should you be careful of?

14   When interconnecting distribution or access layer routers to provide redundancy, what issues should you be careful of?

15   What are the two main goals you must be careful to address when building redundancy into a network?

CHAPTER 4

Applying the Principles of Network Design

The elements of network design—hierarchy, redundancy, addressing, and summarization—have been addressed in relative isolation up to this point. The following list groups them together:

- **Hierarchy**—Provides a logical foundation, the "skeleton" on which addresses "hang."

- **Addressing**—Isn't just for finding networks and hosts; it also provides points of summarization.

- **Summarization**—The primary tool used to bound the area affected by network changes.

- **Stability/Reliability**—Provided by bounding the area affected by changes in the network.

- **Redundancy**—Provides alternate routes around single points of failure.

Figure 4-1 shows the traffic and routing table patterns throughout a well-designed hierarchical network. (You may recognize Figure 4-1 because you have seen pieces of it in previous chapters.) Note that the routing table size is managed through summarization; so, no single layer has an overwhelming number of routes, and no single router must compute routes to every destination in the network if a change does occur.

Figure 4-1   *Traffic and Routes in a Well-Designed Network*

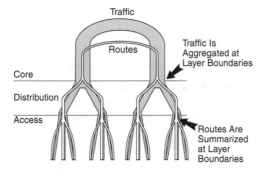

How do you design a network so that the routes and traffic are well-behaved? By managing the size of the routing table. *Managing the size of the routing table is critical in large-scale network design.*

The primary means of controlling the routing table size in a network is through summarization, which was covered in detail in Chapter 3, "Redundancy." Summarization is highly dependent on correct addressing. Therefore, the routing table size, summarization, and addressing (the three basics of highly scalable networks) are closely related.

To illustrate these principles, this chapter begins with a network that is experiencing stability problems and "reforms" it to make it stable and scalable. This exercise applies the principles discussed in the first three chapters of this book.

Reforming an Unstable Network

This section of the chapter reforms the network shown in Figure 4-2. Because this is a rather large network, only one small section is tackled at a time. This chapter covers how to implement changes in the topology and addressing, which can improve this network. Chapter 5, "OSPF Network Design," Chapter 6, "IS-IS Network Design," and Chapter 7, "EIGRP Network Design" address how to implement routing protocols on this network.

This exercise begins with the core of the network and works outward to the distribution and access layers as detailed in the following sections.

Examining the Network Core

As you consider the core of this network, it's good to remember the design goals that you worked through for network cores back in Chapter 1, "Hierarchical Design Principles." As your primary concerns, focus on switching speed and providing full reachability without policy implementations in the network core.

The first problem in the network illustrated in Figure 4-2 is that the core has too much redundancy—this is a fully-meshed design with $5\times(5-1) = 20$ paths. The primary exercise here is to determine which links can be eliminated. To do this, you need to narrow your focus a bit; Figure 4-3 shows only the core and its direct connections.

Network traffic in the network illustrated in Figure 4-3 flows between the common services and external connections to and from the HQ VLANs and the networks behind the distribution layer. A diagram of this network traffic reveals that most traffic flows:

- From the networks behind Routers A, C, and D to the networks behind Router E
- From the networks behind Routers A, C, and D to the networks behind Router B

Figure 4-2   *An Unstable Network*

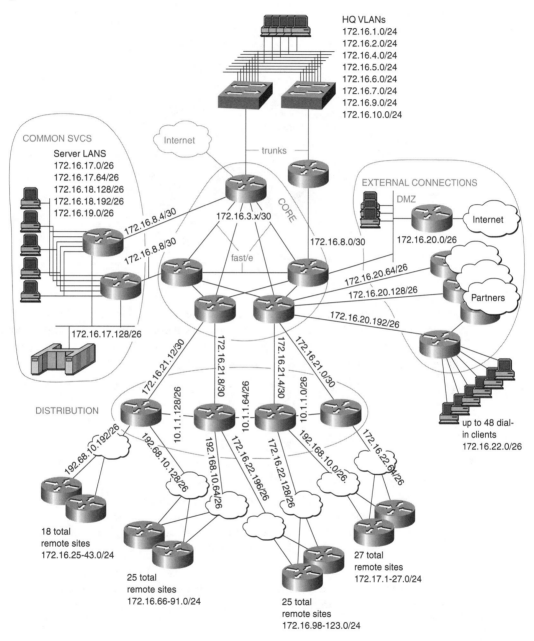

HQ VLANs
172.16.1.0/24
172.16.2.0/24
172.16.4.0/24
172.16.5.0/24
172.16.6.0/24
172.16.7.0/24
172.16.9.0/24
172.16.10.0/24

COMMON SVCS

Server LANS
172.16.17.0/26
172.16.17.64/26
172.16.18.128/26
172.16.18.192/26
172.16.19.0/26

Internet

trunks

EXTERNAL CONNECTIONS

DMZ

Internet

CORE

172.16.8.4/30

172.16.3.x/30

172.16.8.0/30

172.16.20.0/26

172.16.8.8/30

fast/e

172.16.20.64/26

172.16.20.128/26

Partners

172.16.17.128/26

172.16.20.192/26

172.16.21.12/30

172.16.21.8/30

172.16.21.4/30

172.16.21.0/30

10.1.1.128/26

10.1.1.64/26

10.1.1.0/26

up to 48 dial-
in clients
172.16.22.0/26

DISTRIBUTION

192.68.10.192/26

192.68.10.128/26

192.168.10.64/26

172.16.22.196/26

172.16.22.128/26

192.168.10.0/26.

172.16.22.64/26

18 total
remote sites
172.16.25-43.0/24

25 total
remote sites
172.16.66-91.0/24

27 total
remote sites
172.17.1-27.0/24

25 total
remote sites
172.16.98-123.0/24

Figure 4-3   *The Network Core*

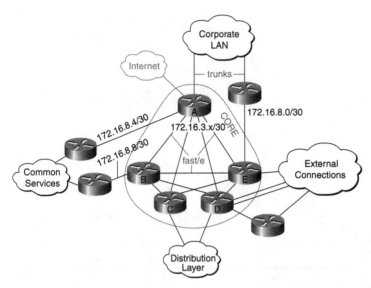

Because there won't be much traffic flowing between Router A and Router C or Router A and Router D, these are the two best links to remove. Removing these two links will reduce the core to a partially-meshed network with fewer paths and more stability. The total number of paths through the core will be cut from 20 to 6, at most, for any particular destination.

Beyond the hyper-redundancy, there are also network segments with hosts connected directly to Router A—the corporate LAN VLAN trunks. Terminating the corporate VLANs directly into Router A means:

- Router A must react to any changes in the status of corporate VLAN.
- Any access controls that need to be applied to hosts attached to one of the corporate VLANs must be configured (and managed) on a core router.

For these reasons, a router will be placed between Router A and the corporate VLANs. Adding this router moves summarization and policy implementation onto the new router, which helps to maintain the goals of the core. Remember, the core's primary function should be switching packets and not summarization or policy implementation.

Finally, after dealing with the physical topology issues, you can examine the IP addresses used in the core of the network; they are all in the 172.16.3.x range of addresses. Can you summarize this address space out toward the distribution layer (and the other outlying pieces of the network)?

To answer this question, you'll need to see if other networks are in the same range of addresses. In this case, 172.16.2.x and 172.16.4.x are both corporate VLANs (refer to Figure 4-2), which effectively eliminates the capability to summarize not only links in and around the core of the network but also the networks within the corporate VLAN.

You have two options: Leave the addresses as they are, which could actually work in this situation, or renumber the links in the core. Because you don't want to worry about this problem again, readdressing the links between the core routers is the preferred option. You need to replace the 172.16.3.x address space that is currently used in the core with something that isn't used elsewhere in the network and that won't affect the capability to summarize in any other area of the network. Unfortunately, choosing a good address space in a network that is already in daily use is difficult.

A quick perusal of the IP addresses in use shows the following:

- 172.16.1.x through 172.16.10.x are corporate VLANs; to make this a block that can be summarized, you can end it at 172.16.15.x, summarized to 172.16.0.0/21.
- 172.16.17.x through 172.16.19.x consist of server farm and mainframe connectivity; to make this a block that can be summarized, you can end it at 172.16.23.x, summarized to 172.16.16.0/22.
- Subnets of 172.16.20.x are all used for connections to external networks.
- 172.16.22.x is used for dial-in clients and other connections.
- 172.16.25.x through 172.16.43.x are used for one set of remote sites.
- 172.16.66.x through 172.16.91.x are used for another set of remote sites.

These are all the 172.16.xx.x's currently in use. The point-to-point links in and around the core use 30-bit masks, so you need a block of only 255 addresses (a block that can be summarized into a single, Class C range). The lowest such block not currently in use is 172.16.21.0/24; therefore, the links in and around the core using this address space need to be renumbered.

If You Didn't Readdress the Core Links. . .

It's possible to rely on the way routers choose the best path to overcome the overlapping address space between the core and the HQ VLANs without readdressing the links in the network core.

You do, however, need to summarize the routes advertised from the HQ VLANs anyway. Because the routers within the core are going to have more specific (longer prefix) routes to any destination within the core, everything will work.

Relying on leaked, longer prefixes to provide correct routing is not recommended because the prefixes can be difficult to maintain, and simple configuration mistakes can cause major side effects. But it is useful to consider this option if you are in a position where networks can't be renumbered to summarize correctly.

Figure 4-4 provides an illustration of what the redesigned core from Figure 4-2 looks like after these changes:

- Removing the excessive redundancy in the core by removing two point-to-point links
- Adding a single router between the core and the HQ VLANs to move policy implementation and summarization out of the core
- Renumbering the point-to-point links in the core

Figure 4-4   *Redesigned Network Core*

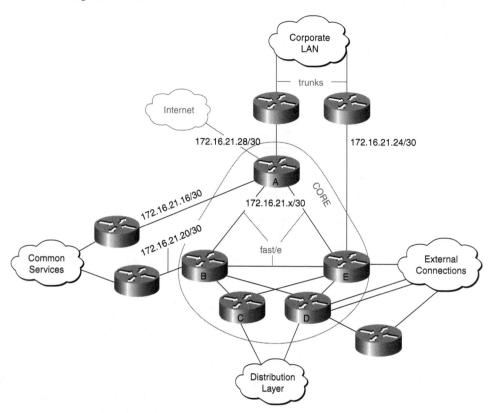

After redesigning the core and improving network stability for the network shown in Figure 4-2, you need to look at the distribution and access layers for possible improvements.

Distribution Layer and Access Layer Topology

As you work through the access and distribution area of this network, keep the goals of the layers in mind. The goals for the distribution layer are as follows:

- Control the routing table size by isolating topology changes through summarization.
- Aggregate traffic.

The goals for the access layer are as follows:

- Feed traffic into the network.
- Control access into the network, implement any network policies, and perform other edge services as needed.

Because the design of the distribution and access layers is so tightly coupled, you need to examine them together. Figure 4-5 focuses on the distribution and access layers and the Frame Relay links that connect them. This way you can more easily understand them in context with the discussion that follows.

Figure 4-5   *Distribution and Access Layers*

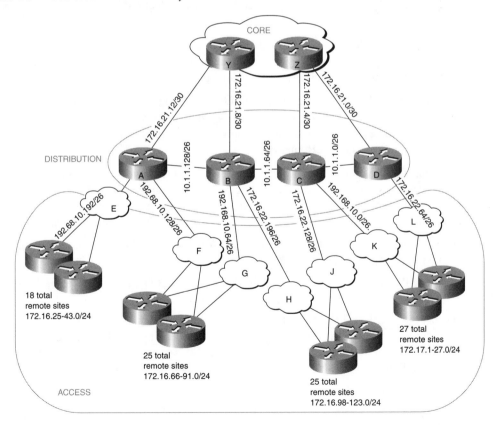

At the distribution layer, Routers A, B, C, and D are currently cross connected, and they each have only one connection to the core. This produces major problems in summarization and the number of paths to a given network within the core. For example, to reach 172.16.98.0/24, a router in the core has the following possible paths:

- Core, Router B, Cloud H
- Core, Router A, Router B, Cloud H
- Core, Router C, Router B, Cloud H
- Core, Router D, Router C, Router B, Cloud H
- Core, Router C, Cloud J
- Core, Router D, Router C, Cloud J
- Core, Router B, Router C, Cloud J
- Core, Router A, Router B, Router C, Cloud J

Furthermore, if a host that is connected to the 172.16.98.0/24 network sends a packet toward the 172.16.66.0/24 network, it will most likely end up traveling across the link between Router C and Router B rather than traversing the core. This can defeat traffic engineering and cause other stability problems.

The most obvious solution is to simply dual home each of the distribution layer routers to the core rather than connecting directly between them. (*Dual home* means to connect each distribution layer router to two core routers rather than one.)

After this change, there is still a single point of failure to consider: *If Router A fails, the remote networks 172.16.25.0/24 through 172.16.43.0/24 will lose all connectivity to the rest of the network.* You can resolve this problem by simply providing these networks with another link to the distribution layer through Router B.

Adding this link means Router B now has three Frame Relay connections; Router A and Router C have two; and Router D has one. Depending on the type of router and traffic handling factors, you may need to even out how many connections each router has. The following adjustments to where the frame links connect leave two connections per distribution layer router:

- Move the link between Cloud H and Router B to Router C; this leaves Router B with only two Frame Relay connections.
- Move the link between Cloud J and Router C to Router D; this leaves Router C with two Frame Relay connections and adds one to Router D for a total of two.

Note that moving these links around is necessary only if there are issues with traffic handling or port density on the distribution layer routers. Load balancing might also be improved by these links. Moving the links uncovers some possibilities in evening out the links attached to each router. Figure 4-6 illustrates what the network looks like after making these link changes.

Figure 4-6   *Modified Distribution and Access Layers*

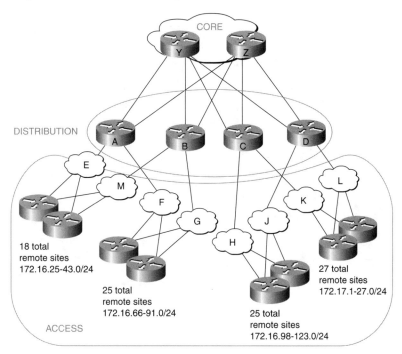

These modifications leave a plethora of paths; normally, there are four ways to reach any access layer network from the core. For example, the 172.16.25.0/24 network has the following paths:

- Cloud E, Router A, Core (through 172.16.21.12/30)
- Cloud E, Router A, Core (through 10.1.1.26/26)
- Cloud M, Router B, Core (through 172.16.21.8/30)
- Cloud M, Router B, Core (through the alternate link)

A single failure (for example, Router A) leaves two paths through Router B. A second failure (Frame Relay Cloud M, for example) isolates the remote networks. If the second failure isolates the remote network anyway, why leave in the extra redundancy?

Figure 4-7 shows the network after removing the extra (redundant) links between the core and the distribution layer routers, which leaves two paths between the core and any remote network.

So far, then, you have moved some links around in between the distribution layer and the core to provide better points of summarization. You have also removed some redundancy, which, it turns out, is overkill. The next step is to make any possible changes in addressing in the distribution and access layers to improve stability.

Figure 4-7 *Final Topology Modifications in Distribution and Access Layers*

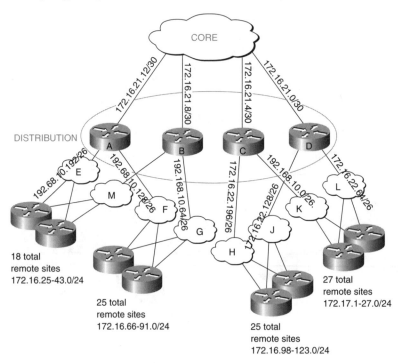

Overhead in Routing Protocols

There are two things engineers yearn for in a good routing protocol: instantaneous convergence and no overhead. Since that is not possible, it is necessary to settle for a low overhead protocol with very fast convergence. But what defines *low overhead*?

One major component of routing protocol overhead is interruption due to updates. You don't want to use a routing protocol that interrupts every host on the network every 30 seconds with a routing update (like Routing Information Protocol [RIP] does). To combat update overhead, routing protocols attempt to reduce the scope and the frequency of interruptions.

One technique used by routing protocols is to reduce the scope of the updates, which means to reduce the number of hosts that will hear the update packet. Broadcast is the worst possible medium for sending updates—every host on the wire is forced to look at the packet and decide whether or not it is interesting. Only a few hosts on a network are interested in the routing updates, so using the broadcast mechanism to send routing updates is a massive waste of time and resources.

To get around this problem, routing protocols use either multicast or unicast routing updates. Open Shortest Path First (OSPF), Enhanced Interior Gateway Routing Protocol (EIGRP), and

Intermediate System-to-Intermediate System (IS-IS) all use well-known multicast addresses for their routing updates so that hosts and other computers that aren't interested in the updates can filter them out at the hardware layer. Border Gateway Protocol (BGP) uses unicast routing updates, which is even better, but does require special configuration to work (**neighbor** statements).

Another technique used to reduce the overhead in a routing protocol is to reduce the frequency of the updates. RIP, which advertises all known destinations every 30 seconds, uses a great deal of bandwidth.

OSPF is periodic, timing its table out every 30 minutes; 30 minutes is much more efficient than 30 seconds. In between these 30-minute intervals, OSPF counts on flooding unreachables as a mechanism for discovering invalid paths. EIGRP and BGP never time their tables out. BGP relies on a *withdraw* mechanism to discover invalid paths, and EIGRP relies on a system of *queries* to discover invalid paths.

Routing protocols reduce network overhead by reducing the number of packets required to provide other routers with the routing information they need. Routing protocols use fancy encoding schemes to fit more information into each packet. For example, whereas RIP can fit 25 route updates in a single routing update packet, IGRP can fit 104.

Routing protocols also use *incremental updates* to reduce the number of packets required to do the job. Rather than a router advertising its full routing table every so often, it only advertises changes in its routing table. This reduces the amount of processing time required to recalculate when changes occur in the network, and it also reduces the amount of bandwidth the routing protocol consumes.

For more information on how OSPF, EIGRP, and BGP operate, please see Appendix A, "OSPF Fundamentals;" Appendix C, "EIGRP Fundamentals;" and Appendix D, "BGP Fundamentals." These appendixes explain in further detail how each of these protocols decides when to send routing updates.

In general, routing protocol overhead should be considered when choosing which protocol to use. Because the design of the network has some bearing on what the overhead will be, there is no absolute answer. You need to understand the burden that every protocol will place on your network before deciding.

Distribution and Access Layer Addressing

Now that you've built good physical connectivity, you need to address the distribution and access layers. The addressing of the links between the core and the distribution layer looks okay; these links are addresses from the core's address space. Because the only real summarization that can take place is the summarization of the entire core into one advertisement for all the outlying areas of the network, the addressing that's in place will work.

The addressing between the access and distribution routers, however, is a mess. Some of the Frame Relay clouds are using 172.16.x.x addresses, which fit into the same address space as the dial-in clients, while other clouds are using address space that isn't used anyplace else in the network, such as 192.168.10.0/26.

How do you make sense out of this? If you number these links from an address space not already in use someplace else, as you did for the core, you won't be able to *summarize them in*, or group them with anything else, at the distribution layer. In this case, not being able to summarize these networks means only six extra routes in the core—but if this network grows (remember that the entire objective of network design is to make it possible to grow), then this a problem.

One solution is to steal addresses from the remote site address space to number these links. The remote sites are grouped into blocks that can be summarized as follows:

- 172.16.25.0/24 through 172.16.43.0/24 can be summarized to 172.16.24.0/21 and 172.16.32.0/20.
- 172.16.66.0/24 through 172.16.91.0/24 can be summarized to 172.16.64.0/20.
- 172.16.98.0/24 through 172.16.123.0/24 can be summarized to 172.16.96.0/20.
- 172.17.1.0/24 through 172.17.27.0/24 can be summarized to 172.17.0.0/20.

Note the first set of addresses can be summarized into only *two* blocks, not *one*. Looking for summarizations when reworking a network like this one is useful because the address space probably wasn't parceled out with summarization in mind.

The easiest way to find addresses for the Frame Relay clouds is to steal addresses from the summarizable blocks cited in the preceding list. For instance:

- Cloud E can be addressed using 172.16.24.0/26.
- Cloud M can be addressed using 172.16.24.64/26.
- Cloud F can be addressed using 172.16.64.0/26.
- Cloud G can be addressed using 172.16.64.64/26.
- Cloud H can be addressed using 172.16.96.0/26.
- Cloud J can be addressed using 172.16.96.64/26.
- Cloud K can be addressed using 172.17.0.0/26.
- Cloud L can be addressed using 172.16.0.64/26.

Whereas stealing addresses from the remote network address space to number the links between the access and distribution layer routers is good for summarization, it does have one possible drawback: You can lose connectivity to a remote network even though all possible paths to that network are not down.

As an example, consider the remote router and its paths to the network core as illustrated in Figure 4-8.

Figure 4-8   *An Individual Remote Router and Its Connections to the Network Core*

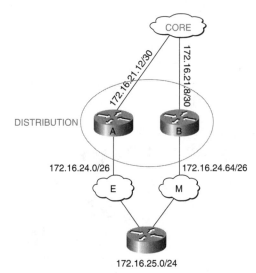

Assume that both Routers A and B are advertising a summary of 172.16.24.0/21, which is the address space from 172.16.24.0 through 172.16.31.0. Therefore, the summary covers the remote network and the links between the access and distribution layer routers shown in Figure 4-8. Furthermore, assume that Router B is used by the core routers as the preferred path to this summary for whatever reason (link speed, and so forth).

Given these conditions, if the remote router's link onto frame Cloud M fails, all connectivity with the remote network 172.16.25.0/24 will be lost, even though the alternate path is still available. It might be very unlikely, of course, that this could happen, but it is possible and worth considering.

The only solution to this type of problem is for Router A to recognize the condition and advertise the more specific route to the remote network. Unfortunately, this capability doesn't exist today in any Interior Gateway Protocol (IGP); you simply have to be aware that this type of problem can occur and know what to look for.

External Connections

This section separately examines the external connections to the network, as was done for the network core and distribution and access layers (see Figure 4-9).

Figure 4-9   *External Connections*

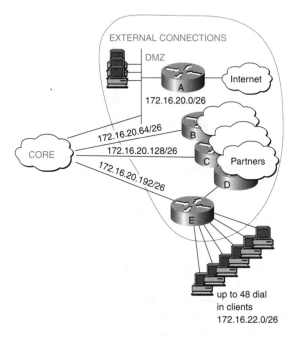

It only takes a quick look to see that there are too many links between the core of this network and the external networks—three connections to four partner networks, an Internet connection, and a bank of dial-in clients. Having this many connections to external networks causes problems in two areas: addressing and routing.

External Connection Addressing

If one of the partners illustrated in Figure 4-9 installs a network that happens to use the same address space as an internal network, how do you handle it? You must either coordinate the use of address space with the other network partners, use only registered addresses, or use Network Address Translation (NAT) (refer to Chapter 2, "Addressing & Summarization"). Because this network uses private address space, you're probably already using NAT to get to the Internet. Therefore, it's logical to use NAT to get to external partner networks as well.

But with this many connections to partner networks, where do you run NAT? It's never a good idea to run it on a core router—don't even consider that. You can run it on Routers B, C, and D, but this connection is very difficult to configure and maintain (especially considering you may need to translate addresses in *both directions*).

It is much easier to connect the external partner networks to the DeMilitarized Zone (DMZ) and put the network translation on the routers there. You can translate the internal addresses to a registered address space on the way out (as you are most likely already doing) and translate the external addresses, if needed, into something acceptable for the internal address space on Routers B, C, and D. From an addressing perspective, the best solution is to attach Routers B, C, and D to the DMZ.

External Connection Routing

The routing side of the equation is this: Even if the internal and external address spaces don't overlap, you don't want to carry routes to these external networks in all your routers. It is much better to carry a single default route from all external networks into the core of the network.

Once again, from a routing perspective, the best solution is to connect Routers B, C, and D to the DMZ.

Dial-In Clients

What about the dial-in clients? Should you connect these to the DMZ as well? Because these clients are assigned addresses within the internal address space, the addressing problems and routing problems outlined for the network partners don't exist for these clients.

Remember that these clients will likely want to connect to internal hosts that other externally connected clients aren't allowed to see, which means special security considerations are necessary on Router A.

All in all, it's better to leave the dial-in clients directly connected to the core. However, you should not allow the link between Router E and the core to be a single point of failure. For this reason, you need to add a dial backup link from Router E to the core.

You also need to renumber the link between Router E and the core so that it fits into the addressing scheme for the core. Figure 4-10 illustrates the network originally illustrated in Figure 4-2 with all the changes covered thus far in this chapter.

Figure 4-10 *The Revised Network with Changes to the Core, Distribution Layer, Access Layer, and External Connections*

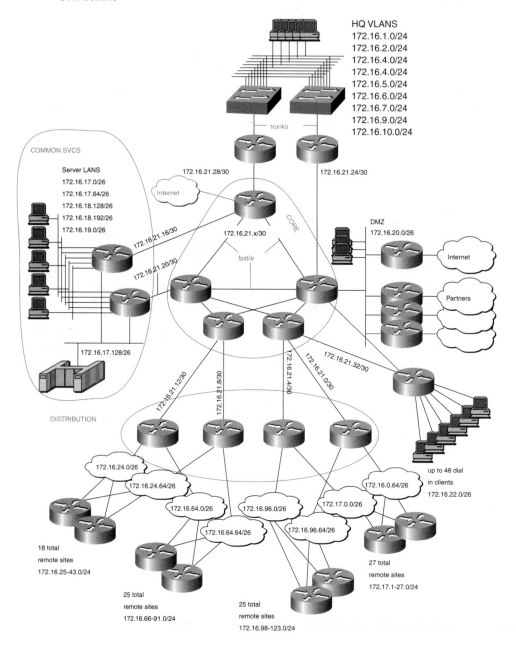

Review

1 What does hierarchy provide in a well-designed network?

2 What is the primary tool used to bound the area affected by network changes?

3 How can you determine which links can be removed from a fully-meshed core network to decrease the number of links?

4 What provides ways around failure points in the network?

5 What two things are most desirable in a routing protocol?

6 What can a routing protocol do to decrease it's burden to hosts that are not running routing on a network?

7 List the addressing problems that are caused by having multiple links to external networks.

8 Given the network shown in Figure 4-10, how many routes do you think a core router will have in its table if no summarization is applied?

9 How many routes do you think a core router will have in its table if all possible summarization is done?

10 Define the core, distribution, and access layers of the network shown in Figure 4-11.

11 Correct any problems in the topology that will affect the stability of the network pictured in Figure 4-11. Explain the changes you make and why.

12 Address the network shown in Figure 4-11 in a way that reduces the routes in the core to a minimum.

Figure 4-11 *Review Exercise Network*

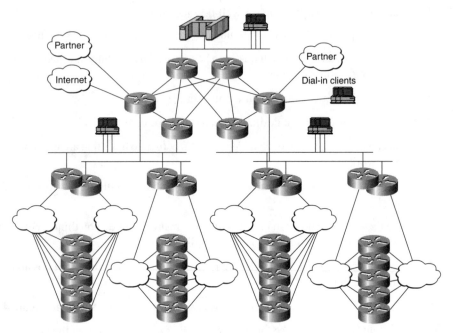

Scaling with Interior Gateway Protocols

CHAPTER 5

OSPF Network Design

Now that you are familiar with the basics of topology and addressing design from the first four chapters in the book, it's time to implement some routing protocols on the network (illustrated in Figure 4-10) to gain a little more practical understanding of the problems and tradeoffs you will be working with. This part of the book begins with Open Shortest Path First (OSPF) because this is a popular protocol. See Appendix A, "OSPF Fundamentals," for a short description of how OSPF works.

This chapter begins by considering how to divide the network up into areas because this decision affects many other design decisions. In this planning, you'll learn where to summarize and deal with some issues common to dial backup—ways of handling the dial-in clients, the problems dial-in links cause, and how to deal with the external connections to the network. Finally, you'll learn about which areas can become stub areas of various types.

Dividing the Network for OSPF Implementation

When implementing OSPF on a network, one design decision affects the implementation of everything else. So, it is important that you figure out how you are going to divide the network before beginning with your implementation of OSPF. Area border points will decide where you can do summarization, what areas can be stubby or not, and how the network can grow in the future. The solution to this dilemma tends to be confusing because OSPF uses a two level hierarchy and, here, you're working with a three level hierarchy.

OSPF's two level hierarchy has a core area and areas hanging off of that core. The network uses a three level design with a core, a distribution layer, and an access layer. The third layer really isn't accounted for in OSPF.

The chapter begins by looking at where to divide the network out toward the remote sites. Should the area borders be at the edge of the core or in the distribution layer?

Distribution Layer Design Issues: The Core Routers as ABRs

First, consider putting the area borders at the edge of the network core, which means defining the core network as area 0. All of the distribution layer routers connected to a given core router will be placed in one area. There are some major advantages to placing the area border routers (ABRs) at the edge of the core; look at Figure 5-1 to see where this will lead you.

Figure 5-1 *Dividing the Areas at the Core/Distribution Boundary*

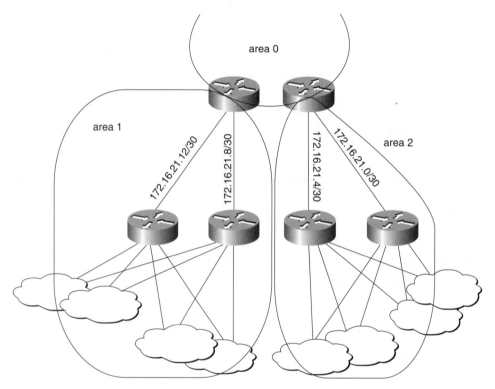

Following are some of the advantages of placing the ABRs at the edge of the core:

- Area 0 is very small.
- There shouldn't be any problems with suboptimal routing because the core routers only receive one route for any given set of destinations (summary). There aren't any distribution layer routers with two connections into the core.
- All the redundant links from the remote sites into the distribution layer are within the same area.
- Because all summarization will be done at the core/distribution layer border, the routing table in the core will be very small—possibly as low as six routes to reach all of the remote sites.

There are some disadvantages to placing the area borders at the core as well. The sections that follow address these disadvantages:

- Summarization at the core
- Dial backup past the summarization point
- Redundancy and router scaling

Summarization at the Core

If you make each of the core routers ABRs, all summarization takes place at the core. As noted in Chapter 1, "Hierarchical Design Principles," this isn't something that should be done in the core. Of course, you can break this rule if the stability of the network doesn't suffer (remember, stability is the goal of this entire exercise); however, you do need to be cautious with summarizing on the core routers.

This can also cause problems with scalability when this network grows because most of the growth is likely to take place in the distribution and access layers. You face the choice of either building a larger number of areas in these layers or having rather large areas, which could be a problem. Making these areas some sort of stub (covered later in this chapter) could improve the scalability.

Dial Backup past the Summarization Point

The rebuild of the network in Chapter 4, "Applying the Principles of Network Design," opted to remove the redundant links between the distribution and core routers in favor of a dial backup link from each distribution layer router and the DMZ-to-Core router (the same router the dial-in terminal server backs up to).

If you summarize at the core routers, the process of dialing in from a distribution layer router to a different core router that it normally attaches to effectively circumvents summarization.

To get a better feel for the problems involved, consider Figure 5-2.

When the link between Router A and Router B fails, Router A is configured so that it automatically dials into Router C, restoring connectivity. But what routes does Router C advertise?

If Router B is summarizing to a relatively short prefix (for example, 172.16.0.0/16), then Router C could summarize to a slightly longer prefix length (for example, 172.16.64.0/20), and this will all work. Because Router C will be advertising a longer prefix length for these routes, the path through Router C will be chosen.

Figure 5-2   *Dial Backup past the Point of Summarization*

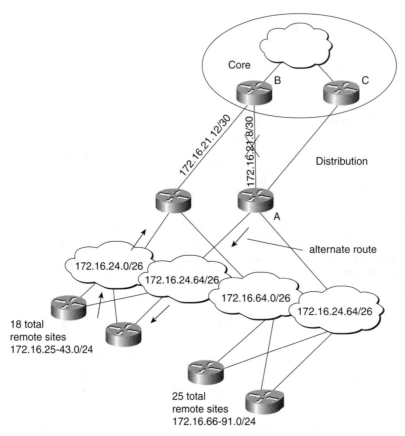

But what if Router B is advertising 172.16.64.0/20? Router C could advertise each route learned through Router B, but this effectively circumvents summarization — not good. The other option is for Router C to summarize to two longer prefixes so that some summarization is taking place. Here you could use 172.16.64.0/21 and 172.16.68.0/21.

Because the distribution layer routers have dial backup links into the core, and the core routers would be doing the summarization if the area border is between the core and the distribution layer, this is a problem in the network. On the other hand, the only time dial backup should be a problem is if the core Router B itself fails.

If the link between Router A and Router B fails, Router A will still have routes to all of the destinations reachable through the core because each remote site is dual-homed. Router A will learn all the routes it needs through some remote site back to the other distribution layer router in this area.

Of course, you don't want these dual-homed remotes to become transit paths. However, the chances of that happening isn't likely because the path through the other distribution layer router would always be better than the path through Router A, through another remote site, and, finally, up through the core.

The Distribution Layer Becomes Extraneous

If you summarize at the core router, you can effectively take the distribution routers out of the network because all they are providing you with is a bit of redundancy. By placing the area borders at the core of the network, you've effectively made this into a two-tier hierarchy.

This isn't to say that distribution layers can't be important in two-layer hierarchies. For instance, it might make sense to have a distribution layer even with a two-tier model. For example, a group of geographically close remote sites might be better off feeding into a distribution router and then to the core instead of running individual links to the core from each remote site.

Another issue is simply the number of links a router should have attached. The distribution layer isolates the core routers, to some degree, from having a large number of remote sites connected. Therefore, it isolates the core routers from various router-scaling issues. Most of these issues deal with queuing and packet forwarding rates and are out of the scope of this chapter.

Distribution Layer Design Issues: The Distribution Layer Routers as ABRs

Rather than putting the border between area 0 and the other areas at the core routers, try putting the links between the distribution routers and the core into area 0. All of the remotes behind one distribution layer router are then in the same area. Look at Figure 5-3 to see where this takes you.

Because summarization of internals can take place at the ABRs, you can summarize at the distribution layer routers. This design solution also avoids having any summarization problems with the dial backup links into the core because you can just have the distribution layer router advertise what it normally does through the dial connection.

The major drawback of this solution is that if the physical topology isn't designed correctly, the distribution layer routers can be drawn into acting as core routers. In other words, distribution layer routers can end up transiting traffic not just for the access layer devices attached to them, but also between two core routers or a core router and another distribution layer router. The physical layer design doesn't allow this to happen because there is only one link between each distribution layer and core router.

Figure 5-3 *The Distribution Layer Routers as ABRs*

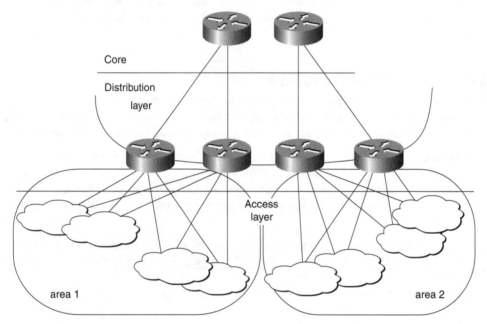

Why wasn't the access layer broken up into to four areas? Because each access layer router is dual-homed into a single distribution layer router. The redundant links between the remote sites and the distribution layer routers would be crossing area borders. See "Case Study: Which Area Should This Network Be In?" later in this chapter to get a better feel for why this is a bad idea in general.

Finalizing ABR Placement in the Distribution Layer Design

Is it better to put the area borders at the edge of the core, or at the edge of the distribution layer? Assume the following criteria:

- Summarization should occur at the distribution layer.

- The physical layer design prevents the distribution layer routers from being pulled into the core.

- No problems exist with dial-in between the distribution layer routers and core.

Given the options and tradeoffs, it seems best to partition the areas at the distribution layer.

Placing the HQ VLAN Routers

Next, move toward the HQ VLANs and figure out where the ABRs should be; Figure 5-4 shows only the core and the HQ VLANs in order to focus on this area.

Figure 5-4   *Examining HQ VLAN Routers for OSPF Implementation*

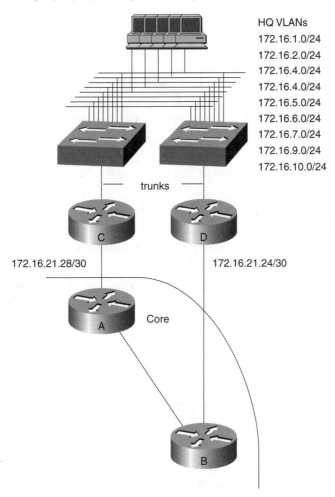

Although it isn't immediately obvious that putting the area border on the HQ VLAN routers versus the core routers to which they are attached is going to make any difference, you should run through the exercise anyway.

If you make Routers A and B the ABRs, then you summarize toward the core from them. Ignore this for now, due to the fact that you are summarizing on a core router, and consider instead what happens if Router C loses its connection to just one of the VLANs. Assume the connection is lost to 172.16.1.0/24.

Routers A and B would be oblivious to this event. They would still be advertising the 172.16.0.0/21 route toward the rest of the core. If, however, a packet were to arrive on Router A with a destination of 172.16.1.10, it will look in its routing table and find that the only route it has to this destination is the summary route.

The critical point to remember here is that when a Cisco router builds a summary route, it puts a route in the routing table to null0 for that entire range of addresses. Router A would forward this packet to 172.16.1.10 to the only route it has for that destination—null0. null0 is the bit bucket, so all traffic to 172.16.1.0/24 would be dropped by Router A.

How would this change if you were to make Routers C and D the ABRs? Go back to the scenario of Router C losing its connection to the 172.16.1.0/24 network. Instead of Router C having only a summary address in its routing table, it will have a specific route through Router D.

Of course, this assumes that all of the parallel VLANs will be running OSPF—but is this really what you want to do? You don't want these VLANs to transit traffic. (It's never a good idea to have transit traffic on a link with hosts attached.) You can configure all of these interfaces as passive and not configure OSPF on all but one of them.

You do need to run OSPF on at least one of these links to prevent packets from being sent to null0 if either Router C or Router D loses its connection to one (or more) of the VLANs. You should set aside a VLAN just for this purpose with no hosts or servers connected to it.

So, with all of the options considered, it's best to put the area border at the routers connected to the HQ VLANs rather than at the edge of the core.

Placing the Common Services Routers

Because the design of the common services networks is so similar to the HQ VLANs, the coverage won't be as in depth in this section. Consider Figure 5-5.

The major issue you face is dropping packets if either Router A or Router B loses its connection to one of the server farm segments, or the segment the mainframe is connected to.

To get around this, include the links between the core routers and the common services routers in area 0 and run OSPF on one of the links between the common services routers. This way you can summarize the parallel LANs between Routers A and B down to one advertisement, 172.16.16.0/22, into the core without risking dropping packets.

Figure 5-5   *Connections to the Common Services*

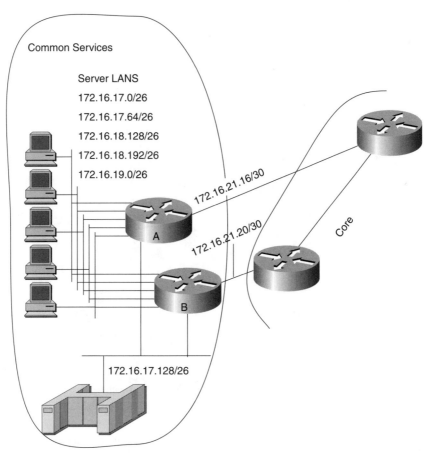

Placing Routers to Dial-In Links

The dial-in links connected to the terminal server are next; Figure 5-6 is reduced to only the links and routers involved for clarity.

The major problem you need to deal with here is that each time a client dials in, the Point-to-Point Protocol (PPP), which is the protocol used on the terminal server for connections to these dial-in users, installs a host route to the client's IP address in the routing table. If there is a network statement that includes that host route, it will be flooded to the entire area.

Likewise, when the client disconnects, the host route is removed from the routing table, and the removal of the route will need to be flooded to the rest of the routers in the area.

Figure 5-6   *Dial-In Links and Terminal Server*

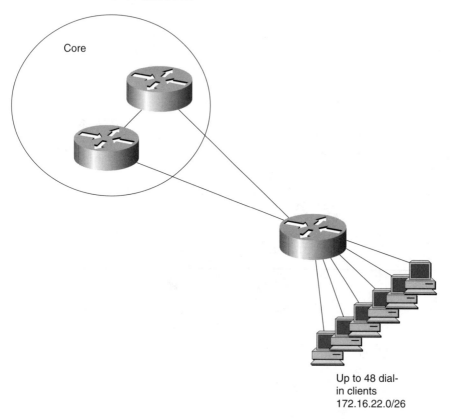

You have a couple different options for reducing flooding in an area caused by dial-in users:

- Make the terminal server an ABR
- Stop PPP from creating the host routes
- Don't run OSPF on dial-in links
- Advertise the dial-in clients off of a loopback interface

The sections that follow analyze each solution before arriving at a conclusion of which solution will work best for the network segment illustrated in Figure 5-6.

Solution 1: Make the Terminal Server an ABR

One of the easiest ways to handle dial-in links in OSPF is to simply summarize these host routes out at the nearest area border—and the closer the area border is, the better. You want to affect the fewest routers possible with these constantly flapping dial-in links.

Another problem you face is that the terminal server dials into another core router for backup. If the ABR is placed on the core router, the second core router must also be an ABR for this same area in case the terminal server ends up dialing into it.

The easiest thing to do, then, is to make the terminal server itself an ABR, and summarize the host routes into one destination, 172.16.22.0/24, toward the core.

Solution 2: Stop PPP from Creating the Host Routes

You can also stop PPP from creating these host routes by configuring **no peer neighbor-route** on the dial interface:

```
interface BRI0
 ip address 192.168.11.6 255.255.255.252
 encapsulation ppp
 dialer-group 1
 ppp authentication chap
 no peer neighbor-route
```

This gets rid of the host routes, but it doesn't provide any method to advertise the dial-in clients. One way you could advertise the dial-in clients is to use a redistributed static route, which leads us to the next solution.

Solution 3: The Static Alternative

It seems silly to make the terminal server into an ABR just to summarize these routes, and **no peer neighbor-route** leaves us without any way of advertising the dial-in clients.

Another way to handle this terminal server, which may or may not be easier (depending on the number of dial-up links and so forth), is to not run OSPF on the dial-in links at all. (In other words, don't cover the dial-in links with a **network** statement.)

Put the links between the terminal server and the core in area 0, create a static route summarizing all of the dial-in clients pointing to null0, and redistribute this static into OSPF. So, on the terminal server, you have:

```
ip route 172.16.22.0 255.255.255.0 null0
!
router ospf 1
 redistribute static
 default-metric 10
```

Solution 4: Advertise the Dial-In Clients Off of a Loopback Interface

Using a "static" means the route to the dial-in clients will be an external route. This may not be a problem in our network, but it could be a problem in a network where there are lots of dial-in clients attaching to terminal servers scattered all over the network because external LSAs are flooded everywhere in OSPF.

It's possible to make the route to the dial-in clients come out as an OSPF internal by assigning the address range of the clients to a loopback interface and including the loopback in OSPF. The key is to keep OSPF from advertising the network attached to the loopback interface as a host route as it normally does.

This can be accomplished by configuring the loopback interface as a point-to-point network type:

```
interface loopback 0
 ip address 172.16.22.1 255.255.255.0
 ip ospf network-type point-to-point
!
router ospf 1
 network 172.16.22.1 0.0.0.0
```

One warning about this approach: If a loopback interface is configured as an OSPF network type point-to-point, the router will not use the loopback address as its router ID. (It normally does.)

Notice that the loopback interface is included only in the **network** statement under **router ospf**. This is so that the individual dial-in client host routes don't get picked up and advertised, as well as the loopback address.

Determining the Best Solution for Dial-In Link Router Placement

If you don't mind the external OSPF route redistributing the static route, it seems this is the least confusing solution with the lowest administrative overhead. If there were a number of terminal servers in the network, and you didn't want externals flooded from each one, advertising the route off a loopback interface is probably better.

The only problem with advertising the route off of a loopback interface is that it can be confusing to understand what's being done with the configuration, and it changes the way OSPF chooses its router ID.

To avoid confusion, use the redistributed static solution. For more information on dial-in for backup, see "Case Study: Dial Backup," at the end of this chapter.

Establishing External Connection Routes

There are two sides to external routers in OSPF. First, they must be flooded throughout the network; they can't be summarized or filtered at ABRs into area 0 at all. Other than stubby areas, external link-state advertisements (LSAs) are flooded throughout the entire network.

Furthermore, each autonomous system boundary router (ASBR) in the network floods a Type 5 LSA, advertising that it, indeed, is an ASBR and any external destinations it advertised can be reached along the path to the ASBR.

On the other hand, losing an external route only produces a partial shortest path first (SPF) run in better implementations of OSPF. Because external routes always represent leaf nodes on the SPF tree, there is no reason to recalculate the entire tree when an external route is lost.

In general, you want to reduce the number of external routes in OSPF. This is something you must consider when trying to decide how to handle links to the partner networks and the Internet. Figure 5-7 presents a better idea of what your options are.

Figure 5-7   *External Network Connections*

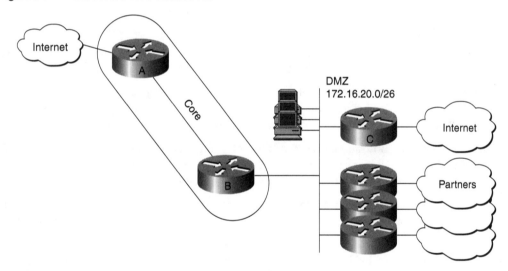

The obvious solution to all of this is to advertise a single default route from Router B into the core, which effectively summarizes all of the partner network's address space into one destination.

The problem occurs in the second link to the Internet off Router A. If you only advertised a default from Router B into the remainder of the core, you would lose connectivity to the partner networks if the Internet link failed from Router C and the alternate Internet link on Router A were to come up.

Although it would be nice to conditionally advertise destinations in the partner networks, OSPF doesn't have any sort of conditional advertisement as BGP does. Because you don't have conditional advertisement for anything but the default route, you need to examine the choices presented in the next few sections:

- Advertise the default and all externals
- Conditionally advertise a default route
- Move the backup Internet connection onto the DMZ

Solution 1: Advertise the Default and All Externals

You could make Router B an ABR, putting all of the external connections into a separate area. Each router that connects to an external network would become an ASBR, redistributing routes as necessary into the rest of the network. Router C would advertise a default route.

This all sounds fine, but for each external connection made, you end up with a new external and ASBR advertisement being flooded throughout your network. You can reduce the number of ASBR advertisements readily enough by a slight change in strategy.

If you run a routing protocol other than OSPF on the DMZ (such as EIGRP, IS-IS, or RIPv2), you can redistribute all of the external destinations into this secondary routing protocol and then redistribute this protocol into OSPF at Router B. What is the advantage of doing this?

Because the DMZ is a broadcast network, when Router B redistributes the external route into OSPF, the forwarding address will be set to the router that Router B heard the advertisement from. See "Case Study: OSPF Externals and the Next Hop," later in this chapter.

As long as Router B is running OSPF on the DMZ (although no other router is running OSPF on the DMZ—it could even be a passive interface on Router B), any addresses on the DMZ will appear to be OSPF internal routes to all the other routers on the network.

This solution converts Router B into a route server for all of the external routes. This cuts down on the number of Type 5 LSAs flooded into the network by cutting down on the number of ASBRs, although the overall number of external routes aren't affected.

To handle the second Internet connection, you would make certain that Router C is actually originating the default route, and Router B is redistributing it. On Router A, you can configure a floating static route so that if the external default route being originated by Router C ever fails, the floating static route configured on Router A would take over.

Solution 2: Conditionally Advertise a Default Route

If the floating static route on Router A seems a little messy, or if you would rather have the default route originated from Router B as an internal route, you can configure a conditionally advertised default route on Router B.

You can set up a **route-map** to make certain the network between Router C and the Internet service provider (ISP) is up, advertising the default route only when it is. You don't have the address for the link between the ISP and Router C, so you can fake it and say it's x.x.x.x:

```
access-list 10 permit x.x.x.x x.x.x.x
!
route-map advertise-default permit 10
 match ip address 10
!
router ospf 1
 default-information originate route-map advertise-default
```

With this configured, Router B will advertise the default route as long as network x.x.x.x exists. You still need some way of advertising a default route from Router A to make this work correctly, either a floating static or another conditional default route. Again, you don't know the link address between Router A and the Internet connection, so use y.y.y.y:

```
!
ip route 0.0.0.0 0.0.0.0 y.y.y.y 200
!
router ospf 1
 redistribute static
 default-metric 10
```

Solution 3: Move the Backup Internet Connection onto the DMZ

One additional solution is to move the alternate Internet connection onto the DMZ. The advantage of this is that it simplifies routing somewhat. You don't need to conditionally advertise anything, nor do you need to advertise any of the external destinations. Just a simple **default-information originate always** configured on Router B will do the trick. On Router B, this looks like the following:

```
!
router ospf 1
 default-information originate always
!
ip route 0.0.0.0 0.0.0.0 x.x.x.x
```

You can run some other protocol within the DMZ, which also provides some routing isolation from the rest of the network. This is the best option because it's the least troublesome to maintain, and it requires that only one link be moved (the alternate Internet connection).

It does leave a single point of failure, but this could be dealt with by adding a second router between the DMZ and the core, or some other strategy. Figure 5-8 shows what the DMZ looks like after implementing these changes.

Figure 5-8 *DMZ Design with a Second Routing Protocol*

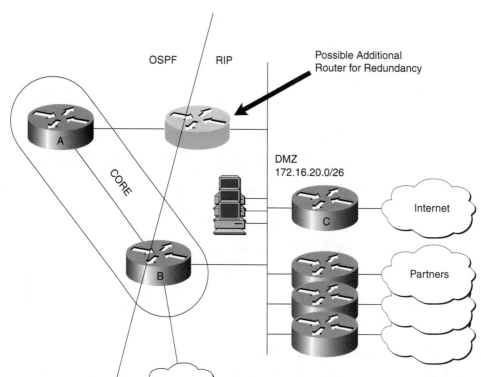

To Stub or Not to Stub

Up to this point in the chapter, it seems as though the dilemma of where to place all of the ABRs in the network has been solved. With OSPF, this leaves just one other question to consider—which areas should be stubbed? There are three types of stub areas in OSPF:

- **Stubby**—External routes are not advertised into stub areas, nor can they be generated from stub areas; routers in these areas rely on the default route to reach all externals.

- **Not-so-stubby areas (NSSAs)**—External routes are not advertised into NSSA areas (unless they originate within the area), but they can be generated within the area.

- **Totally stubby**—Neither external nor internal routes are advertised into a totally stubby area; all routers rely on a default route to reach any destination outside the area.

Refer to Figure 5-9, which presents how the areas are set up, to see if any of them can be stubbed.

Figure 5-9   *OSPF Areas*

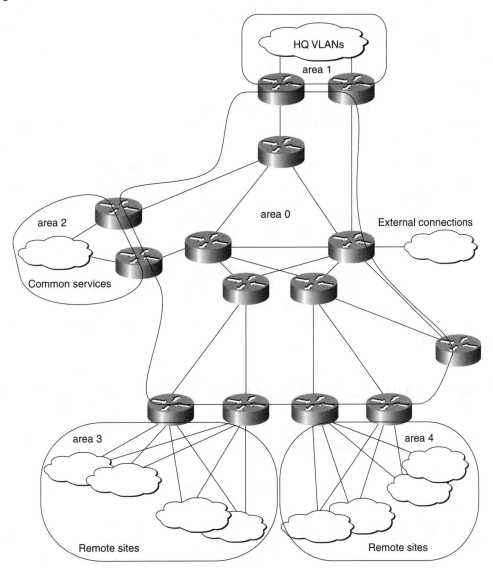

Totally Stubby Areas

Generally you wouldn't make an area totally stubby unless it had only one exit point. None of the areas in Figure 5-9 have only one exit point. Therefore, it doesn't seem useful to totally stub any of them.

Not-So-Stubby Areas

Not-so-stubby areas are generally used for areas that originate externals and don't need any information about the interior of the network. Since you aren't originating any external routes into the network, you probably won't need any NSSAs either.

Stubby Areas

Depending on traffic flow, some of these areas might make good candidates for regular stubs. In each area, it depends on the amount of traffic destined to external hosts and whether optimum routing is important:

- **area 0**—This area cannot be made into any type of a stub in an OSPF network.

- **area 1**—This area probably has a good deal of traffic to external links, although that's not certain. If it does, it should remain a normal area. The number of routers in the area (two) also influences you, here; it's small enough that flooding some externals into area 1 probably isn't going to be a problem.

- **area 2**—This area probably has very little contact with outside networks. If there is some host or service that external hosts will need to contact, suboptimum routing isn't much of an issue because both paths to the DMZ area are two hops. This could be a stub area.

- **areas 3 and 4**—There could be a great deal of traffic to external services from these areas, but there isn't much of a chance of suboptimal routing from them to the DMZ area. These can be stub areas.

Case Study: Troubleshooting OSPF Adjacency Problems

One of the various problems that you often run into with OSPF is when a pair of routers is attached to the same network, but they won't become fully adjacent. If you know the right things to look for, this type of problem can be quickly dealt with.

Before troubleshooting neighbors, which won't bring up an adjacency, you need to make certain that they should become fully adjacent. For example, the routers in Figure 5-10 are connected to the same link, but they will never become fully adjacent.

Assume that Router A becomes the designated router (DR) on this network, and Router B becomes the backup designated router (BDR). Since the DR is responsible for sending Router C any information it learns from Router D, there isn't any reason for Router C and Router D to become fully adjacent.

And, as a matter of fact, they won't. Routers C and D will build their neighbor relationship to the two-way state only, and they will never build a full adjacency.

The routers in Figure 5-11, however, should be building a full OSPF adjacency; they are connected through a point-to-point link, and they are both in area 0.

Figure 5-10   *Neighbor Relationships on a Broadcast Network*

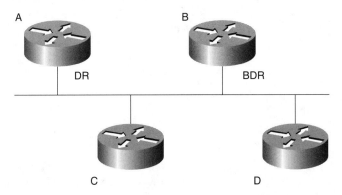

Figure 5-11   *Two OSPF Routers*

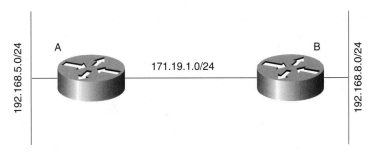

When you look at the **show ip ospf neighbor** output from either router, however, you can see that the adjacency isn't being built.

From Router A the output is as follows:

```
A#sho ip ospf nei
A#
```

The first thing to do when this type of problem occurs is to run **debug ip ospf adj** on one of the routers. Once again, from Router A, the output is as follows:

```
A#debug ip ospf adj
OSPF adjacency events debugging is on
A#
20:12:35: OSPF: Rcv hello from 172.19.10.1 area 0 from Serial0 172.19.1.2
20:12:35: OSPF: Mismatched hello parameters from 172.19.1.2
20:12:35: Dead R 40 C 80, Hello R 10 C 20
```

This output reveals that you have mismatched hello parameters, in this case the Dead and Hello timers are mismatched. The Hello timer on this router (labeled C in the **debug** output) is 20, while the Hello timer on the remote router (labeled R in the **debug** output) is 10. Looking at the configuration on Router A, you see the following:

```
!
interface Serial0
 ip address 172.19.1.1 255.255.255.0
 no ip directed-broadcast
ip ospf hello-interval 20
 no ip mroute-cache
 !
```

The OSPF Hello interval on this interface has been set to 20. Correcting this should fix the problem. The Hello interval, Dead interval, wait time, and link type all have to match for OSPF routers to become fully adjacent.

However, other problems aren't so easy to find quickly, unless you know specifically what you are looking for. Next, correct the timers and see if the neighbors will come up into FULL state. A few executions of the **show ip ospf neighbor** command reveals the following:

```
A#show ip ospf neighbors
Neighbor ID     Pri   State          Dead Time   Address        Interface
172.19.10.1      1    INIT/  -       00:00:35    172.19.1.2     Serial0
A#show ip ospf neighbors
Neighbor ID     Pri   State          Dead Time   Address        Interface
172.19.10.1      1    EXCHANGE/  -    00:00:35    172.19.1.2     Serial0
rp-4700-13A#sho ip ospf nei
Neighbor ID     Pri   State          Dead Time   Address        Interface
172.19.10.1      1    INIT/  -       00:00:35    172.19.1.2     Serial0
A#show ip ospf neighbors
Neighbor ID     Pri   State          Dead Time   Address        Interface
172.19.10.1      1    EXCHANGE/  -    00:00:35    172.19.1.2     Serial0
```

Even though the mismatched timers have been corrected, the routers still won't become adjacent. They just flip-flop between INIT and EXCHANGE modes.

EXCHANGE state means you are trying to exchange databases with the neighbor. So, the logical assumption is that you are getting hello packets across the link, but not database information.

Why would hello packets be okay and database packets not be okay? Well, hello packets are small, while database packets are large. Prove this theory by **ping**ing with some various sized packets across the link between the two routers using an extended **ping** as follows:

```
A#ping
Protocol [ip]:
Target IP address: 172.19.1.2
Repeat count [5]: 1
Extended commands [n]: y
Sweep range of sizes [n]: y
Sweep min size [36]: 100
Sweep max size [18024]: 1500
Sweep interval [1]: 100
Type escape sequence to abort.
Sending 15, [100..1500]-byte ICMP Echos to 172.19.1.2, timeout is 2 seconds:
!...............
Success rate is 6 percent (1/15), round-trip min/avg/max = 1/1/1 ms
```

You can see from the preceding output that the **ping** fails with a packet size of 200 bytes, which seems very small. Take a look at the router on the other end of the link and see how the interface is configured:

```
interface Serial0
 mtu 100
 ip address 172.19.1.2 255.255.255.0
```

So, it looks like you've found the problem—the MTU size is mismatched on the link. One router thinks the MTU is 100 bytes, while the other end thinks it is 1500 bytes. Because the hello packets are only 64 bytes, both routers can send and receive them with no problems. But when it comes time to send and receive maximum sized database descriptor (DBD) packets, Router B, with an MTU of 100 bytes, will drop the 1500 bytes packets generated by Router A.

One side note—Cisco routers running newer software will not have this problem because the routers exchange the MTU size of the link in their hello packets. When they exchange LSAs or DBDs, they limit their packet sizes to the minimum MTU on the link.

Of course, if the MTU of one end of a link is different than the MTU of the other end of the link, larger packets will still fail to cross the link in one direction, regardless of OSPF's ability to bring up an adjacency. This just shifts the problem from building the adjacency to the more esoteric problem of some applications not working across the link, or FTP control sessions working correctly by data sessions failing.

Case Study: Which Area Should This Network Be In?

Sometimes you may find that a given remote router has been, or needs to be, dual-homed to routers in different areas, as shown in Figure 5-12.

Figure 5-12 *Remote Dual-Homed into Two Different Areas*

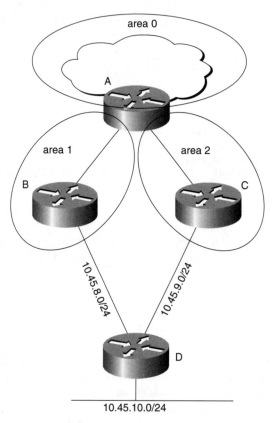

When dual homing a remote site to two routers in different areas, you need to decide which area to put each link in. Begin by putting the serial link between Routers D and B in area 1 and the serial link between Routers D and C in area 2; these changes are illustrated in Figure 5-13. Now that you have those two down, you still have one small enigma to handle: Which area do you put the remote Ethernet in?

If you put the Ethernet link in area 1, Router C will route traffic to the Ethernet link completely through the core of the network to reach it—talk about suboptimal routing! Putting the Ethernet in area 1 also defeats the purpose of dual homing the remote. Since traffic can't travel from area 1 (the Ethernet) through area 2 (the serial link between Routers D and C) to area 0, the dual homing doesn't provide any redundancy.

All of these same problems apply in the opposite direction if you put the remote Ethernet in area 2.

Figure 5-13   *Adding the Two Serials to Areas 1 and 2*

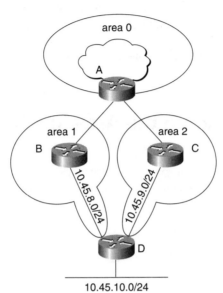

A Third Area and Virtual Links

One possibility is to put this Ethernet in a third area (for example, area 3) and run virtual links between area 3 and area 0 through both area 1 and area 2. This will work, but it also presents a major suboptimal routing problem.

Suppose that a host attached to Router C wants to reach a destination on this remote Ethernet. Because all traffic between areas must pass through area 0, the packets would be passed to area 0 by Router C, then back through the virtual link to Router D, and, finally, to their destination.

Using redistribute connected to Advertise the Remote Network

One possible solution for this type of a problem is to simply redistribute the Ethernet into both areas from Router D. It's simple enough to configure:

```
!
hostname D
!
router ospf 10
 net 10.45.8.0 0.0.0.255 area 1
 net 10.45.9.0 0.0.0.255 area 2
 redistribute connected
```

Don't Dual-Home Remotes into Different Areas

Finally, you could find some way to connect this remote site so the problem doesn't exist. This is the best solution because it doesn't add externals into the mix, and there aren't any problems with suboptimal routing. If possible, avoid remotes that are dual-homed into two different areas. Instead, find a way to connect any remote sites that need to be dual-homed to routers in the same area.

Case Study: Determining the Area in Which to Place a Link

Figure 5-14 presents a situation you might come across from time to time, where Router C and Router D are ABRs, while Router A and Router B are in area 0, and Router E and Router F are in area 1.

Figure 5-14   *What Area Should the Network in the Middle Be In?*

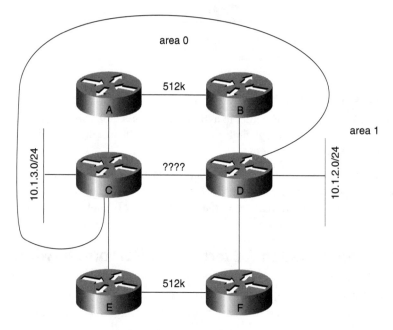

What do you do with the WAN link in the middle? Should it be in area 0, or area 1? Begin by putting the WAN link in area 0—it is a direct link between two core routers, so it's probably supposed to be in the network core.

Assuming no summarization at the area border, Router C will have two routes to 10.1.2.0/24:

- An inter-area route through the WAN link
- An intra-area route through Router E, the 512k link in area 1, Router F, then Router D

Since OSPF always prefers intra-area routes over interarea routes, Router C will choose the path through Router E (the 512k link), Router F, and then Router D, rather than the one hop WAN link through area 0. This is relatively radical suboptimal routing, so try putting the WAN link in area 1.

Placing the WAN link in area 1 presents the same problem—only this time it's for the 10.1.3.0/24 network. Router D is going to prefer the link through Router B (the 512k link), Router A, then Router C, rather than the one hop path over the WAN link through Router C. How do you resolve this?

You could put the WAN link in area 0 and then configure some static routes to get around the problem:

- On Router D, a static route for 10.1.3.0/24 via Router C
- On Router C, a static route for 10.1.2.0/24 via Router D

This doesn't seem like a very scalable solution, though, and you are trying to build a network that will scale. You need another option.

It's also possible to put the WAN link in area 1 and then build a virtual link across it so that it is in both area 0 and area 1; however, a virtual link shouldn't be used unless it's absolutely necessary.

The only other option is to fix the network design. Either this is a bad place to put an area border, or there is something wrong with the design of this network's topology. This is the preferred option: Fix the physical network topology so this isn't a problem!

Case Study: Dial Backup

One of the problems you face when using dial backup in OSPF is where the router dials into versus where the area borders are. Figure 5-15 will be useful in seeing what the problems are and in considering some solutions.

You want Router F to dial up to some other router when Router E loses its connection to Router C. You can either dial into Router D, Router A, or Router B; but the question is which one?

The immediate choice would be to configure Router F to dial into Router D if the remote segment loses all connectivity through Router E, but this still leaves a single point of failure at Router A. The single point of failure could be solved by moving the link between Routers D and A so that the link runs between Routers D and B instead, but this could cause routing problems and so forth in the network. So, you don't want to go with that solution.

Figure 5-15   *Dial Backup in OSPF*

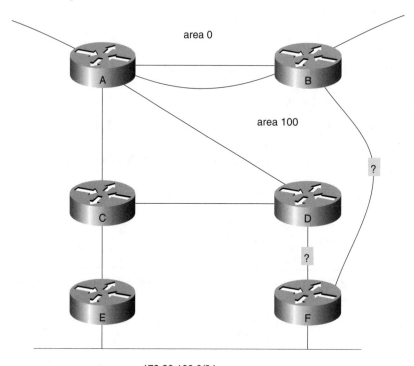

172.30.100.0/24

Dialing into Router A itself isn't going to solve the single point of failure problem, so the only other option is to dial into Router B. But this means that there will appear to be two area 100s connected to area 0—one through Router A, and the other through Router B. Is this legal?

When an ABR begins building LSAs for area 0, it takes the routing information from each of its other areas and bundles them into summary LSAs (Type 3 LSAs, to be exact). The summary LSAs don't contain any area information. Therefore, the other routers on the core simply don't know what areas these destinations are in. The routers only know that to reach these destinations, the next hop is a given ABR.

So, it *is* legal to have multiple areas with the same area ID attached to the same area 0, and to configure Router F to dial into Router B as a backup. The only other issue that remains is any possible summarization that might be taking place on Router A, the normal ABR for area 100.

The trick here is not to just summarize off the dial-in link on Router B. Router B will then advertise specific routes to anything behind Router F, while Router A will continue to advertise the summaries it's configured for.

Case Study: OSPF Externals and the Next Hop

One of the more interesting aspects of OSPF's handling of external routes is the forwarding address. Looking at a **show ip ospf database** for an external site reveals the following:

```
router#sho ip ospf data extern
        OSPF Router with ID (130.30.4.9) (Process ID 3100)
                AS External Link States
   Routing Bit Set on this LSA
LS Type: AS External Link
   Link State ID: 10.1.1.0 (External Network Number )
   Advertising Router: 130.30.0.193
Network Mask: /24
        Metric Type: 2 (Larger than any link state path)
Forward Address: 0.0.0.0
```

A few fields have been deleted from the preceding output to make it easier to see the fields that are important to the discussion at hand. The following three fields are particularly interesting:

- **Routing Bit Set on this LSA**—This means the route is valid and will be in the forwarding/routing table. The routing/forwarding table is what you see in a **sh ip route**.

- **Advertising Router**—This is the router ID of the router advertising this external destination.

- **Forward Address**—This is the address to forward traffic destined to this network.

The output reveals a forwarding address of 0.0.0.0; this means forwarded packets destined to this network are sent to the advertising router. For the routing bit to be set on this LSA, there must be a router LSA for the advertising router in the OSPF database.

But the forwarding address could be different than the advertising router. See Figure 5-16 as an example.

Here, Routers A and B are running OSPF, while B is learning some routes from other routers through RIP and redistributing them into OSPF. If you look at the external LSA for 172.30.0.0/16 on Router A, you will see the following:

```
A#sho ip ospf data extern
        OSPF Router with ID (130.30.4.9) (Process ID 3100)
                AS External Link States
   Routing Bit Set on this LSA
LS Type: AS External Link
   Link State ID: 172.30.0.0 (External Network Number )
   Advertising Router: 10.1.1.1
Network Mask: /16
        Metric Type: 2 (Larger than any link state path)
Forward Address: 10.1.1.2
```

Figure 5-16   *Setting the Forwarding Address in an OSPF External Site*

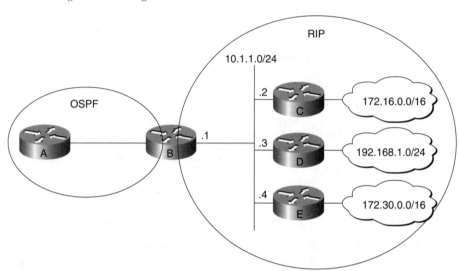

The **Forward Address** field now shows the address of Router C rather than 0.0.0.0. There are times when you will see this and the **Routing Bit Set on this LSA** field won't show up. This is because the forwarding address must be reachable as an internal OSPF LSA.

For example, if Router B were redistributing the 10.1.1.0/24 network into OSPF as well as the RIP routes, then the next hop, 10.1.1.2, would be an external site. OSPF will never forward an external site through an external site. (This is a defense against routing loops.)

Why does OSPF do this, anyway? Why not just use the router ID of the redistributing router all the time? Because in the preceding scenario, Router A could have an alternate path to 10.1.1.0/24, which is much better than the route through Router B.

Review

1   What parameters must be matched for OSPF routers to become adjacent?

2   Is it ever normal for two OSPF routers to reach only a two-way state? When?

3   What is a good way to test for MTU mismatches?

4   Explain why having a router dial backup beyond the point of summarization is bad.

5   What options do you have with a remote dual-homed into two different areas?

6   Explain how you can end up throwing packets away if you summarize on Routers A and B in Figure 5-17 to 172.27.0.0/16?

Figure 5-17   *Diagram for Review Question 6*

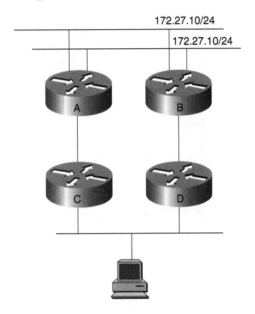

7   Can you have multiple areas with the same area number?

8   What one issue must you design around when dealing with dial-in links?

9   Where are external LSAs flooded?

10   What type of SPF run is required when the state of external links change?

11   How do you inject default routes into OSPF?

12   What does the **always** keyword do on the end of the **default-information originate** command?

13   What is the **Forward Address** in the OSPF database used for?

14   What is the difference between a totally stubby area and a stubby area?

15   Implement OSPF on the network you redesigned for review question 11 in Chapter 4, "Applying the Principles of Network Design." Place the ASBRs, deal with any design issues raised, and decide which areas can be stubbed.

CHAPTER 6

IS-IS Network Design

The Intermediate System-to-Intermediate System (IS-IS) protocol was originally designed to provide routing information for the Open Systems Interconnect (OSI) protocols. IS-IS is a link-state protocol in which Intermediate Systems (ISs), or routers, flood routing information to each other within hierarchical levels.

So why would you want to consider IS-IS for routing in a large-scale IP network? In fact, I'm certain some people out there right now are thinking, "IS-IS—are you crazy? It's so hard to configure."

On the contrary, IS-IS is used in very large-scale IP networks, primarily because of its flexible timers, fast convergence, and capability to handle instability in the IP routing domain very well. It's to IS-IS's advantage, in many cases, that it wasn't originally designed for routing IP, but rather, that it was adapted for IP routing by the Internet Engineering Task Force (IETF). The main advantage is that changes in IP routing information don't affect the core of its functionality, which is to provide Connectionless Network Service (CLNS) routing information.

This chapter works through implementing IS-IS on the network built in Chapter 4, "Applying the Principles of Network Design," so that you can get a feel for the issues involved. There are plenty of case studies in this chapter that cover different aspects of IS-IS's operation, various design options and issues, and some troubleshooting tips.

Dividing the Network

The first question you must always ask when contending with a routing protocol that provides multiple levels of routing (such as OSPF and IS-IS) is: Where do I divide up the network? The answer to this question predetermines many other design problems and solutions, so you must answer it carefully.

In IS-IS the network is divided up into areas, with level 1 (L1) routing taking place *within* the areas and level 2 (L2) routing taking place *between* the areas. L1 routers understand the topology of only the area they are within, whereas L2 routers know how to route packets traveling between these areas. (See Appendix B, "IS-IS Fundamentals," for more information on how IS-IS works.) The critical issue is where to put these boundaries between the L1 areas, or rather, where to place L2 routers in the network.

The following are issues that you need to think about when deciding where to place area borders in the network:

- All L2 routers must form a contiguous core. In other words, two L2 routers cannot be separated by a L1 router someplace in the middle.

- Most IS-IS routers do not automatically repair a partition's L2 area. If the contiguous group of L2 routers is split through a network failure, most IS-IS routers cannot automatically use L1 links to repair the broken core. It's important to leave enough redundancy between the L2 routers so that a single link failure will not cause the core to be partitioned. You should try to reduce the number of routers running both L1 and L2 routing if possible.

- IP network summarization can occur only on L2 routers. Therefore, you need to make certain that L2 routers are placed where summarization will take place.

Given these issues, you need to look at the individual cases in the network and think through where it would be best to place the L2 routers. Figure 6-1 removes some of the detail to make these issues easier to examine.

Start your examination of the network division by assuming all routers in the core are going to be L2 routers.

Analyzing Routers in the Distribution Layer

The first section of the network to look at is the largest section of routers outside the core—the routers in the distribution layer between the core and the remotes. Should these routers participate in L2 routing along with the core? This section examines the issues surrounding this question, including summarization, area size, and routing efficiency.

Configuring the Distribution Layer Routers as L1 Routers

Summarization and eventual area size are two of the main issues to consider when you put these routers in their own areas as only L1 routers.

With regard to summarization (because only L2 routers can summarize IP subnets), the decision not to run L2 routing out to these distribution layer routers means summarization must take place on the core routers, which is contrary to the core's design goals.

With regard to area size, if any distribution layer router eventually has a large number of remote sites attached to it, too many routers could end up being in a single area, making administration and general care and feeding of the network more difficult.

Figure 6-1   *The Network*

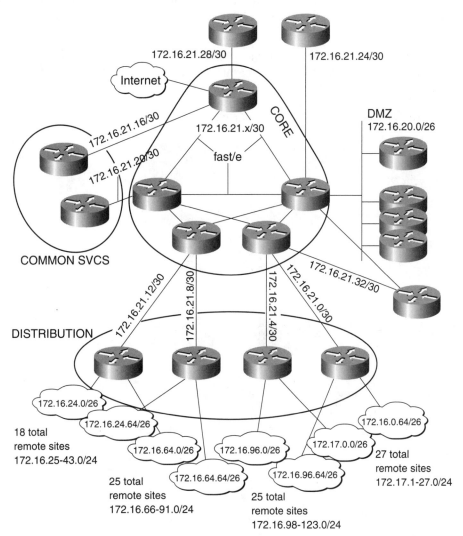

Configuring the Distribution Layer Routers as L2 Routers

However, you might decide to configure these distribution layer routers as part of the L2 core area. There are also some factors to consider here.

With regard to summarization, because the distribution layer routers are running L2 routing, they can summarize toward the core, which is good. This doesn't preclude summarization at the edge of the core (because the core routers are running L2 routing as well), but it lightens the load on these routers in any case.

The disadvantage of this approach is the possibility for traffic from one remote site to another to be routed suboptimally. Consider, for example, the small piece of the network illustrated in Figure 6-2.

Figure 6-2   *Suboptimal Routing with Distribution Layer Routers in the Core*

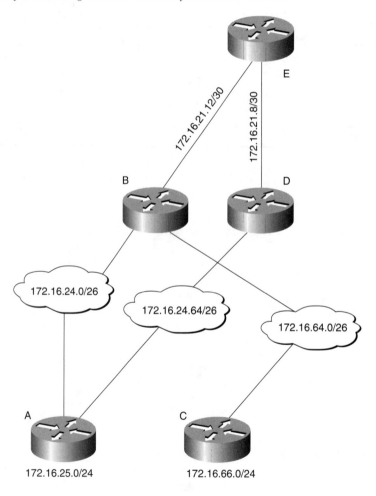

Assume Router A chooses Router D as its nearest L2 router, and Router C chooses Router B as its nearest L2 router. Because all L1 routers choose the nearest L2 router to exit their area and pass all traffic through that L2 router, Router A ends up using the rather long path through Router E to reach 172.16.66.0/24, even though there is a path through its other link.

If traffic flow between remote sites is common, suboptimal routing argues strongly for the distribution layer routers to run L1 routing only.

If the number of distribution layer routers grows large and you run L2 routing down to the distribution layer, it could result in a larger number of routers running both L1 and L2 routing. Because you want to reduce the number of routers running both L1 and L2 routing, this is something you should be concerned with.

Distribution Layer Routers: L1 or L2?

There isn't any real way to make a final decision about whether to configure distribution layer routers as L1 or L2 without knowing more about the growth plans and traffic patterns on this network. The three key things you need to know to make this decision are as follows:

- How much traffic will flow between the remote sites, and how important is it that routing between the remote sites be optimized?
- How many remote routers will eventually attach to a given distribution layer router?
- How many distribution layer routers will there eventually be?

Given that you don't know the answer to these questions, the best option is to reduce the number of routers running L1 and L2 routing and only run L1 routing on these distribution layer routers. It's important to note that doing this results in summarizing IP subnets on the core routers, which was previously stated as something that shouldn't be done.

Remember, however, that network design is a series of tradeoffs; it's important to know the rules and when it's okay to break them. Remember that the final goal isn't to simply follow the rules of good hierarchical network design, but to provide the most stability you can within the constraints of network size, traffic patterns, and other factors.

Analyzing Routers in the Common Services Area

The next part of the network to look at is where the two routers connect the core of the network to the common services. You can run either L2 or L1 routing on these routers. Figure 6-3 removes some of the detail from the network illustration in Figure 6-1 to cut the problem down to size.

Figure 6-3 *Routers Connecting the Network Core to the Common Services*

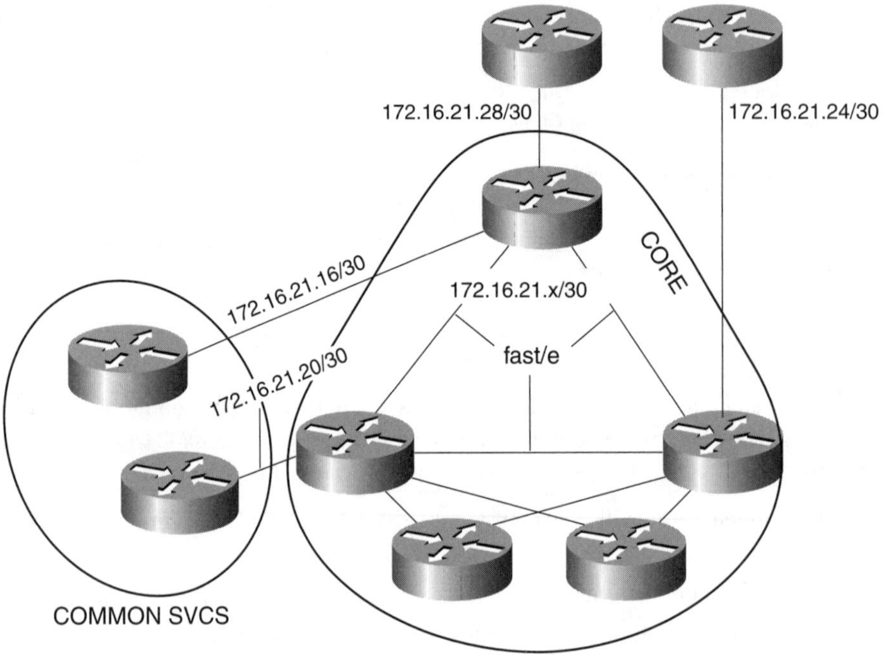

There are three primary issues to consider here—a subset of those that you considered when looking at what to do with the distribution layer routers:

- **Summarization**—If these two routers are running as L1 routers only, then any summarization must be done on the core routers.

- **Suboptimal routing**—If these two routers only run L1 routing, they will choose one exit point from their area. No matter which core router they choose as their exit point, they will sometimes use suboptimal paths over the network core to reach some destinations.

- **Number of routers running L2 routing**—If these routers run L2 routing, it will increase the number of routers in the network running both L1 and L2 routing.

Consider the tradeoffs. If optimal routing is important (which seems to be the case for routers connecting the core to a set of common services), then it's probably important to run L2 routing on these routers.

In fact, any time there are multiple connections to the core (as is the case in both of these situations), you will have these tradeoffs and considerations. However, the answer may not be the same in every situation.

Suboptimal routing is not such an issue if the second link is purely used for redundancy; however, if the second link is to load-share with the first link, suboptimal routing can be a problem.

For the sake of argument, assume that there are business factors in this network which state that the suboptimal routing isn't acceptable. So, these routers are run as part of the L2 core.

Analyzing Routers on the DMZ for External Connections

The decision of whether the routers on the DeMilitarized Zone (DMZ) should only run L1 routing or participate in L2 routing depends on the mechanics of advertising these external networks into the core.

If the only connections to external networks were through this DMZ, it would be relatively simple to advertise a single default route into the core; however, there is a backup Internet connection over on the other side of the network. To get a better handle on this, refer to Figure 6-4.

Figure 6-4   *External Connections*

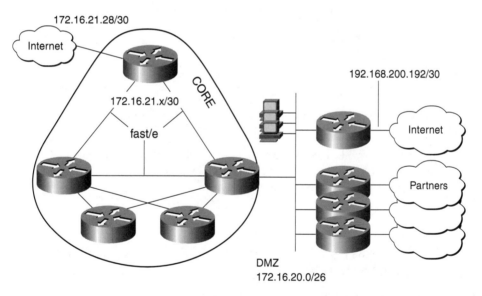

To optimize this portion of the network, you need to be able to do the following:

* Advertise a default route from the router that connects to the Internet, unless this connection to the Internet is down.

* Advertise a default route from the router with the backup connection to the Internet when necessary.

* Advertise a minimal number of external routes to the partner networks.

Because summarization can only occur on L2 routers, you can either run the routers on the DMZ as L1 routers and let the core router attached to the DMZ do the summarization, or you can run all of these routers as L2 routers and allow them to do their own summarization.

Because the preference for this network is to avoid summarization in the core, these routers are run in L2 with the understanding that this decision may need to be changed if a large number of routers end up being connected to the DMZ in the future.

Each router that connects to a partner will advertise the routes available through that partner, and the router that connects to the Internet will advertise a default route.

To advertise a default route in IS-IS, you generally don't redistribute a static route to the 0.0.0.0/0 network; instead, you configure **default-information originate** under the IS-IS routing protocol.

There is only one problem with this approach of advertising the Internet router: How does the Internet router know when to stop advertising its default route and allow the alternate connection to take over? IS-IS handles this by allowing you to conditionally advertise the default route.

Consider the following configuration for the Internet router:

```
route-map advertise-default permit 10
 match ip address 10
 !
access-list 10 permit 192.168.200.192 0.0.0.3
 !
router isis
 default-information originate route-map advertise-default
```

The Internet router will advertise the default route only if the 192.168.200.192/30 route is in its IS-IS database. Note that this means you must run IS-IS on this link, even though you probably aren't going to run IS-IS with the service provider.

An Alternate Internet Connection Backup Solution

An alternate solution is to move the backup Internet connection so that it's behind the router connecting the DMZ to the network core. Figure 6-5 illustrates this link move.

With this alternate connection moved, you can reconsider whether or not to make the routers on the DMZ L1 only, or L2. Because all external connectivity will now pass through this single core router, there is no reason to leak specific information on the partner's networks into the L2 core.

Instead, the router between the core and the DMZ can advertise a single default route to provide reachability to all of these networks using a simple default information originate.

Figure 6-5   *Moving the Alternate Internet Connection onto the DMZ*

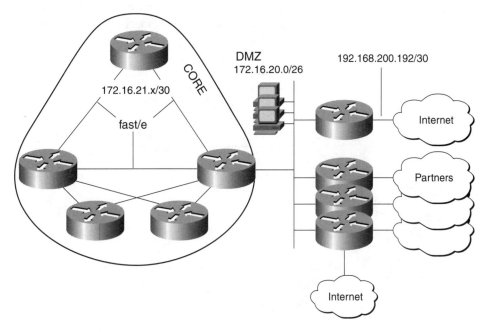

This illustrates an important point about network design—it's very common to see dial backups and redundant links placed on the wrong side of summarization points in a network. It's generally possible to get these types of designs to work, but it's never optimal, and it generally contributes to network instability.

Analyzing Routers on the DMZ for Dial-In Clients

Should the access server that dial-in clients connect to be configured to route L1 or L2? One important thing to remember about access servers is that they automatically generate a host route (32-bit mask) for each dial-in session they accept. You certainly don't want these host routes floating around in the network causing reconvergence each time a client connects or disconnects.

You need to make certain these host routes are either not advertised into IS-IS, or they are summarized down to a single route. So once again, you need to decide if you want the core router to summarize these host routes or the access server itself.

It seems to be harmless enough to allow the core router to do the summarization if it weren't for the dial backup link between the access server and a second core router. Unless you want to configure (and maintain) the summarization on both of these core routers, it's best to go ahead and place the access server in the L2 domain.

The Final IS-IS Network Design

Working out which routers will be L1 and L2 accomplishes most of the design work for this network. The only remaining things to define are the area borders and summarization. Use Figure 6-6 to work through these final issues.

Figure 6-6   *Final IS-IS Network Design*

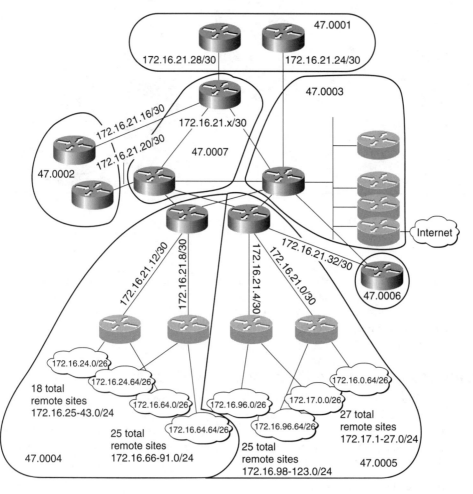

The routers that are lighter gray will be running L1 routing only. This breaks the network up into the areas labeled 47.001 through 47.006. For summarization, you have

- **47.0001**—Both L2 routers will summarize to 172.16.0.0/21 into the core.
- **47.0002**—Both L2 routers connected to the server farm will advertise summaries for 172.16.10.0/22 and any individual 172.16.21.x links.

- **47.0003**—The L2 router bordering the DMZ area will advertise a 0.0.0.0/0 default route.
- **47.0004**—Advertises 172.16.24.0/21, 172.16.32.0/19, 172.16.64.0/19, and any individual 172.16.21.x networks.
- **47.0005**—Advertises 172.16.96.0/21, 172.17.0.0/19, and any individual 172.16.21.x networks.
- **47.0006**—Advertises 172.16.22.0/24 through a summary address.

Other Factors in IS-IS Scaling

There are at least four protocol structure factors that need to be considered when working with IS-IS: SPF flooding, the number of pseudonodes allowed in an area, the possibility of overrunning the IS-IS database on a given router, and metrics.

Link State Flooding

One of the major factors to consider when you're using any link-state protocol is the amount of flooding that occurs. Excessive flooding can cause excessive SPF runs, which eat CPU time and memory on the routers.

IS-IS in an IP network has an immediate advantage because it treats all IP reachability information as leaf nodes in the shortest path tree. Because of this, any change in IP reachability information is always only a partial shortest path first (SPF) run—the leaf nodes of the tree are recalculated, but the remainder of the tree (which represents CLNS reachability) is left alone.

It's easiest to think of this as if there are actually two sections in the SPF tree (although there aren't). The primary part of the SPF tree contains information on the reachability of other routers in the area, whereas the rest of the tree contains information on the reachability of IP destinations within the network. When the reachability of any IP network changes, only the smaller part of the table needs to be changed.

Of course, any time an internal link (between routers) fails, or a router fails, a full SPF run must take place within that area.

Another issue with link-state protocols is the aging of the database. Once a particular link-state packet (LSP) ages out, the originating router must reflood it. This occurs by default every twenty minutes in IS-IS. A full SPF run on every router in the network every 20 minutes with a large number of routes can spell trouble for memory and processor utilization.

Fortunately, there is a way around this. The aging timers are adjustable in IS-IS. You can set the maximum age for LSPs using the **max-lsp-lifetime** command, and the rate at which LSPs are refreshed using the **lsp-refresh-interval** command (and it's probably a good idea to do so on larger networks).

LSP Corruption

It is possible, on certain types of links, for the packet contents to be corrupted, but the data link layer error correction fields not to show it. For example, a switch that translates from Token Ring or FDDI to Ethernet, like the one illustrated in Figure 6-7, could easily corrupt data. But, because the Layer 2 CRC must be regenerated when the packet is rebuilt in the new format, the data corruption could go unnoticed.

Figure 6-7   *LSP Corruption*

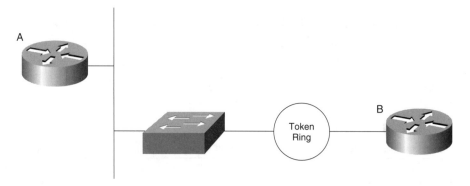

If Router A generates an LSP and multicasts it toward Router B on the Ethernet, the switch (during the translation to Token Ring) can corrupt the packet. When the packet reaches Router B, it would pass the Layer 2 checks in the router and be passed to IS-IS for processing.

When the IS-IS process on Router B discovers the information in the packet is corrupted (by looking at the Layer 3 checksum information), it will change the LSP's remaining lifetime field to 0 and reflood the packet to purge the bad information from the network.

Router A will see this reflooding of an LSP it originated, generate a new copy of the LSP, and flood it again to make certain other routers on the network have current information on its links.

If the switch corrupts the packet again, the entire process will repeat itself, possibly causing an LSP reflood storm in the network. The obvious answer to this problem is to fix the switch—but sometimes it's not that easy. While you're fixing the switch, Routers A and B are flooding this LSP back and forth, causing other problems on your network.

It is possible to turn off the reflooding part of this problem on Router B by configuring the router to ignore LSPs with invalid checksums, rather than attempting to flush them from the network. The command to configure this behavior is **ignore-LSP-errors**.

When would you want to turn off error checking for LSPs? Generally, you wouldn't, but it might be useful when you are receiving a lot of errors, tracking these errors through some other means, and want to provide some stability back into your network.

Maximum Number of Pseudonodes

There is a hard limit on the number of pseudonodes within an area of 255. In other words, you can't have more than 255 multi-access networks within one area.

Overflowing the Database

It is possible (but a very rare condition) to overflow the LSP database on the router when trying to put a large number of routes on a small router. If this happens, the router that is overloaded will set the overload bit in its LSPs.

A router advertising LSPs with the overload bit set is indicating that it doesn't have a complete database. To prevent loops, other routers will use the LSPs generated by this router but will not rely on paths that must pass through this router.

The overload bit can be seen in the IS-IS database:

```
Rtr-A> show isis database

IS-IS Level-1 Link State Database
LSPID                LSP Seq Num  LSP Checksum  LSP Holdtime  ATT/P/OL
1789.6800.A49C.00-00  0x00000006   0x4D70        748           1/0/1  (4)
1789.6800.4513.00-00* 0x00000002   0x356F        541           0/0/0  (1)
1789.6800.6CA5.01-00* 0x00000001   0x50E4        220           0/0/0  (2)
```

Metrics

In IS-IS, internal metrics fall between 0 and 63, whereas external routes fall between 64 and 127. These small ranges of metrics improve the efficiency of the SPF calculations, but they also leave little room to maneuver when assigning metrics to links in your network for optimum routing.

The default interface cost in IS-IS is 10; in larger scale networks, it's obvious that this default metric won't leave you much in the way of number of hops possible.

You'll need to spend some serious time thinking about what costs to assign to various interfaces in your network when implementing IS-IS so that you don't find yourself in a position where the total hop count through the network is severely limited. This is a very important consideration when designing large-scale IS-IS networks.

Troubleshooting IS-IS Neighbor Relationships

There are two instances where IS-IS will not form neighbor adjacencies correctly. The first is with misconfigured NSAPs. For example, Router C has just been attached to the network in Figure 6-8, and it isn't forming L1 adjacencies with Routers A and B as was expected.

Figure 6-8   *IS-IS Neighbors in Different Areas*

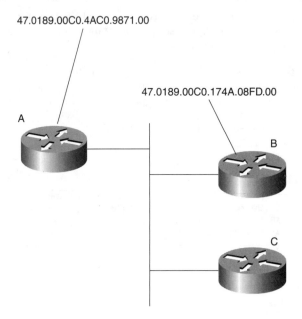

On Router A, you see the following:

```
A#sh clns nei
System Id      SNPA              Interface   State  Holdtime  Type  Protocol
B              00C0.174A.08FD    Et0         Up     27        L1    IS-IS
C              00C0.0c76.f096    Et0         Up     26        L2    IS-IS
```

It's easy to see from this output that Router A has formed a L1 adjacency with Router B, and a L2 adjacency with Router C. This means Router C must have been misconfigured with an incorrect network service access point (NSAP); the area ID is probably wrong.

Another instance where IS-IS routers will not form a neighbor adjacency is if you are running integrated IS-IS across a point-to-point link and the IP addresses on the interfaces the routers are connected through aren't on the same subnet. For an example of this, look at Figure 6-9.

Figure 6-9   *IS-IS Neighbors in Different Subnets*

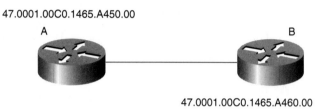

47.0001.00C0.1465.A450.00

47.0001.00C0.1465.A460.00

When you look at Router A's CLNS neighbors, you see the following:

```
A#show clns neighbor
System Id       Interface   SNPA              State  Holdtime  Type Protocol
00C0.1465.A460 Se0         *HDLC*            Up     297       IS   ES-IS
```

Note that the protocol is ES-IS rather than IS-IS; you would expect an IS-IS adjacency between these two neighbors. Because they are ES-IS neighbors, they will not exchange routing tables. Comparing the IP address of the interfaces on the two routers illustrates what is wrong:

```
A#show ip interface brief
Interface               IP-Address      OK? Method  Status        Protocol
....
Serial0                 172.19.2.1      YES manual  up            up
....
```

Serial0 on this router is configured as part of the 172.19.2.0/24 subnet.

```
A#show cdp neighbor detail
....
Device ID: rp-2501-13a
Entry address(es):
  IP address: 172.19.1.2
  CLNS address: 47.0001.00c0.1465.a460.00
Platform: cisco 2500,  Capabilities: Router
Interface: Serial0,  Port ID (outgoing port): Serial0
```

Serial0 on the other router is configured as part of the 172.19.1.0/24 subnet. Let's change the subnet that Router A's Serial0 interface is in to see if it resolves the problem.

```
A#config t
Enter configuration commands, one per line.  End with CNTL/Z.
A(config)#int s0
A(config-if)#ip address 172.19.1.1 255.255.255.0
A(config-if)#end
A#show clns neighbor
System Id      Interface   SNPA            State  Holdtime  Type Protocol
00C0.1465.A460 Se0         *HDLC*          Up     22        L1L2 IS-IS
```

Now, these two routers have correctly formed an IS-IS neighbor relationship, and they will exchange routes. Note that they are forming both an L1 and L2 adjacency; this is the default for Cisco routers running IS-IS.

Case Study: The Single Area Option

As stated at the beginning of this chapter, it would be possible to run this entire network in a single IS-IS area using L1 routing only. The advantage to this is that all routing in the network is optimal. The disadvantage is that you can't summarize any place in the network.

There are three primary areas that you need to consider when choosing the single area option: the HQ VLANs and the common services areas (which have a large number of parallel links with hosts connected to them), and the dial-in clients, or other similar area, where the topology will change regularly.

HQ VLANs and Common Services Areas

The biggest issue with the HQ VLANs and common services areas is the multiple parallel LANs/VLANs. You don't necessarily want these paths to become transit paths in case of some other failure in the network because hosts and through traffic generally don't mix well.

There are two options: Install a summary static route and redistribute it into IS-IS, or just inject the individual routes represented by these parallel links into IS-IS through **redistribute connected** or some other means.

Using a summary static route is a simple strategy. For example, the two routers connected to the server farm could have a single static route:

```
ip route 172.16.10.0 255.255.248.0 null0
```

This single static route then could be redistributed into IS-IS. The rest of the network will only know about 172.16.10.0/22, which is reachable through one of these two routers. Each of these routers will know about the specific subnets (because they are directly attached) and choose the longer prefix (directly connected) routes to actually forward packets to.

The main problem with this idea is if one of these two routers loses its connection to just one of these parallel LANs, it is likely that the router will begin throwing packets destined to that LAN to null0, essentially black holing those packets.

Unfortunately, there isn't much of a way around this. It's just a risk that must be considered if this method is used. Using **redistribute connected** causes each of the LAN's addresses to be injected into the entire routing domain, so this is less of an issue.

Dial-Up Clients Area

The problem with the dial-up clients is the constant flapping of these dial-up links. Each time a customer dials in or drops a dial-in session, the resulting topology change will need to be flooded to the entire network.

Once again, static routes come to the rescue. Instead of advertising these dial-up links, it's best to simply put a static route to null0 in the terminal server and redistribute this static route, which in this case is

```
ip route 172.16.22.0 255.255.255.0 null0
```

Although the terminal server will only be advertising this single route, when a packet for one of these dial-up clients reaches this router, it will have a more specific (host) route in its table. Because longest prefix match always wins, the router will use the host route installed by the dial-up process rather than sending the packet to null0.

Case Study: The Two-Layer Network

If all the access points in a network connect to the same physical location (one building, for instance), it's possible to collapse the core and distribution layer onto a single network (or a set of parallel high speed LANs), producing a design something like that shown in Figure 6-10.

Essentially, this type of network collapses the core and distribution layer into one set of routers, or one area, within the design. Deciding where to place the L1/L2 border in this type of network is much easier because there is such a natural break between the distribution layer and the network core. Figure 6-11 illustrates this.

Figure 6-10 *A Two-Layer Network*

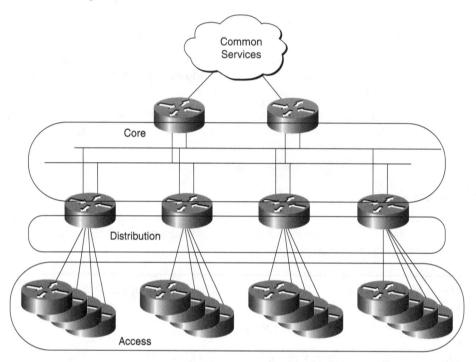

The bottleneck in this design will eventually be the parallel Ethernet links in the core of the network, or the router interfaces on that network. With high enough traffic rates, the parallel Ethernet links will eventually become oversubscribed, or the routers may run into problems buffering the packets between the higher speed links in the core and the lower speed links connecting to the remote sites.

Going to Gigabit Ethernet, or other high speed technologies, will probably resolve the oversubscription problem in the core for most networks to some degree, but adding more parallel links to the two already shown isn't an option.

Why? Because each link added represents a new path through the network from the common services to the remote sites and you run up against the problems with convergence and routing table sizes encountered in Chapter 3, "Redundancy."

Increasing the speed of the links in the network core doesn't help the buffering problems in the routers connected between the core and the access layer; if anything, it could make this problem worse.

Figure 6-11   *Dividing the Two-Layer Network*

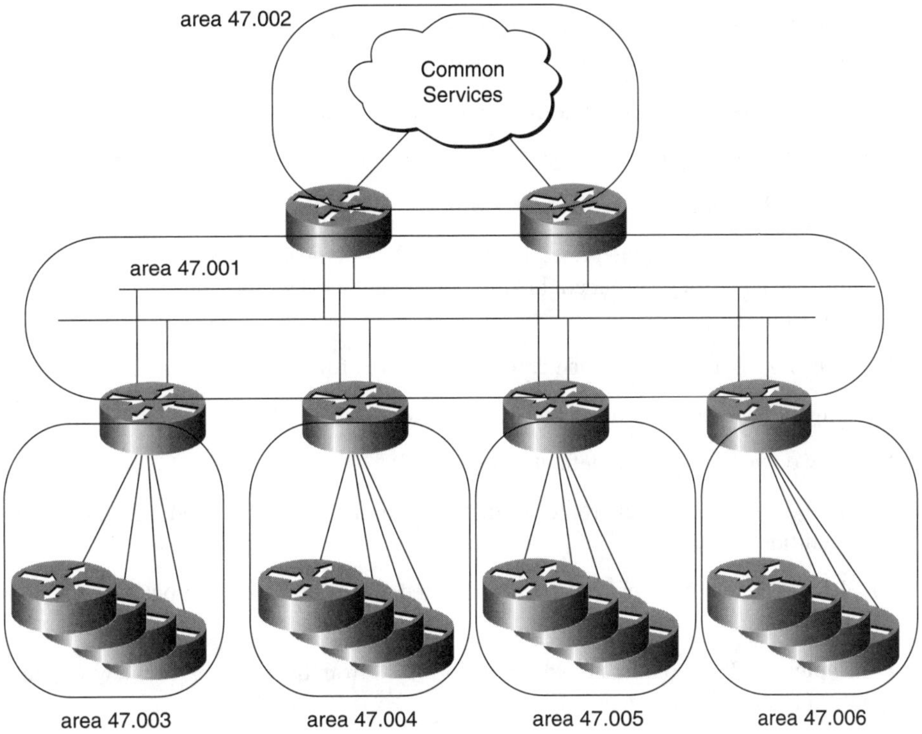

Some form of standard, full mesh point-to-point links could be substituted in the core, but this is worse than the broadcast links currently shown. You will lose IS-IS's capability to handle broadcast networks through the pseudonode process.

Review

1   What protocol was IS-IS originally designed to provide routing information for?

2   Where can summarization take place in IS-IS?

3   How many levels of routing are there in an IS-IS network?

4   How many pseudonodes are allowed in an IS-IS area?

5   Is it possible to overflow the LSP database on a router? What are the indications that this is occurring?

 6 What is the range of internal metrics in IS-IS? What is the range of external metrics in IS-IS? Why is this a problem in a large-scale network?

 7 Why isn't it good to have a dial backup dial in to a router behind a summarization point for the networks behind the dial backup router?

 8 Will routers in different areas form L1 neighbor adjacencies?

 9 Should you just let all the routers in your network run both L1 and L2 routing?

10 Will IS-IS automatically repair a partitioned L2 routing domain?

11 Will routers running integrated IS-IS, which are in the same area but different IP subnets, form an adjacency? What could you look at, and what would you see to determine this is happening?

12 Must all L2 routers form one contiguous group of routers?

13 How often does IS-IS flood link-state packets? Is this adjustable?

14 How do you advertise a default route in IS-IS?

15 How do you configure a router so that a default route is advertised only under some conditions?

16 What is the effect of an LSP that is corrupted at the data link layer, but the error correction codes are correct?

17 Implement IS-IS on the network you corrected from the Chapter 4 review, explaining all design tradeoffs and decisions.

CHAPTER 7

EIGRP Network Design

The previous two chapters looked at implementing two different link-state protocols, Open Shortest Path First (OSPF) and Intermediate System-to-Intermediate System (IS-IS). These are on the network in Figure 7-1, which was originally presented in Chapter 4, "Applying the Principles of Network Design," as Figure 4-10. This chapter follows suit by taking a look at implementing Cisco's advanced distance vector protocol—Enhanced Interior Gateway Routing Protocol (EIGRP).

For more information on how EIGRP functions, refer to Appendix C, "EIGRP Fundamentals." EIGRP has numerous advantages over its link-state counterparts, but it also has limitations and behaviors that a network designer must understand to successfully implement a scalable EIGRP network. This chapter describes some of these behaviors and provides techniques that network designers can use to improve the performance and scalability of EIGRP networks.

This chapter helps you to do the following:

- Analyze summarization at the core, distribution layer, and access layer of an EIGRP network

- Analyze the best way to deal with external connections, common services, and dial-in clients

- Explore case studies on summarization methods, query propagation, excessive redundancy, troubleshooting common problems, and redistribution issues

Analyzing the Network Core for Summarization

The network core in EIGRP has similar requirements to those presented by OSPF and IS-IS. Adequate redundancy and bandwidth must be provided in the core in order to provide rapid, reliable delivery of packets presented to it from the distribution layer and destined to common resources or other distribution layer routers. The core should present as little impediment to the delivery of packets as the geographic distances and budgets will allow. Network designs are much more scalable if it doesn't matter where a packet enters the core from the distribution layer. The core should appear to be a fast cloud that the distribution layer uses to reach common resources and other distribution layer routers.

Figure 7-1   *Large Scale Network*

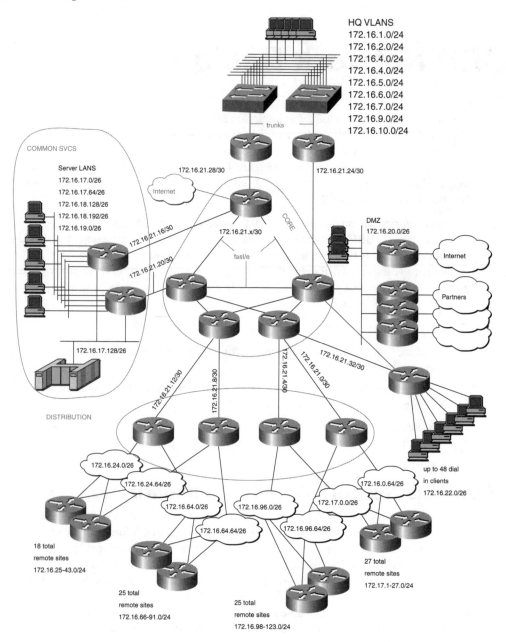

HQ VLANS
172.16.1.0/24
172.16.2.0/24
172.16.4.0/24
172.16.4.0/24
172.16.5.0/24
172.16.6.0/24
172.16.7.0/24
172.16.9.0/24
172.16.10.0/24

COMMON SVCS

Server LANS
172.16.17.0/26
172.16.17.64/26
172.16.18.128/26
172.16.18.192/26
172.16.19.0/26

trunks

172.16.21.28/30

172.16.21.24/30

Internet

172.16.21.16/30

172.16.21.x/30

CORE

DMZ
172.16.20.0/26

Internet

fast/e

172.16.21.20/30

Partners

172.16.17.128/26

DISTRIBUTION

172.16.21.12/30

172.16.21.8/30

172.16.21.4/30

172.16.21.0/30

172.16.21.32/30

172.16.24.0/26

172.16.24.64/26

172.16.64.0/26

172.16.96.0/26

172.17.0.0/26

172.16.0.64/26

up to 48 dial
in clients
172.16.22.0/26

172.16.64.64/26

172.16.96.64/26

18 total
remote sites
172.16.25-43.0/24

27 total
remote sites
172.17.1-27.0/24

25 total
remote sites
172.16.66-91.0/24

25 total
remote sites
172.16.98-123.0/24

If the network core meets these criteria, then summarization can be performed at the core, and you will see significant benefits. The following sections discuss the best ways in which summarization can be implemented at the network core to provide maximum stability and resiliency. These methods include summarizing from the network core to the distribution layer and summarizing within the core itself.

Summarizing from the Core to the Distribution Layer

Chapter 2, "Addressing & Summarization," explained that maximum stability and scalability occurs when maximum summarization is performed. If your network core topology is robust enough to present a minimum of delay to transit packets, you are free to summarize to the fullest from the core to the distribution layer.

In our example network, shown in Figure 7-1, maximum summarization can be performed due to the designed, adequate core bandwidth and redundancy. You can put summarization statements on the serial links connecting the core to the distribution layer, either presenting only the two major network routes (172.16.0.0/8 and 172.17.0.0/8), or just the default route (0.0.0.0/0) to the distribution layer, as shown in Figure 7-2. Refer to "Case Study: Summarization Methods," later in this chapter for an explanation of the different ways that summarization can be performed in an EIGRP network.

Figure 7-2   *Summarizing Outbound from the Core*

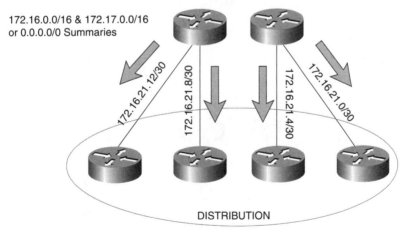

Minimizing the updates sent to the distribution layer routers from the core greatly reduces the query range and simplifies the process of bringing up neighbors across these critical links in the network. Refer to "Case Study: Controlling Query Propagation," later in this chapter for details on how important it is to limit the reach of queries in an EIGRP network.

One possible negative side-effect of summarizing from the network core to the distribution layer is that if the destination subnet is closer in the topology to one core router than another, the shortest path from the distribution layer router to the target network may not be the one taken. If the network core is truly presenting minimal delay to traffic, then the addition of an extra hop will not be significant when compared to increased stability.

Summarizing within the Core

You can summarize between the core routers, but it's only necessary if the distribution layer routers are not summarizing toward the core themselves. As Figure 7-3 illustrates, the core routers could summarize toward the other core routers so that each core router has full component knowledge of the subnets inside of the regions to which it is connected but only summary knowledge of the other regions.

Figure 7-3 *Summarization within the Core*

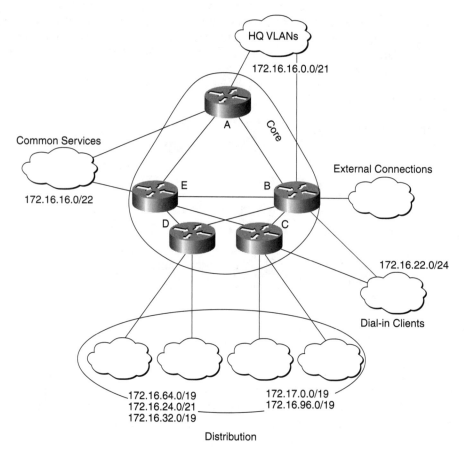

The following list describes the routing advertisements resulting from the setup in Figure 7-3:

- Router A advertises 172.16.0.0/21 for the HQ VLANs and 172.16.16.0/22 for the common services out toward the other core routers.
- Router B advertises 0.0.0.0/0 for the external connections, 172.16.24.0/24 for the DMZ, and 172.16.0.0/21 for the HQ VLANs toward the other core routers.
- Router C advertises 172.16.22.0/24 for the dial-in users, 172.17.0.0/19 for remote sites, and 172.16.96.0/19 for remote sites.
- Router D advertises 172.16.64.0/19, 172.16.24.0/21, and 172.16.32.0/19 for remote sites.
- Router E advertises 172.16.16.0/22 for the common services.

The advantage of this approach is that the core routers have full knowledge about all remote locations in their region and can choose the optimum route from the core router to the remote site. The disadvantage of this approach is that the core routers for each region are directly involved in the query path for any link failure inside of their region.

Should you summarize within the core of the network? Because this makes the configuration of the core more complicated and moves work from the distribution layer into the network core, you probably shouldn't adopt this solution. In any case, you will need to hold off on making a final decision until you have dealt with summarization in the distribution layer.

Analyzing the Network's Distribution Layer for Summarization

The distribution layer's goals in hierarchical networking are to summarize and aggregate traffic. The following sections on summarizing toward the network core and summarizing toward the remote sites will give you a better idea of what you can do with summarization here.

Summarizing toward the Network Core

You can apply summarization to the inbound links toward the core to limit their advertisements to one or more summary routes representing all the subnets off of that distribution router. For example, in Figure 7-4, summarization occurs outbound from Router A and Router B on the serial links toward the core router.

For the setup in Figure 7-4, both Router A and Router B advertise the following routes:

- 172.16.64.0/19
- 172.16.24.0/21
- 172.16.32.0/19

Figure 7-4 *Summarization between the Distribution Layer and Core*

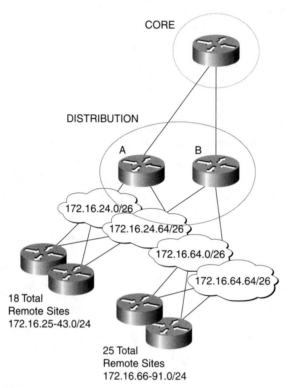

However, there is one problem that can occur with this summarization method unless proper steps are taken. If Router A and Router B both advertise to the core only a summary route representing the same sets of networks at the remotes, you can create a "black hole" should one of the distribution routers lose access to one of the remotes. For example, if Router A advertises 172.16.64.0/19, but loses the Frame Relay permanent virtual circuit (PVC) to one remote in that range, all the packets forwarded to Router A that are destined to a remote site in that range will be dropped. This can be a serious problem.

There are two solutions to this problem. The first solution is to summarize at the core rather than between the distribution and core routers, as covered in the previous section "Summarizing within the Core." This solution defeats the goals of the distribution layer, however, and will cause queries for networks in the branches to be propagated into the core.

A second solution is to have a relatively high-speed and reliable link connecting the distribution layer routers within a region. Routes advertised over this link will not be filtered, but both distribution layer routers will contain all of the components from each other. Note that the link between the distribution layer routers must be robust enough to support remote-to-remote traffic within the region. On most corporate networks, however, remote-to-remote traffic is negligible when compared to remote-to-common resource traffic.

The obvious solution to the summarization toward the network problem is to have a relatively high-speed and reliable link connecting the distribution layer routers within a region, given that there will be very little remote-to-remote-traffic. Figure 7-5 illustrates the new design.

Figure 7-5   *Links between Distribution Layer Routers*

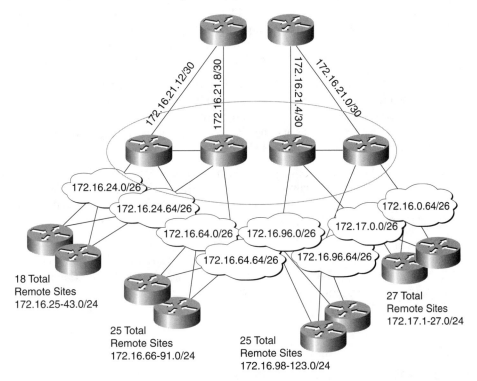

The first thing to note in Figure 7-5 is that no link exists between the two center distribution layer routers because this would cause too much route leakage. You might remember that the original network design had these links in it before reworking the network design in Chapter 4, "Applying the Principles of Network Design." This is a perfect instance of implementation issues forcing compromises in design; the greater goal isn't to meet all of the written goals—it's to produce the most stable network possible with the material at hand.

Summarizing toward the Remote Sites

Summarization should be performed on the interfaces outbound to the remote sites, as well. The purpose of this summarization is to limit the routing updates to the remote routers so that they contain only a default route or major net routes; without the summarization, all the components in the region will be sent to the remote sites. As explained in the Case Study later in the chapter, "Troubleshooting Stuck-In-Active Routes," sending the intra-region component routes unnecessarily to the remotes causes the remote sites to be included in the query process, which is not a good thing. Increasing the range of the query process beyond what is absolutely necessary increases the amount of work required to reach network convergence and the chances that there will be a problem with convergence due to link or router issues. The more devices or links involved in convergence increases the likelihood that you will have a problem with it.

Additionally, if the routes are not summarized from the distribution routers to the remote routers, a significant amount of more work and traffic are required to start up the neighbor relationship between the distribution and remote routers. Because smaller bandwidth links tend to be used between remote sites and the distribution layer, decreasing EIGRP's bandwidth requirements at startup is a wise move.

The method used to summarize the routes to the remote sites can be either the **summary-address** statement or the **distribute-list** statement. Either one of these methods will work fine for this application. For more on how to implement the **summary-address** and **distribute-list** statements, refer to "Case Study: Summarization Methods," later in the chapter.

At the end of the earlier section "Summarizing within the Core," the decision of whether to add summarization within the network core was not made. Based on the decision to summarize from the distribution layer into the core via **summary-address** or **distribution-list** statements, summarization within the core is unnecessary. Because each distribution layer router is sending only summary information to the core, it is probably unnecessary to further summarize between core routers.

Analyzing Routing in the Network's Access Layer

Access layer routers can normally be classified as *stub* or *dual-homed*. The sections that follow present each type along with alternative methods of supporting them.

Stub Sites

Stub sites are those that have only a single path into the rest of the network and typically have very few routes to advertise upstream. True stub sites do not have dial backup or any other way that they could gain an additional path into the distribution layer. As such, true stubs are fairly rare.

There are generally two (obvious) ways to handle stubs: running EIGRP out to them (allowing them to advertise their locally connected networks) or not running EIGRP out to them.

If EIGRP is running out to the stub site's remote router, the remote router can advertise any reachable destinations using EIGRP. In this case, the question is, what should the distribution layer router to which the stub is connected advertise to the remote site?

By definition, a stub site really doesn't have any routing decisions to make; that is, if the address isn't local, it must be reachable through the link to the distribution layer. Therefore, it is particularly appropriate to limit the routes sent from the distribution layer to the remote to the minimum number possible. Believe it or not, the minimum can be one—or even none!

You can either send a single default route from the distribution layer router to the stub remote site or you can filter out all updates from the distribution layer router to the remote site and define a static default route in the remote site pointing back to the distribution layer router, which is more efficient. In this way, the routes from the remote are learned dynamically for delivery of traffic to the remote, but a static route is used for the traffic inbound from the remote.

If EIGRP is not running between the stub's router and the distribution layer router to which it connects, you use static routes at both the remote site and the distribution layer router. Because EIGRP is not running between the remote router and the distribution layer router, there isn't any way for the distribution layer router to learn dynamically about destinations reachable at the remote site.

To provide the rest of the network with information about destinations available at this stub site, static routes are defined in the distribution layer router pointing to the appropriate access router for each remote network. This is ideal for situations where the links to the remote sites are not very robust; because EIGRP isn't running over the link, it isn't affected a great deal if the link often fails and, therefore, cannot create any problems for the remainder of the network due to SIAs.

The disadvantage of this approach is the administrative overhead of defining a large number of static routes and then maintaining them when the network topology changes. Typically, this approach should be used only if you are trying to eliminate problem links from the query and update path for EIGRP.

Dual-Homed Remotes

The second category of access layer routers, dual-homed remotes, is much more common than stubs. Some are "permanent" dual-homed remotes, like the example network, with low-speed (or low-CIR) connections to two different distribution routers from each remote site. The purpose of the two connections from the remote could be for load balancing, but they are usually for redundancy. These important remote sites are connected in such a way that a Frame Relay PVC failure or distribution layer router failure will not cause them to lose access to the core of the network.

Another type of remote connection that needs to be treated as if it were dual-homed is a stub site with dial backup capability. Even though stub sites with dial backup capabilities don't have two permanent paths into the core of the network, the dial connection will come up in the event of Frame Relay failure. When the Frame Relay connection comes back up, for a brief period of time both the Frame Relay and dial connection will be functional and, thus, make the remote appear as if it is dual-homed.

Distribution layer routers that are attached to these dual-homed remotes will see each of the remotes as an alternative path to reach elsewhere in the network; they will appear to be transit paths or alternate paths through the network. For an example, look at Figure 7-6.

Figure 7-6   *A Dual-Homed Remote as a Transit Path*

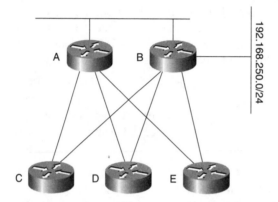

With a default configuration of EIGRP running between all the routers shown in Figure 7-6, Router A sees four paths to the 192.168.250.0/24 network:

- Router C to Router B
- Router D to Router B
- Router E to Router B
- Router B

Router A would normally choose the route directly through Router B to reach this destination, but if that route fails, Router A will choose between the remaining three routes or, possibly, load share between them. This may be fine from a traffic standpoint; the links can be sized to handle the load, and so forth.

The problem is that Router A will see each of these paths as a path through which it must query if the 198.162.250.0/24 network fails, and it will hold each of these paths in its topology table, consequently wasting memory.

Summarizing outbound from the distribution layer, as discussed in the section "Summarizing toward the Remote Sites," effectively limits the number of paths Router A sees to reach the 192.168.250.0/24 network. Because the remote routers won't have routes to this specific network through Router B, they cannot advertise it back to Router A.

This is an important concept for the EIGRP network because there are so many remotes that are dual-homed. It's important that you summarize to the greatest possible extent from the distribution layer into these remote site routers. You should configure the distribution layer routers with distribution lists or summary address statements so that the access layer routers receive only a default route.

Dual-Homed Remotes and Best Next Hop

In some networks, there may be a requirement that the remote sites use the path through the distribution router that is closest to the target network instead of sending to whichever distribution router is next in the load-sharing scheme. For example, if a remote router is connected to one distribution router in Los Angeles and another distribution router in New York, it may be very desirable to choose the distribution router that is topologically closest to the target network. This requires a slightly different approach than the one discussed previously.

If a dual-homed remote site needs to select the best next hop to reach certain destinations (typically data centers or common services areas), specific routes to those destinations must be propagated to the remote routers so that path selection can take place. Of course, allowing these additional routes will increase the work required to bring up the adjacency between the distribution router and the remote router and possibly allow the feedback of routes from distribution router to remote router to distribution router as described in a preceding paragraph. So how do you deal with this situation?

If a limited number of routes are being allowed from the distribution layer router to the remote router, the additional overhead of bringing up the link should not be severe. Care must be taken to keep the number of routes advertised to the remotes to a bare minimum.

The second action that should be taken is to eliminate the possibility of the distribution layer routers seeing the remote routers as transit paths to the routes that are allowed in the advertisements to the remote routers. This can be accomplished by putting distribution lists in the remote routers, allowing only the routes at that remote site in routing updates. In other words, the routes permitted are only those originating at the remote site, not routes learned via the links to the distribution layer. This will stop the remote routers from "reflecting" routes back to the distribution layer.

Another reason that the distribution lists in the remote routers, as described in the preceding paragraph, may be a good idea is that they will act as an insurance policy against disaster due to misconfiguration of a distribution router. If a summary address statement or distribution list is accidentally left off of a distribution router, any interface that is no longer getting filtered routes may learn many more routes than desired. The extra routes may be an annoyance, and they may create havoc, as well.

Depending on the summarization strategy used in the network, it is possible that these inadvertently leaked routes could be the most specific routes to the target networks learned by the other distribution router. Without the distribution lists limiting updates from the remote routers to only those routes originating at the remote site, the remote learns these extra routes and then advertises them to the other distribution router to which it is connected. This may cause the other distribution router to use the remote to reach those target networks because IP routing always follows the most specific route. This could be a disaster because it is very doubtful that the links to the remote routers are provisioned to support the amount of traffic that may occur if the remote were used as a transit site.

In the sample network shown previously in Figure 7-6, the distribution lists in the remote are not really necessary because every distribution router will know the same level of summarization. To be safe, however, you should put the distribution lists in.

Analyzing Routes to External Connections

Another area to be concerned with in the EIGRP network implementation concerns the method of propagating routing information for external destinations; that is, sites that are not part of the AS, such as the partner networks attached to through the DMZ shown in Figure 7-7. You can classify these external sites in two ways: those that have a limited scope of addresses and those that don't. An example of the first type is connections from the AS into either another company's network, or other divisions of the company that fall under other administrative control. An example of the second type is the Internet connection.

This section describes several methods that EIGRP offers to propagate information about these external destinations. First, if the external AS has a limited number of IP networks, you can redistribute the routes into EIGRP from the other AS. Redistributing routes into EIGRP can be a reasonable choice if done correctly. If done poorly, however, redistribution can create a disaster. Refer to "Case Study: Redistribution," later in the chapter for more information on how to resolve the problem of redistributing routes from EIGRP into other protocols and vice versa. The "Case Study: EIGRP/IGRP Redistribution" focuses more exclusively on redistribution between IGRP and EIGRP for combining networks and for transitioning from IGRP to EIGRP.

If the external connection is to the Internet, redistributing the routes into EIGRP is not appropriate. There are entirely too many routes in the Internet; you will overpopulate the routing tables in the AS! Besides, as mentioned earlier, you should limit your routing knowledge to the minimal set that enables you to route traffic properly. Typically with an Internet connection, if the address isn't contained within the AS, it's out there, and you could simply follow a default route to reach it.

In EIGRP, there are two ways to propagate information about the default route. You could define a static route to 0.0.0.0/0 and redistribute this route into EIGRP from the DMZ router. This route matches any target IP address that the router does not have a more specific route to. One problem with this approach is that if there are any routers that are summarizing to 0.0.0.0/0 with **ip summary-address eigrp <AS> 0.0.0.0 0.0.0.0** statements on their interfaces, they will not accept this default route.

Figure 7-7   *Network Setup for Propagating Routing Information to External Connections*

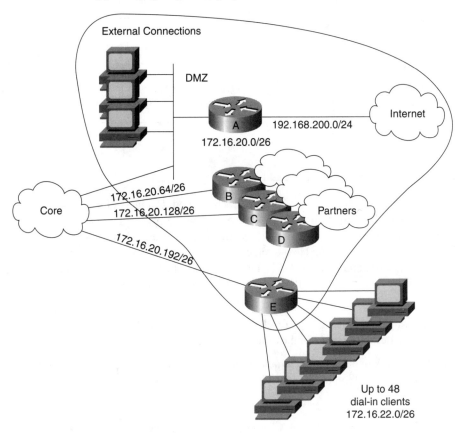

A local summary route has a default administrative distance of 5 and the external default route will have an administrative distance of 170 and will, thus, fail to be installed in the routing table. Either the local router must have a static route with a better administrative distance than the summary, or the summary must be configured with a administrative distance higher than 170. (Chapter 1, "Hierarchical Design Principles," covers administrative distances in greater detail if you need to review.)

An alternative to using a 0.0.0.0/0 route is to define a default network by configuring **ip default-network x.x.x.x** on the DMZ router. The destination configured as the default must be reachable from all other routers in the network.

In the case of the example network in Figure 7-7, you could use the address of the link that connects the network to the Internet, which would look something like this:

```
!
ip default-network 192.168.200.0
!
```

You could also install a static route on the DMZ router for a destination that doesn't exist anyplace else in the network and point it to the other side of the link to the Internet.

```
!
ip route 10.0.0.0 255.0.0.0 192.168.200.1
ip default-network 10.0.0.0
!
```

There are positive and negative aspects of each method. Using a default network allows you to learn the default destination through some other routing protocol and adjust your default routing in response to losing that route. Static default routes can be recursive (can point to a network not directly attached to the router in which they are configured), but they don't provide the flexibility of default networks. Default networks also work correctly with IGRP if there is any IGRP in your network. IGRP can't carry the default route of 0.0.0.0/0.

On the other hand, the default route is more common and can be passed to, or learned from, other routing protocols, such as Border Gateway Protocol (BGP) or OSPF. Cisco routers also converge faster for changes in the default route than they do for changes in a default network.

For the network in this chapter, which has no IGRP, stick with a default route of 0.0.0.0/0. This is the preferred method unless you have some reason to use a default network.

Analyzing Routes to the Common Services Area

The common services are connected to the core through two distribution routers and are also connected via multiple, parallel Ethernet links (or Fast Ethernet links), as illustrated in Figure 7-8. Whether these are truly separate physical links or VLANs connected through switches, to EIGRP they present the appearance of multiple parallel paths connecting the "back side" of the two distribution routers. One of the more typical errors made by network designers is to include all of these parallel paths as alternative paths for routes to reach much of the rest of the network. This section addresses how to avoid this condition.

Ideally, the servers on these segments point their default gateway to a Hot Standby Routing Protocol (HSRP) address shared by the two distribution routers. This design allows the servers on these segments to adapt to a router failure almost immediately.

Figure 7-8   *Common Service Connections*

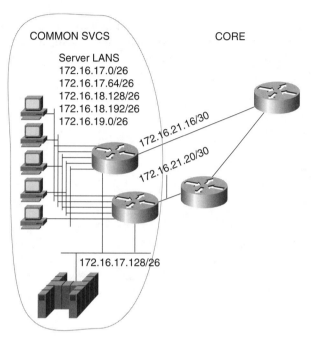

These networks are not designed for transit traffic; that is, traffic is not expected to enter the common services distribution router from the core, go through one of the Fast Ethernet links used by the common services, and then exit through the other distribution router back to the core. EIGRP, however, won't know this by default. It will treat each of these links as an alternate path, storing information about them in the topology table, and propagating queries through them. These alternate paths complicate EIGRP's convergence.

To eliminate the possibility of these networks being used for transit traffic, the network manager shouldn't run EIGRP on any of these parallel Ethernet links. (Well, one or two should run EIGRP, but this is discussed following Figure 7-9.) Configuring **passive-interface** {*interface*} for an interface or subinterface will remove EIGRP from these interfaces.

To prevent the rest of the routers in the network from going active on individual segments supporting these servers, you should use the same strategy that is used everywhere else in the network. Summarize the subnets that reside on the common service Ethernet connections in both distribution layer routers so that they will send only a single summary route out to the core.

If a single Ethernet connection goes down in the common services area, the remainder of the network will not start the query process to find an alternative path. The query will stop at the first router that doesn't have knowledge of the specific subnet that has failed, which will be a core router.

There is one problem with this strategy though—it can create routing black holes in the same way that dual-homed remotes can. To understand why, examine Figure 7-9, which has all but two of the common services networks removed.

Figure 7-9   *Simplified Common Services*

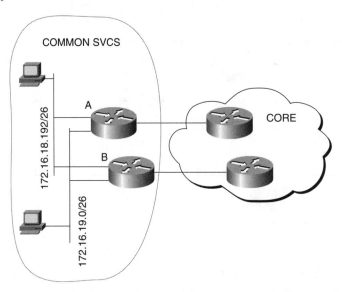

Router A and Router B will both be advertising a summary of 172.16.16.0/22, which covers the entire address range but doesn't overlap with any other addresses in the network. (See Chapter 4 for more details.)

If Router A's interface on the 172.16.18.192/26 network fails, Router A will continue advertising the 172.16.16.0/22 summary toward the core. If, however, one of the core routers forwards a packet destined to the 172.16.18.192/26 network toward Router A, Router A will drop it because it has no route for this destination—or even worse, it will send the packet back toward the core along its default route.

To resolve this situation, Router A must know that 172.16.18.192/26 is reachable through Router B. This is why EIGRP should be run over at least one of these parallel Ethernet links. In order to do this, a **passive-interface** statement should NOT be put into the configuration for at least one Ethernet link. It would be even better if there were one or two links between these routers dedicated to redundancy (with no servers or other devices on them) to account for just this situation.

Analyzing Routes to Dial-In Clients

There are a number of issues and complications that dial-in access creates. This section discusses host routes created by the dial process and EIGRP bandwidth concerns.

Host Routes

Typically, dial in is handled through the Point-to-Point Protocol (PPP). When a PPP session is initiated, a host route (/32) is created on the access server for the remote site, and the host route is removed when the call is dropped. If there is a large number of dial-in clients, this can create a significant amount of network activity as the network reacts to these host routes appearing and disappearing.

There are two methods of eliminating this influx of network activity in EIGRP. First, you can define the command **no ip peer host-route** on the interface(s) of the access server, which will stop the host route from being created in the first place.

The second method you can use to eliminate the host routes is to summarize the host routes learned via the dial interfaces and allow only this summary route to be advertised toward the core. This summarization can be done by either configuring an **ip summary-address** *autonomous system* **eigrp** statement, or by using a **distribute-list out** statement, as discussed in "Case Study: Summarization Methods" later in the chapter.

If the client dialing in is normally included as part of a summary elsewhere in the network (for instance, a PC with an address that is normally part of one of the remote sites that dials into the access server), the more specific component that dialed in will need to be sent out nonsummarized.

It's impossible to get around advertising this host route because the access server can't advertise the same summary that the remote site router (or some router between the access layer and the core) is advertising without causing other routing problems.

If hosts will be dialing in using addresses that are summarized elsewhere in the network, the only way to resolve this is to place an access server for each region behind the summary point. An example of this technique is shown in Figure 7-10; the addresses for the dial-in clients will fall into the summaries that the distribution layer routers are already advertising. Some network administrators use this strategy to minimize components being advertised in the network, but many of them are content with the components being advertised.

Figure 7-10 *Addressing Dial-In Clients*

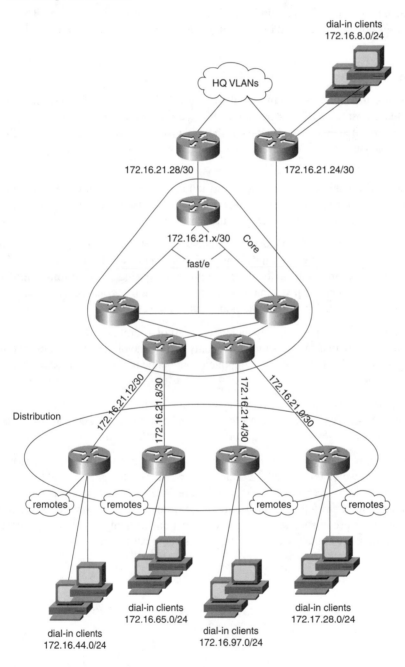

Bandwidth Issues

Bandwidth can be an issue when routers are dialing into an access server (rather than individual hosts). EIGRP uses the bandwidth configured on the interface (using the **bandwidth** command) to determine the rate to pace EIGRP packets. EIGRP paces its packets so that it won't overwhelm the link by using 50% of the defined bandwidth by default. Because EIGRP relies on the bandwidth configured on the interface for packet pacing, it's very important for the interface to be configured correctly. (It should reflect the real bandwidth available on the link.)

If EIGRP believes that the interface has more bandwidth than is really available, it can dominate the link and not allow other traffic to flow. If EIGRP believes that the interface has much less bandwidth than it actually does, it may not be able to successfully send all of the updates, queries, or replies across the link due to the extended pacing interval.

To make things more complicated, the bandwidth is divided by the total number of remote peers on ISDN Primary Rate Interface (PRI) and dialer interfaces in an attempt to fairly distribute the available bandwidth between the neighbors that are reachable through that interface.

With Frame Relay multipoint interfaces, this works fine. With ISDN or dialer interfaces, however, you never know how many neighbors will be dialed in. If there is only one Basic Rate Interface (BRI) dialed in, the bandwidth should be defined as 64 K. If 23 BRIs are dialed in, then the bandwidth should be 1.544 M. Because the defined bandwidth doesn't change with the number of neighbors dialed in, you should set the bandwidth to make it work for both extremes by doing the following:

- Define the dial-in interfaces as dialer profiles instead of dialer groups or dialer interfaces; this allows you to set the bandwidth per dialed-in peer. However, this is a very intense administrative approach.

- Summarize the EIGRP updates out of the dial link to make the amount of traffic so insignificant that it can fit across the link regardless of how much bandwidth is actually available.

Summary of EIGRP Network Design

The previous sections explored how the best summarization techniques can be applied to an EIGRP network to improve its scalability. A number of techniques were discussed and numerous recommendations were made to summarize routes at various points in the network. These points include the following:

- Summarizing from the network core to the distribution layer

- Summarizing from the distribution layer to the network core

- Summarizing from the distribution layer to the remote sites

- Placing distribution lists on the remote routers to limit their advertisements to contain only those routes originating at the remote site
- Summarizing from the common services area to the network core
- Implementing passive interfaces on all but one or two common services Ethernet/Fast Ethernet links
- Summarizing from the dial access servers into the network core

By taking these steps, the network will be robust and scalable. Adding additional sites requires only that the same techniques be applied to the new routers. New regions can be added by using the same summarization/distribution list techniques to minimize the scope of queries and updates in the EIGRP network and providing the most robust, stable possible networking environment.

Case Study: Summarization Methods

There are two basic tools used to summarize routes in EIGRP: **summary-address** statements and **distribute-list** statements. These two methods provide significantly different approaches to limiting the routing updates to a summary of the information and each is uniquely useful. The best solution to a summarization problem is often a mixture of both approaches. One or both of these basic tools will be applied in all three layers—core, distribution, and access—in order to provide the maximum in summarization and, thus, the maximum in stability and scalability. Next, you can look at each tool in order to understand the pros and cons of each.

summary-address **Statements**

The first summarization tool is the **summary-address** statement. This command is in the form **ip summary-address eigrp** *AS network mask distance* and is applied to an interface of a Cisco router out of which you want to advertise a summary route. The **summary-address** command provides two related functions:

- It creates a summary route in the routing table (identified as a summary route with a next-hop address of null0). It will then propagate to any neighbors out of the interface with the summary address statement defined.
- It filters out the components of the summary that would normally have been sent out of the interface with the summary address statement. In this way, it sends ONLY the summary information.

While the summary address method of summarization is extremely flexible and powerful, it can also be administratively wearisome and possibly error-prone. As mentioned previously, the **summary-address** statement needs to be applied to each interface that you want to advertise the summary. On routers that contain dozens or even hundreds of interfaces and subinterfaces, there can be a large number of **summary-address** statements that must be defined correctly.

There are also a couple of issues that need to be understood about the summary address implementation in order to make proper use of the tool. First, a summary route will be created and sent only if EIGRP has an internal component of the summary. This means that if all components that make up the summary disappear, or only external (redistributed) components exist, the summary route is not installed and advertised. This is proper behavior because a router should not be advertising that it can reach a range of addresses if there are not any components of that range reachable through the advertising router.

One unfortunate side-effect of using the summary address method is that if you are receiving a route that matches the summary (same network and mask) from another source, you won't accept it. This is because the summary route generated by the **summary-address** command has an administrative distance of five by default, which will be better than the administrative distance of any dynamically learned route.

To illustrate, suppose that you have a router that is learning its default route through an external source:

```
router#show ip route
....
Gateway of last resort is 172.19.1.1 to network 0.0.0.0
....
D*EX 0.0.0.0/0 [170/2195456] via 172.19.1.1, 00:00:09, Serial0
```

You want to configure a **summary-address** statement that will advertise the least number of routes possible out of interface serial 1. So, you will configure the following:

```
router(config)#int serial 1
router(config-if)#ip summary-address eigrp 100 0.0.0.0 0.0.0.0
```

Now, you have:

```
rp-2501-13a#show ip route
....
Gateway of last resort is 0.0.0.0 to network 0.0.0.0
....
D*    0.0.0.0/0 is a summary, 00:00:49, Null0
```

This is a problem. Any packets that should follow the default route and be directed toward 172.19.1.1 will actually be sent to null0 (the bit-bucket). Essentially, you will throw these packets away.

To resolve this, you can use a new addition on the **ip summary-address** command:

```
router(config-if)#ip summary-address eigrp 100 0.0.0.0 0.0.0.0 200
```

The final 200 sets the administrative distance of this summary route to 200. Although the downstream router will still receive only the 0.0.0.0/0 route, the summary won't be installed in this router's routing table because the administrative distance is higher than the external EIGRP route you currently have. This feature isn't available in all versions of IOS software. (It was integrated in 12.0(5)T, so the version must be later than this.)

distribute-list **Statements**

The second method used to filter and summarize routes in EIGRP is to define distribute lists under the EIGRP configuration. This method uses a totally different approach than the **summary-address** statements, but it provides very similar functionality. With the distribute list approach, you explicitly tell EIGRP which routes are allowed to be advertised out of any or all interfaces. The command is of the form **distribute-list** {*access-list-number\name*} **out** [*interface-name\routing-process*] and is entered in EIGRP configuration mode. The access list associated with the distribute list (access list 1 in the example) describes the route, or routes, that can be sent out the interface defined under the **distribute-list** command. A wildcard mask can be supplied in the access list in order to have more than one route permitted under the same access list.

Note that a key difference between distribute lists and summary addresses is that distribute lists do not automatically create the summary route you need to advertise. If the route permitted by the access list does not exist, then the route is not sent, of course. Typically, the network manager will define a static route to match the access list so that the route will always be there to advertise. This static route can be floating (that is, with a high administrative distance) so that if the same route is learned from elsewhere, it will be accepted and used. The static route will be used only if the dynamically derived route disappears.

Case Study: Controlling Query Propagation

Not only do **summarization** statements and/or distribute lists limit the size and content of the updates sent to neighbors from a router, they also control the scope of EIGRP query propagation. (See Appendix C for further details on the query process.) Look at Figure 7-11 and consider a query propagating through this network.

Figure 7-11   *Controlling Query Propagation*

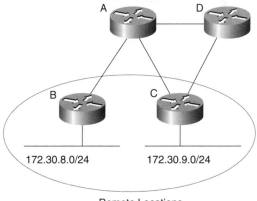

Remote Locations

If Router B loses its route to 172.30.8.0/24, which is directly attached, it will query each of its neighbors in search of a different path to reach this destination. Because Router B has only one neighbor, the only router that will receive the query is Router A. Router A will then query each of its neighbors, Router C and Router D, looking for an alternative path to 172.30.8.0/24. Router C will then query Router D. Therefore, Router D will receive two queries: one from Router A, and one from Router C.

You know from looking at the network topology that Router D will not have a route to 172.30.8.0/24 unless Router A does—so why should you bother Router D with two queries about this network? Well, you can configure Router A so that Router D doesn't receive two queries.

A query will stop propagating when it reaches a router that doesn't have any knowledge of the route that has gone active. (See Appendix C for further information on the active process within EIGRP.) Therefore, if you remove Router C's knowledge of 172.30.8.0/24, Router C will not propagate a query it receives from Router A to Router D. This is where summarization and distribution lists come into play; they keep Router C from knowing about the 172.30.8.0/24 destination.

On Router A, you can advertise a summary of all the routes available in remainder of the network, 172.30.0.0/16, to Router C. When Router C receives a query for the 172.30.8.0/24 network, it will note that it does not have a topology table entry for this particular destination network and will immediately reply to Router A that it does not have any alternative paths.

Case Study: A Plethora of Topology Table Entries

One of the common problems in an EIGRP network is the sheer number of alternate paths through which a given destination can be reached. Each alternate path in the topology table also represents a query that must be generated if the path currently being used fails for some reason. But these alternate paths aren't always obvious when you look at the topology table:

```
router#show ip eigrp topology
IP-EIGRP Topology Table for process 100

Codes: P - Passive, A - Active, U - Update, Q - Query, R - Reply,
       r - Reply status

P 172.19.2.128/25, 1 successors, FD is 2297856
        via 172.28.1.2 (2297856/128256), Serial0.1
P 172.19.10.0/24, 1 successors, FD is 2297856
        via 172.28.1.2 (2297856/128256), Serial0.1
```

The preceding topology table shows what appear to be two destinations, each with a single path to reach them. However, the paths shown here are only a subset of what is known by EIGRP. This output doesn't show all the paths available. It shows only the ones that the Diffusing Update Algorithm (DUAL) has calculated to be loop free.

To get a more accurate picture of what paths are available, you can do a **show ip eigrp topology all** or a **show ip eigrp topology** for a particular destination:

```
router#show ip eigrp topology all
IP-EIGRP Topology Table for process 100
 Codes: P - Passive, A - Active, U - Update, Q - Query, R - Reply, r - Reply status

P 172.19.2.128/25, 1 successors, FD is 2297856
        via 172.28.1.2 (2297856/128256), Serial0.1
        via 172.28.2.2 (3879455/2389454), Serial0.2
        via 172.28.3.2 (4893467/2389454), Serial0.3
        via 172.28.4.2 (4893467/2389454), Serial0.4
        via 172.28.5.2 (4893467/2389454), Serial0.5
        via 172.28.6.2 (4893467/2389454), Serial0.6
        via 172.28.7.2 (4893467/2389454), Serial0.7
        via 172.28.8.2 (4893467/2389454), Serial0.8
        via 172.28.9.2 (4893467/2389454), Serial0.9
        via 172.28.10.2 (4893467/2389454), Serial0.10
P 172.19.10.0/24, 1 successors, FD is 2297856
        via 172.28.1.2 (2297856/128256), Serial0.1
        via 172.28.2.2 (3879455/2389454), Serial0.2
        via 172.28.3.2 (4893467/2389454), Serial0.3
        via 172.28.4.2 (4893467/2389454), Serial0.4
        via 172.28.5.2 (4893467/2389454), Serial0.5
        via 172.28.6.2 (4893467/2389454), Serial0.6
        via 172.28.7.2 (4893467/2389454), Serial0.7
        via 172.28.8.2 (4893467/2389454), Serial0.8
        via 172.28.9.2 (4893467/2389454), Serial0.9
        via 172.28.10.2 (4893467/2389454), Serial0.10
```

```
router#show ip eigrp topology 172.19.10.0 255.255.255.0
IP-EIGRP topology entry for 172.19.10.0/24
  State is Passive, Query origin flag is 1, 1 Successor(s), FD is 2297856
  Routing Descriptor Blocks:
  172.28.1.2 (Serial0.1), from 172.28.1.2, Send flag is 0x0
      Composite metric is (2297856/128256), Route is Internal
 ....
  172.28.2.2 (Serial0.2), from 172.28.2.2, Send flag is 0x0
      Composite metric is (3879455/2389454), Route is Internal
 ....
  172.28.3.2 (Serial0.3), from 172.28.3.2, Send flag is 0x0
      Composite metric is (3879455/2389454), Route is Internal
 ....
  172.28.4.2 (Serial0.4), from 172.28.4.2, Send flag is 0x0
      Composite metric is (3879455/2389454), Route is Internal
 ....
  172.28.5.2 (Serial0.5), from 172.28.5.2, Send flag is 0x0
      Composite metric is (3879455/2389454), Route is Internal
 ....
  172.28.6.2 (Serial0.6), from 172.28.6.2, Send flag is 0x0
      Composite metric is (3879455/2389454), Route is Internal
 ....
  172.28.7.2 (Serial0.7), from 172.28.7.2, Send flag is 0x0
      Composite metric is (3879455/2389454), Route is Internal
 ....
  172.28.8.2 (Serial0.8), from 172.28.8.2, Send flag is 0x0
      Composite metric is (3879455/2389454), Route is Internal
 ....
  172.28.9.2 (Serial0.9), from 172.28.9.2, Send flag is 0x0
      Composite metric is (3879455/2389454), Route is Internal
 ....
  172.28.10.2 (Serial0.10), from 172.28.10.2, Send flag is 0x0
      Composite metric is (3879455/2389454), Route is Internal
```

From the preceding output examples, you can see that although there is only one successor for this particular destination, there are many different possible paths. This almost always indicates a topology with too much redundancy; this router has at least ten neighbors, and each of them has a path to this destination.

Unfortunately, there aren't any definite rules on how many paths are too many in the topology table. The number of alternative paths, however, indicates how many query paths there are in the network and, therefore, how much work the routers in the network will need to do when converging on a topology change.

In general, you should avoid running EIGRP over multiple parallel links between two routers unless you intend transit traffic to be passed over all of them, summarize as much as possible, and use distribute lists to reduce the amount of routing information a router needs to deal with whenever possible.

Case Study: Troubleshooting EIGRP Neighbor Relationships

There are numerous reasons why EIGRP may have problems establishing neighbor relationships. In order to determine the source of the problem, the first thing to do is to add the command **eigrp log-neighbor-changes** under the router process in the configuration of every router. This will give you much more information about the cause of any neighbor problems.

This Case Study describes two common problems that cause EIGRP not to establish neighbors successfully. The first problem occurs when the primary addresses used by the routers trying to be neighbors do not belong to the same subnet. The second common problem occurs when the underlying media is failing to deliver either unicast or multicast traffic in one direction or both. The two sections that follow discuss each of these error conditions in more detail.

Common Problem 1

Because Cisco routers permit the definition of both primary and secondary IP subnets on the same interface, many network implementers will treat the primary and secondary addresses as equal. As Figure 7-12 reveals, this isn't necessarily the case.

Figure 7-12 *EIGRP Neighbors with Different Primary Addresses*

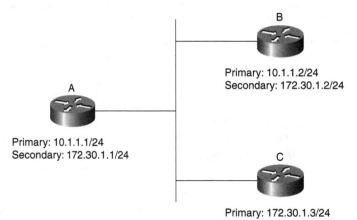

From Figure 7-12, you can see that Router C has its primary (and only) IP address in the subnet with the secondary addresses of Router A and Router B. You can determine this easily by the output of **show ip eigrp neighbors** on all three routers.

```
A#show ip eigrp neighbors
IP-EIGRP neighbors for process 1
H    Address                 Interface    Hold Uptime    SRTT    RTO   Q  Seq
                                          (sec)          (ms)         Cnt Num
1    172.30.1.3              Et0          13 00:00:15      0    5000  1  0
0    10.1.1.2                Et0          13 00:09:56     26     200  0  323
B#show ip eigrp neighbors
IP-EIGRP neighbors for process 1
H    Address                 Interface    Hold Uptime    SRTT    RTO   Q  Seq
                                          (sec)          (ms)         Cnt Num
0    172.30.1.3              Et1          11 00:00:03      0    3000  1  0
1    10.1.1.1                Et1          11 00:11:09     23     200  0  3042
C#show ip eigrp neighbors
IP-EIGRP neighbors for process 1
C#
```

As the preceding output indicates, Router A and Router B see Router C as a neighbor (a neighbor with a problem, however—note the Q count and lack of SRTT), but Router C doesn't see Router A or Router B as neighbors. This is because Router A and Router B match the IP address of the source of the hello packet with *any* of its addresses on that interface. Because Router C falls in one of the subnets, Router A and Router B will accept Router C as a neighbor.

NOTE	The *Q count*, shown in **show ip eigrp neighbor**, indicates the number of items from the topology table that need to be sent to this neighbor. Some (or all) of these items may never be sent due to split-horizon, distribution lists, summaries, or other things; so this doesn't indicate the number of packets that need to be sent or the number of routes that are being sent.
	The *Smoothed Round Trip Time (SRTT)*, shown in **show ip eigrp neighbor**, indicates the average amount of time it takes for a neighbor to respond to packets that require an acknowledgement. It is a smoothed (or weighted) average over multiple transmit/ acknowledgement cycles.

On the other hand, when Router C compares the source address of the received hellos, it doesn't match any of the addresses on that interface and will, therefore, reject them. In some versions of IOS, the message "neighbor not on common subnet" will be a definite indication of this problem.

Common Problem 2

Another problem that is often seen with EIGRP neighbor establishment occurs when the underlying media fails to deliver either unicast or multicast traffic in one direction or both. The remainder of this Case Study describes how it looks when you are missing multicast traffic in one direction using the network diagramed in Figure 7-13.

Figure 7-13 *EIGRP Neighbors with Multicast Delivery Problems*

When looking at Router A's **show ip eigrp neighbors** output, you will see the following:

```
RouterA#show ip eigrp neighbors
IP-EIGRP neighbors for process 1
H   Address                   Interface    Hold Uptime    SRTT    RTO  Q  Seq
                                           (sec)          (ms)         Cnt Num
0   192.168.10.2              Se1             13 00:00:10     0  5000  1  0
```

Notice that Router B is seen in the neighbor table of Router A, but the Q count is not zero and the SRTT is not set to a value. If you have **eigrp log-neighbor-changes** configured (as you should!), you will also get messages on the console, or syslog, reporting that this neighbor is being restarted due to **retransmit limit exceeded**. These symptoms indicate that you are not able to get updates delivered and acknowledged to this neighbor, but you are able to see the neighbor's hellos.

Now look at Router B's **show ip eigrp neighbors** output:

```
RouterB#show ip eigrp neighbors
IP-EIGRP neighbors for process 1
RouterB#
```

Here you will notice that Router B doesn't have Router A in its neighbor table at all! This indicates that the multicast packets sent by EIGRP as hellos are not being delivered to this neighbor. Common reasons for this are a missing **broadcast** keyword on a **dialer map** or **frame-relay map** statement, misconfiguration of Switched Multimegabit Data Service (SMDS) multicast groups, or some other problem with the delivery mechanism.

For example, a correct configuration for a multipoint Frame Relay interface would look like the following:

```
!
interface Serial 0
 encapsulation frame-relay
 ip address 172.30.14.1 255.255.255.0
 frame-relay map ip 172.30.14.2 100 broadcast
 frame-relay map ip 172.30.14.3 104 broadcast
 frame-relay map ip 172.30.14.4 210 broadcast
```

Note the broadcast keyword inserted at the end of each **frame-relay_map** configuration command.

This symptom could also indicate that traffic from Router A is not being delivered to Router B. You can determine whether this is the case by **ping**ing Router B from Router A. If the unicast **ping** works, but EIGRP is unable to see Router A from Router B, you should **ping** 224.0.0.10 (EIGRP's multicast address) from Router A and see if Router B responds.

A multicast **ping** to 224.0.0.10 should be forwarded onto every interface by the router and be responded to by every adjacent EIGRP neighbor:

```
router#show ip eigrp neighbors
IP-EIGRP neighbors for process 1
H   Address               Interface   Hold Uptime    SRTT   RTO  Q   Seq
                                      (sec)          (ms)        Cnt Num
4   192.168.10.2          Se1          14 00:00:05      0  3000  8   0
3   10.31.1.2             Se0.1        12 00:00:11    132   792  0   1668
2   10.31.2.2             Se0.2        12 00:00:12    131   786  0   1670
1   10.31.3.2             Se0.3        11 00:00:12    166   996  0   1669
0   10.1.2.1              Et0          10 1w4d         13   200  0   60131
router#ping 10.31.1.2
Type escape sequence to abort.
Sending 5, 100-byte ICMP Echos to 10.31.1.2, timeout is 2 seconds:
!!!!!
Success rate is 100 percent (5/5), round-trip min/avg/max = 16/16/20 ms
router#ping 224.0.0.10

Type escape sequence to abort.
Sending 1, 100-byte ICMP Echos to 224.0.0.10, timeout is 2 seconds:

Reply to request 0 from 10.1.2.1, 12 ms
Reply to request 0 from 10.31.3.2, 112 ms
Reply to request 0 from 10.31.2.2, 104 ms
Reply to request 0 from 10.31.1.2, 100 ms
Reply to request 0 from 10.250.1.1, 12 ms
Reply to request 0 from 10.200.1.1, 12 ms
Reply to request 0 from 10.1.3.2, 12 ms
```

Case Study: Troubleshooting Stuck-in-Active Routes

Stuck-in-active (SIA) routes can be some of the most challenging problems to resolve in an EIGRP network. For more detail on EIGRP's active process, refer to Appendix C. In summary, a route becomes active when it goes down or its metric worsens, and there aren't any feasible successors. When a route goes active on a router, that router sends out queries to all of its neighbors (except through the interface where the route was lost) and awaits the replies. A 3-minute timer starts when the router marks the route as active; if the timer expires without getting all of the replies, the route that was active is considered stuck in active processing (thus the label "stuck-in-active" routes) and requires drastic actions.

Three minutes is an incredibly long time to a router. The reason that the replies could take longer than 3 minutes should be explained. Figure 7-14 shows a simple network that is reacting to a lost route in order to understand how to troubleshoot it.

Figure 7-14   *SIAs*

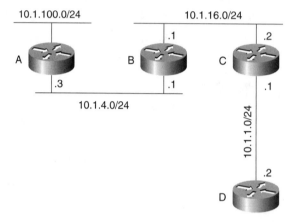

Router A loses network 10.1.100.0/24 due to shutting down an interface to simulate a failure. Router A then goes active on the route and sends a query to Router B, which looks in its topology table for another successor, or feasible successor, for 10.1.100.0/24. In this case, Router B will not have other successors or feasible successors. So, it will also go active on the route and send a query to Router C. Router C will go through the same decision process, and the query will continue on to Router D (and farther if there were farther to go).

During this entire process, Router A's 3-minute timer has been running because a reply is not sent back from Router B until it receives an answer from Router C, which is waiting on Router D. If something happens somewhere downstream (as it will in this Case Study) the timer on Router A may expire, and Router A will consider the path through Router B unreliable. When that happens, Router A resets its neighbor relationship with Router B and tosses all routes previously learned through Router B (relearning these routes requires rebuilding the neighbor relationship). This can be brutal if the link between Router A and Router B is a core link in your network!

Now, you can see how to troubleshoot SIA routes on the example network in Figure 7-14. First, how do you know you are getting stuck-in-active routes? You will see messages in your log such as the following:

```
Jan  19 14:26:00: %DUAL-3-SIA: Route 10.1.100.0 255.255.255.0 stuck-in-active
state in IP-EIGRP 1. Cleaning upJan  19 14:26:00: %DUAL-5-NBRCHANGE: IP-EIGRP
1: Neighbor 10.1.4.1 (Ethernet1) is up: new adjacency
```

The DUAL-3-SIA message identifies which route is getting stuck—10.1.100.0/24 in this case—but it doesn't reveal which neighbor didn't answer. You will need to have **log-neighbor-changes** configured (as recommended earlier) in order to get the message immediately after the DUAL-3-SIA message, stating new adjacency for the neighbor (or neighbors) which was reset due to the SIA. You can also tell which neighbors have been recently reset by looking for a short uptime in **show ip eigrp neighbors**, but you cannot be sure that their reset condition was due to the SIA. Again, make sure **log-neighbor-changes** is configured on every router.

Because the log captured SIA messages, you need to try to determine where the source of the problem is. There are two questions to ask about SIA routes:

- Why are the routes going active?
- Why are they getting stuck?

Both aspects of the problem should be worked on, but the second is the most important by far and probably the most difficult to resolve. If you determine why a route is going active and resolve this part of the problem without determining why it became stuck, the next time a route goes active it could also become stuck. Therefore, finding the cause of the *stuck* is more important than finding the cause of the *active*.

Even though it is more important to find the cause of routes becoming stuck rather than why they went active, that doesn't mean you should ignore why routes are going active. Using the DUAL-3-SIA messages, you can determine if the routes going active are consistent; that is, are they all /32 routes from dial-in clients coming and going, or are they all the result of poor quality lines at the fringes of the network? If they are all host routes caused by dial-in users, you should try to minimize these active routes through summarization or other methods. If the active routes are due to unstable links, you need to get these Layer 2 problems resolved.

How do you troubleshoot the stuck part of the SIA? If the SIA routes are happening regularly, and you are monitoring the routers during the time of the problem, this is a fairly straightforward job. If the problem happens infrequently, and you were not monitoring the routers when the problem happened, it is extremely difficult (actually, it's almost impossible) to find the cause. For this Case Study, assume that the problem is happening regularly enough for you to catch the routes having problems.

On Router A (where you are receiving the DUAL-3-SIA messages for 10.1.100.0/24) you look for active routes using the command **show ip eigrp topology active**. Looking at the following output reveals a lot about the state of the active route:

```
routerA#show ip eigrp topology active
IP-EIGRP Topology Table for process 1
 Codes: P - Passive, A - Active, U - Update, Q - Query, R - Reply,
        r - Reply status

A 10.1.100.0/24, 1 successors, FD is Inaccessible
    1 replies, active 00:01:23, query-origin: Local origin
        via Connected (Infinity/Infinity), Loopback0
    Remaining replies:
        via 10.1.4.1, r, Ethernet1
```

The **A** on the left side of the address shows that this is an active route. The **active 00:01:23** reveals the duration of the wait on a reply to this query. It is normal in a fairly large network to see routes go active, but if the amount of time they stay active is more than a minute, then something is certainly wrong, and SIAs may occur soon.

Notice the field **Remaining replies**; any neighbors listed under this field have not yet replied to this query. Depending on the timing when the command is issued, you will often see neighbors who haven't replied with a lowercase **r** beside the address but not under **Remaining replies**. For example (but not directly related to this Case Study), refer to the following:

```
router#show ip eigrp topology active
IP-EIGRP Topology Table for process 1 Codes:
P - Passive, A - Active, U - Update, Q - Query, R - Reply,
r - Reply status A 10.1.8.0 255.255.255.0, 1 successors, FD is 2733056
    1 replies, active 0:00:11, query-origin: Multiple Origins
        via 10.1.1.2 (Infinity/Infinity), r, Ethernet0
        via 10.1.5.2 (Infinity/Infinity), Serial1, serno 159
        via 10.1.2.2 (Infinity/Infinity), Serial0, serno 151

Remaining replies:
        via 10.1.1.1, r, Ethernet0
```

The first entry in the preceding output for **show ip eigrp topology active** identifies a neighbor that you are waiting on but isn't under the **Remaining replies** section. Keep your eye out for both forms.

Now, back to the troubleshooting. Because the **show ip eigrp topology active** on Router A revealed that you were waiting on neighbor 10.1.4.1 for 1 minute and 23 seconds, you know which neighbor to look at next—Router B. Log into Router B and issue **show ip eigrp topology active** again to see why you haven't gotten an answer from it. The results of this command are as follows:

```
RouterB#show ip eigrp topology active
IP-EIGRP Topology Table for process 1 Codes:
P - Passive, A - Active, U - Update, Q - Query, R - Reply,
r - Reply status
A 10.1.100.0/24, 1 successors, FD is Inaccessible
    1 replies, active 00:01:36, query-origin: Successor Origin
        via 10.1.4.3 ((Infinity/Infinity), Ethernet
    Remaining replies:
        via 10.1.1.1, r, Ethernet0
```

You'll note that Router B is still waiting on a reply from 10.1.1.1, which is Router C. So the next logical step is to log into Router C and see why it isn't answering. Once on Router C, you issue the command **show ip eigrp topology active** again and get the following results:

```
RouterC#show ip eigrp topology activeIP-EIGRP Topology Table for process 1
Codes: P - Passive, A - Active, U - Update, Q - Query, R - Reply,
r - Reply status A 10.1.100.0/24, 1 successors, FD is Inaccessible, Q
     1 replies, active 00:01:49, query-origin: Successor Origin
          via 10.1.1.2 (Infinity/Infinity), Ethernet1
     Remaining replies:
          via 10.1.16.1, r, Serial0
```

Router C is in the same condition as Routers A and B. Router C has not answered Router B because it is still waiting on an answer as well. Now log into 10.1.16.1, which is Router D, to see if this router is having the same problem. The output of **show ip eigrp topology active** on Router D provides different results:

```
RouterD#show ip eigrp topology active
IP-EIGRP Topology Table for process 1
```

So, Router D isn't waiting on anyone! Router C is waiting on Router D, but Router D isn't waiting on replies from any other router. This indicates the link between Router C and Router D is unreliable, and you need to start exploring why the communications between Router C and Router D aren't working correctly. The first thing you need to establish is whether the neighbor relationship is up by issuing the **show ip eigrp neighbor** command:

```
RouterD#show ip eigrp neighbor
IP-EIGRP neighbors for process 1
H    Address                  Interface    Hold Uptime     SRTT   RTO   Q  Seq
                                           (sec)           (ms)         Cnt Num
0    10.1.16.2                Se0            14 00:10:27    1197   5000  1  741
RouterD#
%DUAL-5-NBRCHANGE: IP-EIGRP 1: Neighbor 10.1.16.2 (Serial0) is down: retry
limit exceeded
%DUAL-5-NBRCHANGE: IP-EIGRP 1: Neighbor 10.1.16.2 (Serial0) is up: new
adjacency
```

The Q count of 1 isn't a promising sign. Then, you get the error message **retry limit exceeded** on the console because you configured **eigrp log-neighbor-changes** on this router. The **retry limit exceeded** message is an indication that acknowledgements are not being received for reliable packets. Now you need to determine why they aren't being received. By going back to Router C and checking the state of the neighbor relationship with Router D, you will find the following information:

```
RouterC#show ip eigrp neighbor
IP-EIGRP neighbors for process 1
H   Address                 Interface   Hold Uptime    SRTT   RTO  Q  Seq
                                        (sec)          (ms)       Cnt Num
0   10.1.16.1               Se0          14 00:10:33   479   5000  1  1388
1   10.1.1.2                Et1          11 00:11:46    28    300  0  5318
RouterC#
%DUAL-5-NBRCHANGE: IP-EIGRP 1: Neighbor 10.1.16.1 (Serial0) is down: retry
limit exceeded
%DUAL-5-NBRCHANGE: IP-EIGRP 1: Neighbor 10.1.16.1 (Serial0) is up: new
adjacency
```

So, Router C is also complaining about the inability of exchanging reliable traffic with Router D. Now you need to use your normal troubleshooting skills to resolve this packet delivery problem. You will need to issue **ping**s, look at interfaces, and take the other normal steps needed to find the true cause of the problem.

Other common problems that can cause a router to not answer queries include the following:

- Low memory
- Congestion on the link—too many routes for pipe or queue drops that are too small
- MTU problems—small packets are delivered over the link but not large packets

Without taking the steps following the chain of waiting routers with the **show ip eigrp topology active** command, you never would have been able to find the failing link and start troubleshooting it.

Case Study: Redistribution

You will often find yourself wanting to redistribute routes from EIGRP into other protocols and routes from other protocols into EIGRP. The main problem with redistribution between protocols is that it's very easy to create redistribution routing loops. Look at Figure 7-15 to see why.

Given the setup in Figure 7-15, the following events will occur:

1   Router C will advertise the 172.16.20.0/24 network to Router B; assume it has a metric of 3 hops when it reaches Router B.

2   Router B will now advertise this route with a metric of four hops to Router A.

3 Router A will redistribute the route into EIGRP with some metric and advertise it to Router D.

4 Router D will redistribute it back into RIP with a default metric of 1 hop, for example, and advertise it to Router E.

5 Router E will advertise this route to Router B with a metric of 2 hops, which is better than the route through Router C (which is, in fact, the correct route).

Figure 7-15   *Redistribution Routing Loop*

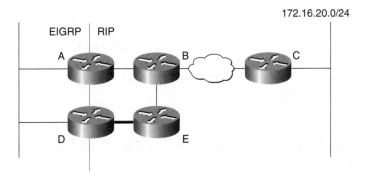

With EIGRP's use of an administrative distance of 170 for external sites, the preceding problem shouldn't happen; should it? The example is simplified to make it clear. In reality, when Router D gets the route from Router A, Router D should prefer the route it had already received from RIP because it has an administrative distance of 120. So what is the problem?

The problem occurs if Router E temporarily loses the route to 172.16.20.0/24 and withdraws it from Router D. If this happens, Router D advertises to Router E the route to 172.16.20.0/24 due to the redistribution from EIGRP. This means that the alternative path is working fine. Unfortunately, because the hop count on the redistribution is set to 1 due to the default metric, when Router E gets the "real" route back from Router B, it will not use it because the one it received from Router D is better. This is not what you want to happen!

This is a classic redistribution routing loop. How do you solve it? The easiest thing to do is to filter the destinations redistributed from RIP into EIGRP and from EIGRP into RIP.

Using Distribute Lists to Troubleshoot Redistribution Routing Loops

The first, and simplest, way to handle this is to set up a distribute list specifically blocking the routes that you don't want to redistribute. For example, on Router D, you could build the following distribute list:

```
access-list 10 deny 172.16.20.0 0.0.0.255
access-list 10 permit any
!
router rip
 redistribute eigrp 100
 distribute-list 10 out serial 0
```

Assuming that serial 0 is the link between Router D and Router E, this will resolve the problem. RIP will not advertise the 172.16.20.0/24 route from Router D to Router E. If you have more than one connection back into the RIP side of the network, it can be difficult to manage the distribution lists that must be maintained.

Using Route Maps to Troubleshoot Redistribution Routing Loops

Another alternative to distribution lists is to use a route map; in which case, you would configure the following on Router D:

```
access-list 10 deny 172.16.20.0 0.0.0.255
access-list 10 permit any
!
route-map kill-loops permit 10
 match ip address 10
!
router rip
 redistribute eigrp 100 route-map kill-loops
```

This configuration allows only those networks permitted by access list 10 to be redistributed into RIP. This has the same effect as the distribute list used in the preceding solution, but it applies the filter in the redistribution rather than in the advertisement to Router D.

Another alternative is to match all external EIGRP routes in the route map, like this:

```
route-map kill-loops deny 10
 match route-type external
route-map kill-loops permit 20
```

But this will also "kill off" any external EIGRP routes learned from a protocol other than RIP. In other words, it will prevent external destinations elsewhere in the EIGRP network from being reached by the hosts attached on the RIP side of the network.

Using Prefix Lists to Troubleshoot Redistribution Routing Loops

In addition to using route maps to troubleshoot redistribution routing loops, you can also use prefix lists. For example, you could configure Router D with the following:

```
ip prefix-list loop-list 10 deny 172.16.20.0/24
ip prefix-list loop-list 10 permit 0.0.0.0/0 le 32
!
route-map kill-loops permit 10
 match prefix-list loop-list
!
router rip
 redistribute eigrp 100 route-map kill-loops
```

The big advantage of prefix lists is that they allow you to match based on prefix length (the subnet mask) as well as the prefix (destination network) itself. There are a lot of possibilities for filtering when this application is considered, but they won't be covered here.

Setting the Administrative Distance to Troubleshoot Redistribution Routing Loops

Another way to block these routes that is completely different and doesn't rely on the manual configuration of an access list, is to set the administrative distance of all external routes learned by Router D from Router A. You can accomplish this configuration using the **distance** command. On Router D, you would configure the following:

```
router eigrp 100
 distance 255 172.16.21.1 0.0.0.0
```

Assuming that Router A's address is 172.16.21.1, Router D assigns an administrative distance of 255 to any routes it receives from Router A. A route with the administrative distance of 255 will never be inserted in the routing table; therefore, they will not be redistributed into RIP from EIGRP (because redistribution always occurs from the routing table rather than any private databases that the various routing protocols use).

The only problem with this approach is that Router D will refuse all routes learned from Router A, including any legitimate ones. You can remedy this by adding the access list back into the equation:

```
access-list 10 permit 172.16.20.0 0.0.0.255
!
router eigrp 100
 distance 255 172.16.21.1 0.0.0.0 10
```

Using External Flags to Troubleshoot Redistribution Routing Loops

All of the previously mentioned troubleshooting methods will work, but they all require either configuring a list of networks or removing the alternative route through the other protocol as a possible backdoor route in the case of failure. Tagging EIGRP externals to block routing loops resolves these two problems and is fairly straightforward to configure.

The two networks in Figure 7-16 have recently been merged by connecting Router A to Router B and Router C to Router D. At some point in the future, the network administrators intend to replace RIP with EIGRP; for now, they are redistributing between RIP and EIGRP on Routers A and C.

Figure 7-16 *Complex Redistribution Routing Loop*

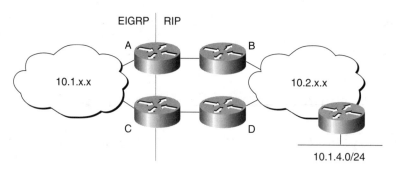

This setup produces a classic redistribution routing loop. Router B learns about some destination, for example 10.1.4.0/24, through RIP, and then advertises this route to Router A. Router A redistributes this route into EIGRP and advertises it to Router C. Then, Router A redistributes this route back into RIP and advertises it to Router D, which will then advertise it back to Router B (possibly with a better metric than Router B learned in the original advertisement).

Almost all of the EIGRP network uses addresses from the 10.1.0.0/16 address space, and almost all of the RIP network uses addresses from the 10.2.0.0/16 address space. However, there are some exceptions, such as the 10.1.4.0/24 network.

If it weren't for the exceptions, this redistribution routing loop would be easy to resolve. You would simply prevent Router A and Router C from advertising routes in the 10.2.0.0/16 address range to Router B and Router D and prevent Router B and Router D from advertising routes in the 10.1.0.0/16 address range to Router A and Router C. Distribution lists combined with summarization would make this configuration very easy. (See the previous Case Study, "Redistribution," in this chapter for more information.)

Because there are exceptions, though, preventing this redistribution routing loop becomes more of a problem. You could build distribution lists around the subnets present on each side and apply them on Router A, Router B, Router C, and Router D, but this adds some serious administrative overhead if there are a lot of exceptions. Specific distribution lists would also require modification for each new exception added.

It is easier to use an automatic method to flag the routes learned through RIP on Router A and Router C, and then you can prevent any route that is flagged from being redistributed back into RIP. For example, Router A will still learn about the 10.1.100.0/24 network through EIGRP and advertise this destination to Router B through RIP.

Router B will still advertise 10.1.4.0/24 to Router A, which will then redistribute it into EIGRP and advertise it to Router C. But Router A will flag this route as coming from the RIP domain so that Router C won't advertise it back into RIP. Using some sort of tag like this means that adding a new network in the RIP AS shouldn't require any reconfiguration on the routers doing the redistribution. This type of routing loop is a good use for EIGRP's *administrator tags*.

Administrator tags are applied and matched using route maps. On Router A and Router C, first you create the route maps and then you apply them to the redistribution between EIGRP and RIP by issuing the following:

```
route-map setflag permit 10
  set tag 1
route-map denyflag deny 10
  match tag 1
route-map denyflag permit 20
```

The **setflag** route map sets the administrator tag on any route to 1, whereas the **denyflag** route map denies routes with a flag of 1 and permits all others. On both Router A and Router C, you apply these route maps to the redistribution between EIGRP and RIP by issuing the following:

```
router eigrp 4000
  redistribute rip route-map setflag
router rip
  redistribute eigrp 4000 route-map denyflag
```

As routes are redistributed from RIP to EIGRP, the route map **setflag** is applied, setting the EIGRP administrative tag to 1. As the routes are redistributed from EIGRP to RIP, the administrative tag is checked; if it is 1, the route is denied so that it won't be redistributed.

Case Study: EIGRP/IGRP Redistribution

One issue commonly faced with EIGRP is redistribution between IGRP and EIGRP for combining networks and for transitioning from IGRP to EIGRP. Use the network in Figure 7-17 as an example.

Figure 7-17   *Redistribution between IGRP and EIGRP*

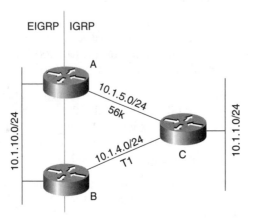

In this network, Router A and Router B are redistributing between EIGRP AS 1 IGRP AS 2. They have similar configurations:

```
hostname A
!
router eigrp 1
 redistribute igrp 2
 network 10.0.0.0
!
router igrp 2
 redistribute eigrp 2
 network 10.0.0.0
!
```

Looking at the routing table, you can see that Router A prefers the IGRP route through Router C, rather than the EIGRP external site through Router B, which is actually the better route (through a T1 rather than a 56k link):

```
A#show ip route
I       10.1.1.0 [100/2000] via 10.1.5.2, 00:00:39, Serial0
```

Looking at the topology table on Router A, you can see the entry through Router B:

```
A#show ip eigrp topology 10.1.1.0 255.255.255.0
IP-EIGRP topology entry for 10.1.1.0/24
   State is Passive, Query origin flag is 1, 1 Successor(s), FD is 256000
   Routing Descriptor Blocks:
   10.1.5.2, from 10.1.5.2, Send flag is 0x0
       Composite metric is (256000/25600), Route is External
```

The EIGRP metric is 256,000, which you can divide by 256 to directly compare to the IGRP metric. 256000/256 is 1000, so the EIGRP external metric is actually better. The redistribution is causing you to choose the worst route rather than the best.

You are choosing the IGRP route because of the administrative distance of the two protocols; whereas IGRP has an administrative distance of 100, EIGRP external sites have an administrative distance of 170.

If you reconfigure Router A and Router B so that EIGRP and IGRP are using the same AS, something odd happens in the routing table:

```
hostname B
!
router eigrp 1
 network 10.0.0.0
!
router igrp 1
 network 10.0.0.0
!
B#show ip route
DEX     10.1.1.0 [170/256000] via 10.1.10.2, 00:00:39, Ethernet0
```

Now the EIGRP external route learned from Router B is the preferred route! When comparing an EIGRP external (redistributed from IGRP in the same AS) and an IGRP route from the same AS, you ignore the administrative distances of the routes and compare only the metrics.

Case Study: Retransmissions and SIA

Two timers that can interact in EIGRP to cause a SIA route in EIGRP are the SIA timer and the hold timer between two peers. But how do these two relate? This section looks at the two independently and then it looks at how they interact.

The Hold Timer

The obvious use for the hold timer is to determine how long you will holdup a neighbor relationship without hearing any EIGRP hellos. Each time a router receives a hello packet from a neighbor, it resets the hold timer to the hold time contained in the hello packet and decrements it once for each second that passes.

Once the hold timer reaches zero, the neighbor is assumed dead. All paths through that neighbor are marked unusable (DUAL is run over these destinations to determine if the route needs to go active), and the neighbor is marked down.

But the hold timer is also used by the EIGRP's reliable transport mechanism as an outer bound on how long to wait for a neighbor to acknowledge the receipt of a packet. As mentioned in

Appendix C, EIGRP will attempt to retransmit 16 times or until retransmission has been occurring for as long as the hold timer, whichever is longer.

So, in the network depicted in Figure 7-18, assume that Router D's hold timer is 240 seconds. (Ignore the Hello timer because these are separate timers).

Figure 7-18   *Interactions between Hold Timers and SIA Timers*

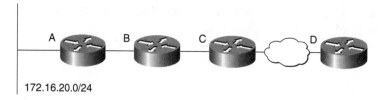

172.16.20.0/24

If Router C sends a packet to Router D, and Router D doesn't acknowledge the packet, Router C will continue retransmitting until it has retransmitted 16 times. Then, it will check to see if it has been retransmitting for 240 seconds. If it hasn't, it will continue sending the packet until it has been retransmitting for 240 seconds. Once it has attempted retransmission for 240 seconds, it will assume that Router D is never going to answer and clear its neighbor relationship.

SIA Timer

The other timer you need to concern yourself with is the SIA timer because it determines how long a query can be outstanding before the route is declared SIA and the neighbor relationship with the router that hasn't answered is torn down and restarted.

This timer is, by default, 3 minutes (although there has been talk of changing it). This means a router will wait 3 minutes once it has declared a route active until it decides that any neighbor that has not replied for this active route has a problem and restarts the neighbor.

Going back to Figure 7-18, this means that if Router A loses its connection to 172.16.20.0/24, it will send a query to Router B. If it doesn't receive a reply to that query within 3 minutes, it will restart its neighbor relationship with Router B. Note that two completely different things are being discussed here—one is how long to wait before getting an acknowledgement for a packet, and the other is how long to wait for a reply to a query.

Interaction between the Hold Timer and the SIA Timer

You can work through an example of how these two timers interact. Assume, in Figure 7-18, that Router A loses its connection to 172.16.20.0/24. Because it has no other paths to this destination, it will mark the route as active and send Router B a query.

Router B will acknowledge the query and then send a query to Router C; Router C will, in turn, acknowledge the query and send a query to Router D. But Router D, for some reason, never acknowledges the query. Router C will begin retransmitting the query to Router D, and attempt to do so until it has retransmitted for the length of the hold timer.

For the entire time that Router C is trying to get an acknowledgement from Router D, Router A's SIA timer is running. Because the SIA timer is 3 minutes, and Router D's hold timer is 4 minutes, it is safe to assume that Router A's SIA timer will go off before Router C gives up retransmitting the query to Router D and clears the neighbor relationship.

Therefore, Router A will register an SIA and clear its neighbor relationship with Router B. So, it's important to remember when designing your network that the hold timer for any given link should never be more than or equal to the SIA timer for the entire network.

In this case, there are two possible solutions:

- Reduce Router D's hold time to something less than the SIA timer (90 seconds, for example) by using the interface level command **ip eigrp hold-time**.

- Increase the SIA timer to something greater than the hold timer (5 minutes, for example) by using the command **timers active** under the **router eigrp** configuration.

It's difficult to know which option to pick without more information. If the link between Router C and Router D is congested often enough that an acknowledgement takes 4 minutes to get through, then it's probably going to be necessary to increase the SIA timer.

On the other hand, if it seems unreasonable to wait 4 minutes for a simple acknowledgement across a single link, then it's better to decrease the hold timer on Router D. (Remember to decrease the Hello timer, too.) The two tradeoffs are as follows:

- The hold timer should be a reasonable amount of time, given the nature of the link and the likelihood of an EIGRP packet being delayed for a given period of time.

- The SIA timer bounds the time the network is allowed to remain unconverged.

These two tradeoffs need to be balanced for your network. There are no magic numbers (although there are defaults).

Case Study: Multiple EIGRP ASs

One design used commonly in EIGRP to limit query range and improve stability is multiple ASs—but is this really effective? Look at Figure 7-19 for some answers.

Begin by assuming that Router D is redistributing all the routes from AS 100 into AS 200 and all the routes from AS 200 into AS 100. If Router C loses its direct connection to 172.30.9.0/24, it will note that it has no feasible successor, place the destination in active state, and query each of its neighbors.

Figure 7-19   *Multiple EIGRP ASs*

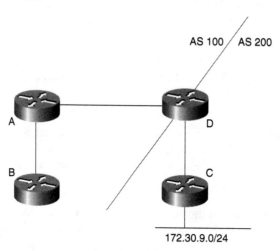

When Router D receives this query, what action will it take? It will look through its topology table and, seeing no other routes to this destination within this AS, immediately send a reply to Router C that this route is no longer reachable. Router C will acknowledge the reply and send an update to Router D that the route is no longer reachable. (So far, so good.)

Return to Router D once more. Router D was redistributing this route into AS 100. When Router D loses the route, it will go active on the AS 100 topology table entry and query its neighbors (in this case, Router A). Router A will, in turn, query Router B; the entire query process runs in AS 100 for this route.

In short, AS boundaries don't really stop queries in EIGRP. The query itself may stop, but a new query is generated at the AS border and propagated through the neighboring AS.

So it won't help with query range issues, but can it really harm anything? Take a look at Figure 7-20 for a moment.

Figure 7-20 reveals that not only does Router D redistribute between AS 100 and AS 200, but an autosummary for the 10.0.0.0/8 network on Router D is being advertised toward Router C, and an autosummary for 172.30.0.0/16 is being advertised toward Router A. Because of these autosummaries, the query range will be bound at Router A for 172.30.9.0/24. In other words, Router B will never receive a query about this network because Router A shouldn't have any information about it in its topology database.

The problem is that EIGRP doesn't autosummarize externals unless there is also an internal component in the topology table. Router D won't build summaries for the 10.0.0.0/8 and 172.30.0.0/16 networks automatically; it will advertise all of the components.

Figure 7-20   *Autosummarization across an AS Boundary*

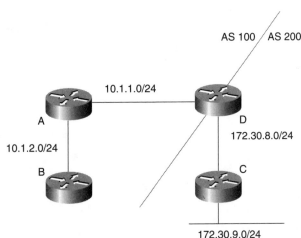

The really confusing part comes in if you decide to add something in the 10.0.0.0 network on Router B. Suppose that you add an Ethernet link to Router B and address it as 10.1.5.0/24. Router B will summarize this to be 10.0.0.0/8 and advertise it toward Router A (remember that this is an internal component), and Router A will advertise it to Router D.

When Router D sees that there is an internal component in the 10.0.0.0 network within AS 100, it will begin summarizing the external sites toward Router A, advertising only the 10.0.0.0/8 route. This means that Router A will have two routes to 10.0.0.0/8—a confusing situation at best.

What if you don't try to put a major net boundary on an AS boundary and rely on manual summarization? There aren't any other problems with multiple ASs, are there? As a matter of fact, yes. Take a look at Figure 7-21 for a third problem.

In the setup in Figure 7-21, Router B and Router D are redistributing between AS 100 and AS 200. Router E is redistributing from RIP into EIGRP AS 200. Router B will receive two routes for 172.30.9.0/24—an internal through Router C and an external through Router A—which route will it choose? The route through Router A probably has a better metric, but Router B will choose the path through Router C because the administrative distance of internal routes is better than the administrative distance of externals.

If all of these routers were in a single AS, Router B will choose the shortest path to 172.30.9.0/24; using multiple ASs causes the routers to choose suboptimal routes.

Consider the route to 172.30.11.0/24 next. Which route will Router B choose for this destination? It seems logical that Router B should choose the route through Router A because both routes are externals. (The administrative distances are the same for both routes.)

Figure 7-21   *Discontiguous ASs*

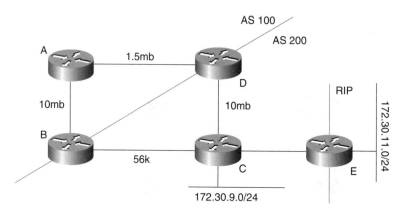

However, the behavior in this instance is undefined. In other words, Router B could choose either route, regardless of which one has the better metric.

All in all, it's best to stick to one AS unless you've carefully thought out all of the issues involved in multiple AS designs. With good design, you can limit the query scope within the network through summarization and distribution lists.

If an EIGRP network grows large enough to need splitting, it's better to use a protocol other than EIGRP to do so (preferably BGP, or possibly NHRP or MPLS).

Review

1 What are the two basic tools you can use to summarize routes (or hide destination details) in EIGRP?

2 How can you tell that a route is a summary when you look at the routing table?

3 What is the default administrative distance for a summary route? What is the problem with this?

4 What bounds a query?

5 How far beyond one of the possible query bounds will a query travel?

6 What is the primary advantage to summarizing between core routers rather than between the distribution layer and core?

7 How is it possible to "black hole" packets when summarizing destinations behind dual-homed remotes into the core?

8 Why should summarization be configured outbound from the distribution layer routers toward access layer routers at remote sites?

9 What is the most common problem with dual-homed remotes? What options are available to resolve it?

10 What methods can be used to break a redistribution routing loop?

11 Under what conditions is the administrative distance ignored between EIGRP and IGRP?

12 What options do you have for generating a default route in EIGRP?

13 How can you prevent multiple parallel links within a network from being used as transit paths?

14 What does EIGRP use to pace its packets on a link?

15 Implement EIGRP on the network you redesigned for Review Question 11 in Chapter 4, "Applying the Principles of Network Design." Discuss decisions on summarization points and be careful of non-transit paths and other design flaws.

PART III

Scaling beyond the Domain

CHAPTER 8

BGP Cores and Network Scalability

Border Gateway Protocol (BGP) is the routing protocol that (literally) glues the Internet together. It falls under the External Gateway Protocol (EGP) category—unlike the protocols described in previous chapters, which are Internal Gateway Protocols (IGPs). BGP4 is the current version, but throughout this chapter, it will be referred to simply as BGP.

Traditionally, BGP has been utilized to exchange routing information between different ASs. In the typical configuration, BGP is used to tie Internet service providers (ISPs) to their customers and each other. This chapter does not deal with connections to the Internet or inter-ISP operations—even though most of the experience in this area comes from the ISPs. Instead, it presents the proven, robust, and scalable BGP features that will allow your network to grow past any IGP limitations. The only portion where Internet connectivity is dealt with explicitly is in the "Case Study: Dual-Homed Connections to the Internet."

This chapter is not about BGP itself, but how it can be used to scale your network even further. It is assumed that you are familiar with the basic operation of the protocol. If you need a quick review, read Appendix D, "BGP Fundamentals," before continuing.

As described in previous chapters, hierarchy, addressing, summarization, and redundancy are essential components of a good network design. The way that the IGP of your choice is placed on top of these elements is equally important. However, all protocols have limitations, and as the network grows, you will unavoidably hit them. The main limitation is the amount of routing information that the protocol can handle, no matter how good your addressing scheme and summarization strategy is. On the other hand, BGP is currently deployed worldwide and carries more than 55,000 routing entries at the core of the Internet. (This number is growing at the time of this writing.) Some providers have been known to carry closer to 80,000 routes!

Policies are hard to define and enforce with an IGP because there is little flexibility— usually, only a tag is available. In the age of continuous mergers and acquisitions, it may be cumbersome and difficult to connect two networks while keeping instability isolated and managing multiple IGPs. BGP offers an extensive suite of knobs to deal with complex policies: communities, AS_PATH filters, local preference, and Multiple Exit Discriminator (MED), to name a few. BGP also counters instability by implementing a *route dampening* algorithm. This is when the advertisement of a route is suppressed if it is known to change regularly over a period of time. (All the parameters from the periodicity of the flaps to the type of routes suppressed are configurable.) Although you will follow the structural recommendations given in this book when building networks with the different IGPs studied, BGP is not tied to a set hierarchical model. In fact, the topology can take any form, and the protocol will adapt to it. Look at the Internet, it has no discernible hierarchical structure; it is impossible to pinpoint a core or a distribution layer (for the Internet as a whole)—and it works!

Neighbors, Routes, and Propagation Rules in BGP

A router using BGP exchanges routing information by forming a neighbor relationship with other routers. BGP routers can either establish internal or external peerings. BGP peers in the same AS are called iBGP peers, while peers in a different AS are called eBGP peers. An AS may have more than one external connection (on different routers); in which case, there is a need to have several BGP speakers in the network to maintain routing consistency. Unlike other protocols, the rules of when and if a prefix is advertised to a neighbor depend on the type of neighbor the prefix was learned from. There are three possible combinations:

- **Routes learned from an eBGP peer**—Propagated to all peers.
- **Routes learned from an iBGP peer**—Propagated only to eBGP peers.
- **Routes originated locally**—Propagated to all peers.

Because routes learned from iBGP peers are not sent to other iBGP peers, it is clear that a full logical mesh is needed between them to ensure consistent routing information.

This chapter is a discussion of the use of BGP as a way to scale your network even further. The discussion starts with a description of the implementation in the core of the network (where full routing is required) and then expands the concepts to be used in the network as a whole.

BGP in the Core

The core is the place in your network where the scalability pains will be felt first. The core needs to have full knowledge of all the destinations in the network—full routes. The task is to configure BGP on all the core routers, and let it handle the routes that are external to the core. The IGP will carry only the information about local destinations. See Figure 8-1.

A simple way to shift the burden of carrying the routing information to BGP is to implement a full iBGP mesh in the core. In this case, the routing information from the distribution layer is redistributed into BGP, which carries it as internal routes. IGP routes have a lower administrative distance than iBGP and, hence, are favored. Therefore, it is necessary to filter all the IGP routes coming from the distribution layer into the core. Another solution is to use a different IGP in the core (or at least use a different instance or process). In addition, iBGP synchronization needs to be turned off. For details on synchronization, see Appendix D, "BGP Fundamentals."

Figure 8-1   *The Network Core*

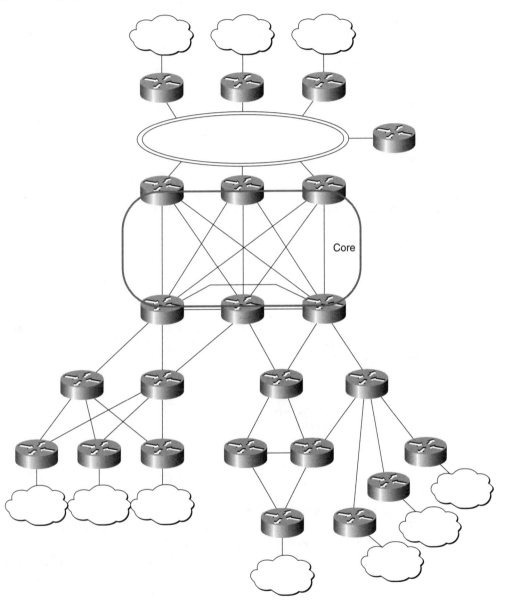

This approach provides an instant scalable core. In terms of migration, you should overlay BGP on the IGP that is currently in use. Once the routes have been redistributed into BGP, and its consistency is verified (in other words, make sure that all the routes are present in the BGP table), you can start filtering the IGP information at the border. If two or more distribution routers are introducing the same summary, then changing iBGP's administrative distance to favor its routes over the IGP's is a safer approach.

It is very important to highlight the fact that BGP was not conceived as an IGP; its main objective when it was designed was to carry external routes—routes learned from other ASs or routing domains. BGP cannot detect routing loops within an AS; it can detect loops only in eBGP routes.

Because of this, you cannot redistribute iBGP routes (routes originated in the local AS) into your IGP. In other words, the BGP routes cannot be passed on to the distribution layer. This leaves you with a single choice: to only carry a default pointing back to the core. If your distribution layer needs at least partial routing information from the core, then you will need to have an eBGP connection. This approach is explored in the following sections. Another advantage of using eBGP to glue your network together is the added flexibility (in filtering and decision making) that BGP provides.

Case Study: Sample Migration

Consider the network core in Figure 8-1. The first task is to overlay BGP on the existing network without any other changes taking place. The configuration is simple and can be standardized for ease of deployment:

```
router bgp 109
 no synchronization
 redistribute ospf 1 route-map routes-to-core
 neighbor x.x.x.x remote-as 109
 no auto-summary
!
route-map routes-to-core permit 10
 set metric-type internal
```

Note that synchronization and autosummary are turned off. This last action allows BGP to carry the routing information with the same granularity as the IGP does (not only the major networks). Also, the MED is set using the **set metric-type internal** command with the purpose of being able to choose the best exit point (shortest IGP distance) in case of multiple options. Remember: One **neighbor** statement is required for each of the other routers in the core.

As discussed in Chapter 5, "OSPF Network Design," the ABRs may or may not be located at the edge of the core. The preceding configuration assumes that the ABRs are not the border routers—so redistribution of OSPF into BGP takes place. Keep in mind that the redistributed routes are the ones present in the routing table.

If the border routers are ABRs, then summarization takes place at these routers. The summarized routes, however, are not present in the routing table at the ABRs. It is necessary to manually create the summaries and then redistribute them. The sample configuration changes to something like this:

```
router bgp 109
 no synchronization
 neighbor x.x.x.x remote-as 109
 redistribute static route-map routes-to-core
 no auto-summary
!
router ospf 109
 area 0 range y.y.y.y t.t.t.t
 area 0 range t.t.t.t t.t.t.t
!
ip route y.y.y.y y.y.y.y null0
ip route t.t.t.t t.t.t.t null0
!
route-map routes-to-core permit 10
 set metric 20
```

An advantage of this method is that the routes are "nailed" to the null0 interface (which means it never flaps and never goes down), which will ensure stability in the core regardless of the state of any of the areas. One major difference in the approach is the use of the metric; in this case, the metric may be set either with a route map, or on each route at the time that they are defined.

To verify the consistency of the information in the BGP table, a comparison must be made between the data in the routing table (learned via OSPF, in this case) and the one in the BGP table. The following configuration presents an example of what you need to see (for network 20.1.1.0/24, in this case):

```
rtrC#show ip route 20.1.1.0
Routing entry for 20.1.1.0/24
  Known via "ospf 109", distance 110, metric 65, type intra area
  Redistributing via ospf 109
  Last update from 140.10.50.6 on Serial0, 00:00:28 ago
  Routing Descriptor Blocks:
  * 140.10.50.6, from 20.1.1.1, 00:00:28 ago, via Serial0
      Route metric is 65, traffic share count is 1

rtrC#show ip bgp 20.1.1.0
BGP routing table entry for 20.1.1.0/24, version 47
Paths: (1 available, best #1)
  Local
    140.10.50.6 from 140.10.50.6 (20.1.1.1)
      Origin incomplete, metric 20, localpref 100, valid, internal, best
```

If these two tables are not uniform, then you will need to revisit your redistribution points and check your filters (if any). Because LSA filtering can be tricky (at best) or impossible, changing the administrative distance for the iBGP routes will be explored next. To achieve the change, the following command is used:

```
router bgp 109
 distance bgp 20 20 20
```

This command sets the administrative distance for internal, external, and local BGP routes to 20. In Cisco routers, the default administrative distance for OSPF routes is 110—and the lowest value is preferred. To verify the effectiveness of the change, take a look at the routes again:

```
rtrC#show ip route 20.1.1.0
Routing entry for 20.1.1.0/24
  Known via "bgp 109", distance 20, metric 20, type internal
  Last update from 140.10.50.6 00:00:09 ago
  Routing Descriptor Blocks:
  * 140.10.50.6, from 140.10.50.6, 00:00:09 ago
      Route metric is 20, traffic share count is 1
      AS Hops 0

rtrC#show ip bgp 20.1.1.0
BGP routing table entry for 20.1.1.0/24, version 47
Paths: (1 available, best #1)
  Local
    140.10.50.6 from 140.10.50.6 (20.1.1.1)
      Origin incomplete, metric 20, localpref 100, valid, internal, best
```

Now, the BGP route is the one in the routing table.

Scaling beyond the Core

As your network grows toward becoming an international Juggernaut, you will find that taking the load off the core routers is not enough—it is time to extend the use of BGP to the rest of the network. Three different approaches may be followed in general:

- You can divide your network into separate routing domains—connect them using eBGP.
- You can use confederations.
- You can use route reflectors.

iBGP requires a full internal mesh to ensure routing consistency. This internal mesh grows larger as BGP extends throughout the network and, of course, as the network grows. The last two approaches in the preceding list present a scalable way to reduce the number of neighbors while maintaining consistency. Dividing your network up into separate ASs and reducing the number of internal neighbors will be covered first.

The first two approaches are very similar. In fact, both require that you follow these three "easy" steps:

1 Divide the network into multiple regions/areas.

2 Select and configure an IGP for each region/area.

3 Connect each region using BGP.

The "divide and conquer" option that you chose will depend on a combination of the topology (resulting from the division) and the external connectivity. The following "rule of thumb" is offered to aid in the decision:

1 Is your network connected to the Internet or are you planning to connect it?

   — If no, then connect the pieces using eBGP.

   — If yes, then go to the next step.

2 Did the division result in a two level hierarchy with a core AS and all the others connecting to it (and not among themselves)? (See Figure 8-2.)

   — If no, then use confederations.

   — If yes, then go to the next step.

3 Where are the connections to the Internet located?

   — If at least one is not in the core AS, use confederations.

You have reached the end of the "magic formula" and no clear decision may have been made. The next couple of pages examine the general case, concentrating on using eBGP connections to tie the pieces together. The operation of a network using confederations is described later in this chapter.

Dividing the Network into Pieces

Depending on the topology (both logical and physical) of your network, the division may take place along geographical boundaries, departmental lines, or the hierarchical structure itself. Figure 8-2 shows a proposed partition of the sample network.

The most straightforward partition is along hierarchical lines. (The same principles can be extended to networks fragmented along different lines.) The distribution layer will always connect to the core at different points. This, along with the fact that it is at these junctions where summarization takes place, makes implementation of a BGP core ideal. In this case, the local BGP process in the distribution router will originate the summarized routes. An eBGP connection will carry the routes into the core, allowing for detailed control regarding which routes make it through and their attributes. The core routers should be configured in a full iBGP mesh.

Figure 8-2 *Divided Into Regions*

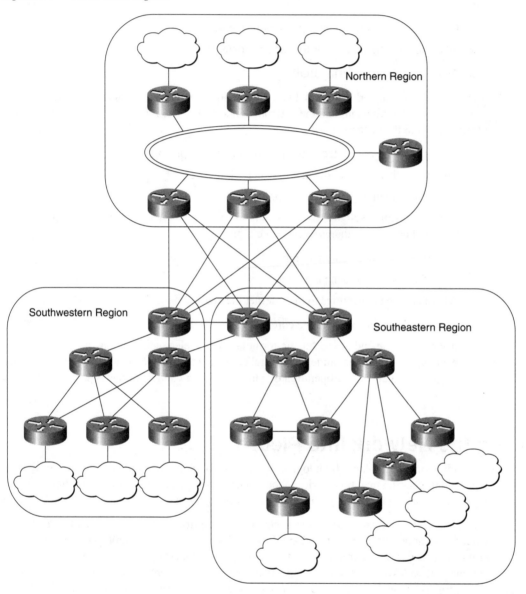

At this point, you have managed to effectively split the network up into several independent units. From the BGP point of view, the core has a full iBGP mesh and eBGP connections to all the other subnetworks. The subnetworks need to have only a few *BGP speakers*, which are the routers that connect to the core. However, there are two situations where you should consider creating an iBGP mesh inside any of these subnetworks:

- **Most of the routes from the core are needed**—In this case, you will have the same scalability issues as you encountered in the core before.

- **The need exists to provide transit to reach other subnetworks**—Clearly, the number of routes will considerably increase and will need to be transported to the core. This scenario will occur only on networks either resulting in more than one layer of hierarchy or without a clear core AS.

Until now, you have been dealing with a straight hierarchical network where there is a core network with all the other pieces connected to it. BGP, however, allows the flexibility to connect the subnetworks anyway you want! BGP will take care of finding the best path to any destination for you.

Connections to the Internet, and/or other networks, should take place at the core, and Private Autonomous System Numbers (ASNs) should be removed at the point where you attach to the outside world. It is important to distinguish the regional eBGP connections from the "real" external ones.

In the case where multiple connections to the Internet exist, these should be located in the core region. If this is not possible, then confederations must be used.

Regional IGPs

After dividing the network into regions, you will effectively have created several "independent" networks. Each one may be designed to have its own core, distribution layer, access layer, addressing scheme, and internal redundancy. In addition, each region may use its own IGP.

The decision whether to use different IGPs or not is up to you. Link state protocols may be tricky in the implementation of filters. If anything, you might end up at least using different instances of the same protocol in the different regions.

BGP Network Growing Pains

Even BGP may experience some growing pains as the core or the regions grow. Keep in mind that a full iBGP mesh is required. Most likely, the core will have a pervasive BGP configuration (which means that all the routers run BGP). Some of the issues that need to be kept in mind with a large number of neighbors include the following:

- BGP update generation
- Loss of information due to aggregation
- Scaling BGP policies
- Scaling IBGP mesh
- Route flaps

Update Generation Issues

BGP sends only incremental updates. If the network is stable, why is update generation a problem? One update needs to be formed for every peer. In other words, each time a prefix changes, the router needs to generate the same amount of updates as neighbors that it has. In routers with a high number of neighbors (even those that experience sporadic changes), this could represent impairment in the form of high percentage processor utilization, which may result in the router not having enough cycles to process traffic. There are two ways to prevent this problem:

- Reduce the number of updates generated
- Reduce the number of neighbors

Reducing the Number of Updates Generated

To reduce the number of updates generated, it's not obligatory to reduce the number of neighbors. The amount of updates may be decreased with the use of Peer Groups.

A *Peer Group* is a set of BGP neighbors that shares the same outbound policy, but their inbound policies may be different. You may configure your router to filter out routes sent to some of the departments in the company (the routes to reach the payroll servers, for instance). In general, iBGP peers receive the same updates all the time, making them ideal to be arranged in a Peer Group. The main advantage, besides ease of configuration, is the fact that the updates are generated only once per Peer Group.

Reducing Neighbor Count

At first glance, the reduction of the number of neighbors does not seem to be possible. After all, you already know that a full iBGP mesh is required for proper operation of the protocol. As far as eBGP peers are concerned, if external information is needed, they have to be there. Two methods can be used, however, to achieve a reduction in the number of neighbors—iBGP neighbors, that is:

- Confederations
- Route reflectors

The next two sections cover these methods in greater detail.

Confederations

In short, this method of reducing the number of neighbors consists of breaking up the AS into smaller units by following the same procedure that was outlined before: assigning a separate ASN to each new piece instead of using a private ASN for each one. In other words, make it look like one AS to the eBGP peers.

The AS will be divided into pieces, each piece will be its own AS (using private numbering) complete with iBGP as well as eBGP peers. The iBGP peers will be the other BGP speakers in the same sub-AS, whereas the eBGP peers will be the BGP speakers both in the other sub-AS and outside the main AS. Each router is configured with the new sub-ASN, but it is given information about which other ASs belongs to the same confederation. In general, eBGP peers between the sub-ASs and the AS are treated as ordinary eBGP peers with one exception: local preference and MED are passed across AS boundaries. This behavior allows the main AS to function as one to the outside. If you are confused, look at Figure 8-3.

Figure 8-3   *Confederations*

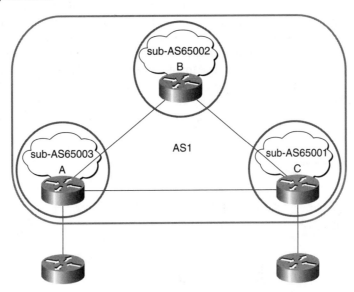

The real ASN is 1; external neighbors will see all three of the ASs as one AS. Internally, the network has been divided into three new sub-ASs. Routers A, B, and C are all eBGP neighbors inside the confederation.

The main advantage of using confederations is the fact that now policies can be more easily controlled inside the network by having multiple ASs. However, the whole network needs to be migrated to this scheme at the same time, and leaving one or more routers without a proper confederation configuration may cause routing loops. At all times each member of a confederation (that is, all the BGP routers in the network) should know what the real ASN is, which sub-AS it belongs to, and what other sub-ASs belong to the same confederation. If any of this information is missing, then improper information propagation may result.

Route Reflectors

One of the big advantages of route reflectors is that you can stage your migration to them, which means that you can configure one router at a time without disrupting normal operation of the whole network.

In short, the iBGP forwarding rules are broken; route reflectors are capable of forwarding iBGP-learned routes to other iBGP peers. It is important to understand that only the routers configured as route reflectors will forward routes to other iBGP peers. Therefore, only the route reflectors need any special configuration.

Because route reflectors may be deployed throughout the network at any given time, study their implementation in parts of the network illustrated in Figure 8-1. The core will maintain a full mesh configuration as long as all the routers at its edge are route reflectors. Some parts of the network may have a two-tier route reflection structure. In general, the best way to place clusters in the network is to follow the physical topology. A router configured as a route reflector will categorize its iBGP neighbors as clients and non-clients (refer to Figure 8-4). Clients are routers that depend on the route reflector to receive internal routing information; clients do not need any type of special configuration—in fact, all they need is an iBGP session to the route reflector. A route reflector and its clients are collectively known as a *cluster*.

Figure 8-4   *Two-Tier Route Reflector Mesh*

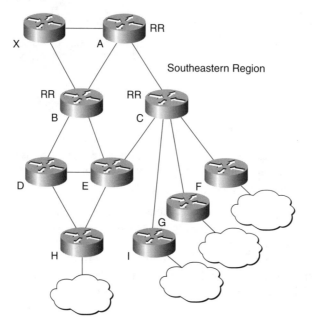

Figure 8-4 shows two separate clusters; each one will be covered here. Router C is a route reflector with four clients (Router I, Router G, Router E, and Router F). If both Router I and Router G have external connections, the prefixes are forwarded as follows:

1 Routers I and G receive an external route. (Assume it's for the same prefix.)

2 Both routers announce this prefix to their iBGP neighbor—Router C is their only iBGP peer.

3 Router C compares the routes and selects one best path.

4 Because it is a route reflector, Router C propagates its best path to all its other clients and non-clients. (Router A is the only non-client peering with Router C, in this case.)

Note that in Router C's case the clients don't have iBGP sessions between them. Router B is a route reflector with three fully-meshed clients (Router D, Router E, and Router H). The full mesh at the client level yields two different results. First, the route reflector doesn't have to reflect the information between clients. Although you might be thinking that a fully-meshed configuration defeats the purpose of having a route reflector, it isn't true! Keep in mind that the objective is to reduce the number of iBGP peers: the clients have a full mesh, but they don't have to peer with the rest of the network! If Router H has an external connection, the prefixes are forwarded as follows:

1 Router H receives an external route, and it propagates it to all of its iBGP peers (Router D, Router E, and Router B).

2 Routers D and E don't do anything more—they follow the rules!

3 Router B will propagate the path information (if it is the best path) to its non-clients (Router A and Router X).

As a side note, if Router B were to reflect the best path back to its clients, there would be redundant information. The issue here is not the redundant information that the clients would receive but the processing that is required by the route reflector. In other words, it is recommended to have a cluster with a full mesh of clients if clients are present in a significant number or if the physical topology dictates this to be so.

Route Reflector Redundancy

As you may have noticed, a route reflector may become a single point of failure. In many cases, this situation is unavoidable because of the physical topology of the network (as discussed in Chapter 3, "Redundancy").

There are a couple of ways to achieve route reflector redundancy. The "classical" case is when the route reflectors are put in the same cluster. Each cluster has a cluster ID (usually the router ID of the route reflector). So, you need to configure all the reflectors to have the same cluster ID. The limitation (but also where the additional redundancy is present) is that all the clients need to have iBGP sessions with both reflectors. The route reflectors should be iBGP peers of each other; if a prefix has already been forwarded by one of the reflectors, the others will not forward it. (This is where the cluster ID comes into play.)

The "modern" approach is to have only one route reflector per cluster. In this case, not all the clients need to connect to all the route reflectors (only the ones that need/want the redundancy). Refer back to Figure 8-4; Router E is a client of two different route reflectors.

Route Reflector Deployment

What is the best way to deploy route reflectors? Where should the reflectors be placed? Before these questions are answered, refer back to Figure 8-4. A third cluster could have been defined with Router A as the route reflector and Router B and Router C as clients, creating a two-level, route reflector architecture.

Keeping in mind the initial objective of using BGP to help scale the network, a route reflector architecture would be deployed in two layers with a full mesh core. Referring back to Figure 8-1, the routers at the network core should be configured in a full iBGP mesh. The routers that border with the distribution layer act as an upper layer of route reflectors. A lower layer may be put at the border between the distribution and access layers. These second level route reflectors would be clients of the first layer ones. A rule of thumb to comply with is this: follow the physical topology. In other words, define the iBGP peering—between clients, reflectors, and/or normal internal peers—to match the physical connectivity of the network. This will provide simplicity to the network and not present a false sense of redundancy.

Figure 8-5 shows another part of the network where route reflectors may be used. In this case, Routers A and B are configured as route reflectors, and Routers C, D, and E are clients of both; note the dual connections. Both the physical topology and the logical BGP connectivity clearly indicate that the packets between clients will go through one of the reflectors, which of the reflectors depends on the IGP metrics.

Case Study: Route Reflectors as Route Servers

Sometimes route reflectors are confused with route servers (and vice versa). Route servers are generally used at Internet exchange points. The objective is for routers to only peer with the route server (not all the other routers in the exchange) and obtain all the routing information from it. The route server has the capability of propagating information in a transparent fashion—as if the advertisements were received directly from the router originating it.

Route reflectors also try to reduce the number of peers needed in an iBGP cloud, whereas the route server is typically used with eBGP neighbors. The route server itself processes no traffic, whereas the route reflectors do. In fact, route reflectors are usually placed at traffic aggregation points. It is clear that route reflectors and route servers satisfy different needs in the network.

Figure 8-6 illustrates a place in the network where a route reflector may be used as a route server.

Figure 8-5   *Dual Connections into Reflectors*

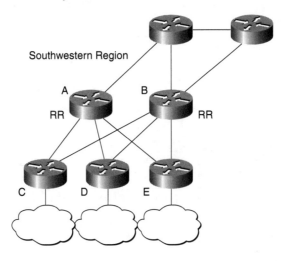

Figure 8-6   *Route Server*

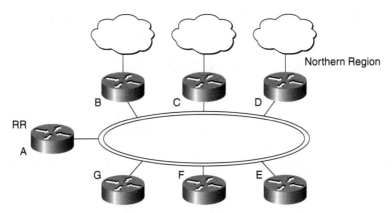

Router A is the route reflector, and it peers with all the other routers on this shared media. The other routers don't peer among themselves. Note that the route reflector is a "router on a stick." In other words, it only has one interface. (This is not necessary, but it makes the example clearer.) All the routes reflected would have a next hop that is reachable through one of the other routers so that Router A will not process the data packets. Keep in mind that the route reflector doesn't change the attributes in the prefixes.

To illustrate this, assume that an external route is learned through Router B. The route is propagated through Router A (the route reflector) to Router E (and all the other clients). This is what the prefix looks like from Router E:

```
E#show ip bgp 30.0.0.0
BGP routing table entry for 30.0.0.0/8, version 7
Paths: (1 available, best #1)
  200
    200.200.200.2 from 10.105.1.71 (200.200.200.1)
      Origin IGP, metric 0, localpref 100, valid, internal, best
      Originator : 200.200.200.1, Cluster list: 140.10.245.1

E #show ip route 200.200.200.2
Routing entry for 200.200.200.0/24, Hash 196
  Known via "isis", distance 115, metric 20, type level-1
  Redistributing via isis
  Last update from 10.105.1.76 on Ethernet0, 00:04:25 ago
  Routing Descriptor Blocks:
  * 10.105.1.76, from 200.200.200.1, via Ethernet0
      Route metric is 20, traffic share count is 1
```

Note that the prefix was learned from the route reflector (10.105.1.71), but the next hop is reachable via Router B (10.105.1.76). In this case, the traffic destined for 30.0.0.0/8 will be forwarded directly to Router B from Router E without going through the route reflector.

Case Study: Troubleshooting BGP Neighbor Relationships

Because BGP is designed as an EGP, rather than an IGP, there isn't much to BGP neighbor relationships. The primary thing to keep in mind is that all communications between BGP peers are based on TCP. So, a valid IP connection must be in place between the peers before a relationship can be established. Take a look at Figure 8-7, which is only three routers, to see what problems are possible.

Figure 8-7   *Simple Network with BGP Peers*

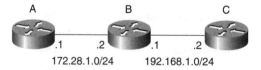

Begin by looking at what Router A would look like with a good, "up and running" eBGP neighbor relationship with Router B. Issuing **show ip bgp neighbor** results in the following output:

```
A#show ip bgp neighbor
BGP neighbor is 172.28.1.2,  remote AS 2, external link
....
  BGP version 4, remote router ID 10.1.1.1
  BGP state = Established, table version = 1, up for 00:00:33
....
Connections established 2; dropped 1
  Last reset 00:01:01, due to : User reset request
  No. of prefix received 0
Connection state is ESTAB, I/O status: 1, unread input bytes: 0
Local host: 172.28.1.1, Local port: 11001
Foreign host: 172.28.1.2, Foreign port: 179
....
SRTT: 710 ms, RTTO: 4442 ms, RTV: 1511 ms, KRTT: 0 ms
```

One main point in the output tells you that this neighbor relationship is up and running fine—the state is established. Other states of interest are

- **Idle**—No BGP neighbor relationship exists with this neighbor.
- **Connect**—BGP is waiting for the transport protocol (TCP) to establish a connection.
- **Active**—BGP is trying to connect to a peer by starting a transport protocol (TCP) connection.
- **OpenSent**—BGP has established a TCP connection, sent an OPEN message, and is now waiting for an OPEN message from its peer.
- **OpenConfirm**—At this point the OPEN message has been received and verified; BGP is not waiting for a Keepalive (or a Notification) message.
- **Established**—BGP can exchange routing information at this point.

No IP Connectivity

When neighbors cycle through the Idle, Connect, and Active states, it generally means that there is no IP path between them. There isn't much to do here but try and figure out why the IP connectivity isn't good. Generally, pings and trace routes can be used to find problems at this level. A **show ip bgp neighbor** may show:

```
A#show ip bgp neighbor
BGP neighbor is 172.28.1.2,  remote AS 2, external link
  Index 1, Offset 0, Mask 0x2
  BGP version 4, remote router ID 0.0.0.0
  BGP state = Active, table version = 0
  Last read 00:00:17, hold time is 180, keepalive interval is 60 seconds
  Minimum time between advertisement runs is 30 seconds
  Received 3 messages, 0 notifications, 0 in queue
  Sent 3 messages, 0 notifications, 0 in queue
  Connections established 1; dropped 1
  Last reset 00:00:19, due to : User reset request
  No. of prefix received 0
  No active TCP connection
```

There are a couple of items that should be highlighted from the preceding output:

- **The "BGP state"** — In this case it indicates "Active." This state was chosen (over Connect or Idle) because it is the most confusing one. "Active" doesn't indicate that the connection is working; it indicates that the router is actively attempting to establish a connection.

- **The last line in the display** — "No active TCP connection" is a clear indication of what is going on.

eBGP Multihop

eBGP is designed to run only between directly connected neighbors, such as between Routers A and B in Figure 8-7. When attempting to configure Routers A and C as eBGP neighbors, Router A will show the following:

```
A#showip bgp neighbor
BGP neighbor is 192.168.1.2,  remote AS 1, external link
 Index 1, Offset 0, Mask 0x2
  BGP version 4, remote router ID 0.0.0.0
  BGP state = Idle, table version = 0
  Last read 00:00:18, hold time is 180, keepalive interval is 60 seconds
  Minimum time between advertisement runs is 30 seconds
  Received 0 messages, 0 notifications, 0 in queue
  Sent 0 messages, 0 notifications, 0 in queue
  Prefix advertised 0, suppressed 0, withdrawn 0
  Connections established 0; dropped 0
  Last reset never
  0 accepted prefixes consume 0 bytes
  0 history paths consume 0 bytes
  External BGP neighbor not directly connected.
  No active TCP connection
```

Note that there is no active TCP connection, and the display states the External BGP neighbor isn't directly connected. If you configure both of these routers for **ebgp-multihop**, the following illustrates what happens:

```
A#conf t
Enter configuration commands, one per line. End with CNTL/Z.
A(config)#router bgp 2
A(config-router)#neighbor 192.168.1.2 ebgp-multihop
A#show ip bgp neighbor
BGP neighbor is 192.168.1.2,  remote AS 1, external link
 ....
   BGP state = Established, table version = 93, up for 00:00:19
 ....
   External BGP neighbor may be up to 255 hops away.
 Connection state is ESTAB, I/O status: 1, unread input bytes: 0
 Local host: 172.28.1.1, Local port: 179
 Foreign host: 192.168.1.2, Foreign port: 11008
```

Note the output of **show ip bgp neighbor** now states the external neighbor may be up to 255 hops away.

Other BGP Neighbor Problems

There are a couple of other problems you can run into with BGP neighbor relationships, which will be quickly mentioned here. The first is that BGP neighbor relationships will not build at all if the AS numbers are configured incorrectly. For instance, two routers with the following configurations will not ever build a neighbor relationship:

```
hostname routerA
!
router bgp 100
 neighbor <B> remote-as 100

hostname routerB
!
router bgp 200
 neighbor <A> remote-as 100
```

Also, you can set the hello and hold intervals for a BGP router:

```
router(config-router)#neighbor 10.1.1.1 timers ?
  <1-4294967295>  Keepalive interval
router(config-router)#neighbor 10.1.1.1 timers 100 ?
  <1-4294967295>  Holdtime
router(config-router)#neighbor 10.1.1.1 timers 100 100 ?
  <cr>
```

These values are not negotiated between routers. They are calculated depending on the local settings and the value received in the Open message (which only carries the Hold Time). Therefore, they can be set to almost anything you want, as long as they are over 3 seconds. The algorithm used to calculate the timers is such that even if the configuration does not match, both routers (for a given BGP session) will use the same values. As you can tell, this is not really a problem, but a common cause of confusion. Luckily, the output of **show ip bgp neighbors** includes a line that indicates the timers used for that particular session:

```
router#show ip bgp neighbor
BGP neighbor is 192.168.1.2,  remote AS 1, external link
...
Last read 00:00:18, hold time is 180, keepalive interval is 60 seconds
...
```

Logging Neighbor Changes

Although there aren't a lot of things that can go wrong with BGP neighbor relationships, it is useful to log changes in the states of neighbors anyway so that you can tell what happened after any type of event occurs. The configuration for logging neighbor changes is simple:

```
router#conf t
Enter configuration commands, one per line. End with CNTL/Z.
router(config)#router bgp 2
router(config-router)#bgp log-neighbor-changes
```

Case Study: Conditional Advertisement

It's often useful to conditionally advertise some routes to upstream neighbors—particularly if you are trying to control which link is crossed by traffic destined to a particular network. (Refer to "Case Study: Dual-Homed Connections to the Internet" for an example.)

BGP has the capability to conditionally advertise routes; look at Figure 8-8 and work through the example that follows.

Figure 8-8   *Conditional Advertisement*

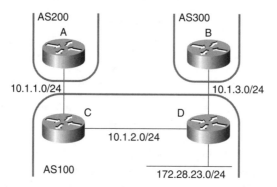

In this case, you want to advertise 172.28.23.0/24 to Router B as long as that link is up, but if it fails, you want to advertise this route to Router A from Router C.

Here, you would build a normal eBGP neighbor relationship between Routers B and D and a normal iBGP neighbor relationship between Routers C and D. The only magic is on Router C. Take a look at Router C's configuration:

```
C#sho running-config
Building configuration...
....
!
router ospf 100
 network 0.0.0.0 255.255.255.255 area 0
!
router bgp 100
 network 172.28.23.0 mask 255.255.255.0
 neighbor 10.1.1.1 remote-as 200
 neighbor 10.1.1.1 distribute-list 20 out
 neighbor 10.1.1.1 advertise-map toadvertise non-exist-map ifnotexist
 neighbor 10.1.2.2 remote-as 100
!
access-list 10 permit 172.28.23.0 0.0.0.255
access-list 20 deny   10.1.3.0 0.0.0.255
access-list 20 permit any
access-list 30 permit 10.1.3.0 0.0.0.255
....
route-map ifnotexist permit 10
 match ip address 30
!
route-map ifnotexist deny 20
!
route-map toadvertise permit 10
 match ip address 10
!
```

The magic is in the **neighbor 10.1.1.1 advertise-map toadvertise non-exist-map ifnotexist** configuration statement. This tells BGP to advertise those networks permitted by the route map **toadvertise** if the networks matched by route map **ifnotexist** aren't in the BGP table.

To see if it works, you need to shut down the link from Router B to Router D and see if Router A picks the 172.28.23.0/24 network up in its routing table:

```
D(config)#int s1
D(config-if)#shut
D(config-if)#
%LINEPROTO-5-UPDOWN: Line protocol on Interface Serial1, changed state to down
%LINK-5-CHANGED: Interface Serial1, changed state to administratively down

A>sho ip route
....
172.28.0.0/16 is subnetted, 1 subnets
B       172.28.23.0 [20/60] via 10.1.1.2, 00:00:25
....
```

Case Study: Dual-Homed Connections to the Internet

Because it's becoming common to see networks dual-homed to the Internet through two service providers, one of the questions people ask is how to load share between these multiple connections. There are two sides to this equation: inbound traffic and outbound traffic. Because asymmetric routing is very common throughout the Internet, the two traffic flows need to be dealt with separately. Along with these two issues, the effects of the use of default routing versus receiving partial/full routing from the providers will also be explored. The last section in this case study deals with the danger of becoming a transit AS.

For the discussion that follows, use Figure 8-9 as a network to work with.

Figure 8-9   *Dual-Homed to the Internet*

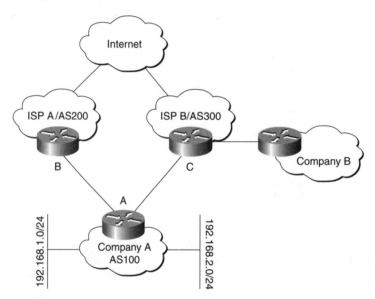

Load Sharing on the Inbound Side

Load sharing on the inbound side is a difficult proposition to start with because you really don't have any control over the decisions made by the routers in other ASs. You, essentially, have three choices:

- Prepend entries to your AS path.
- Set your Multi-Exit Discriminator (MED) outbound.
- Set communities on your outbound advertisements.

The last two options apply only if you are dual-homed to the same provider as in Figure 8-10.

Figure 8-10   *Dual-Homed to the Same ISP*

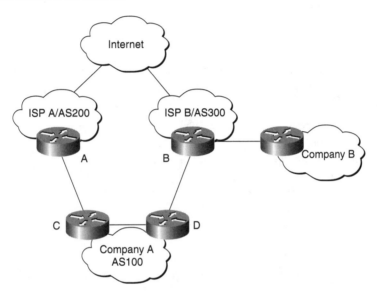

The one thing to remember is that ISPs often aggregate the address space you are advertising through them, and routers always choose the path with the longest prefix length. Before implementing any of these methods, you need to have a discussion with your providers about their aggregation policies. If there is a strong aggregation policy, there may not be much you can do about controlling inbound load, except, perhaps, controlling what you advertise out each link. (See "Case Study: Conditional Advertisement.")

Prepending AS Path Entries

Prepending AS path entries is usually fairly effective in controlling traffic inbound to your network. It's rather simple to configure, as well. If you want the traffic destined to 192.168.2.0/24 to come through ISP A and the traffic destined to 192.168.1.0/24 to pass through ISP B, you could configure the following:

```
router bgp 100
 neighbor <B> remote-as 200
 neighbor <B> route-map add-to-200 out
 neighbor <C> remote-as 300
 neighbor <C> route-map add-to-300 out
route-map add-to-200 permit 10
 match ip address 5
 set as-path-prepend 100 100
route-map add-to-300 permit 10
 match ip address 10
 set as-path-prepend 100 100
access-list 5 permit 192.168.1.0 0.0.0.255
access-list 10 permit 192.168.2.0 0.0.0.255
```

Making the AS_PATH length longer for 192.168.1.0/24 when it is advertised to ISP A, and vice versa, will achieve the objective.

Setting MED Outbound

The MED is an indication (to your neighbor AS) of which path you prefer for incoming traffic. As mentioned previously, the MED should be used only when dual-homed to the same AS (as in Figure 8-10).

The value that should be used for the MED is the metric of your IGP to reach the advertised destination. In other words, you will be giving an indication of the internal topology of your network so that the provider can make an informed decision. The configuration is straightforward:

```
router bgp 100
 neighbor <B> remote-as 200
 neighbor <B> route-map set-MED out
 neighbor <C> remote-as 200
 neighbor <C> route-map set-MED out
 !
route-map set-MED permit 10
 set metric-type internal
```

Setting Communities

If you refer to Appendix D, "BGP Fundamentals," you will notice that the decision algorithm will not compare the MED until after looking into the local preference and the AS_PATH (among others). This means that the MED value that was set up in the last section may be overridden by those other attributes. It would be nice to be able to change the local preference value of your routing information as seen by your provider. The only downside is that you don't have access to change the configuration of your provider's routers.

Don't despair, it is possible to make an arrangement with your ISP to set a given community string on your routes, which will cause the ISP to set their local preference so that you can control which destinations will use a given inbound link. Just call them up!

Load Sharing on the Outbound Side

Keep in mind that BGP will choose only one best path for each destination. Therefore, load sharing will have to be done manually by changing the configuration of the router. For the outbound case, there are three variations that should be explored depending on the number of routes learned from the eBGP peers:

- No routes received; that is, use a default.
- Full routing received.
- Only partial routes received.

The decisions made will change for each case. The problem being addressed is: "How do I load share my outgoing traffic between different providers given that there is always only one best path for each destination?" All of the answers can't be offered in this short case study, but hopefully, you realize the fact that each situation has to be examined separately and that there is no easy and straightforward solution to this problem.

Using Default Routes Out

The most obvious, easiest solution is to use static default routes outbound toward both providers and let the router worry about balancing between the two service providers. Of course, when you use this solution, there is a chance that the outbound router will choose to send traffic destined for a network in Company B through ISP A.

This means the traffic to Company B will actually pass through the entire Internet core to reach its final destination rather than passing just ISP B's network; this is slightly suboptimal routing.

Accepting Full Tables

Another solution is to accept the full Internet routing table from both ISPs and choose the best route based on the BGP attributes for each prefix. This will clearly work for destinations like Company B because the router attached to Company A will choose the shortest AS path by selecting the path through ISP B rather than the longer path through ISP A.

For a possibly significant number of networks within the Internet cloud, though, (if both providers are Tier One ISPs with a similar distribution of customers) there will not be any clear way to choose one path over the other. All the selection criteria down to the router ID of the BGP peer will result in a tie. Therefore, the router IDs will be used to choose the path. This may result in a large amount of traffic being forwarded over the same link because the same router will always win, and the same path will always be chosen.

Note that the preceding paragraph has many conditions that need to be met for the statements to be true. Experience should tell you that only a low percentage of dual-homed networks would satisfy them. In the general case, you will most likely use a Tier One (or national) provider and a Tier Two (or regional/local) provider. If this is the case, then the number of routes for which no clear selection criteria exists will have considerably diminished. The purpose of this book is not to delve into how to select your ISP or other topics along that line.

Accepting a Partial Table

One final way of controlling the traffic outbound from your network is to accept only those routes from each provider that are directly attached to them and use a default route to reach the rest of the network in the Internet. In other words, Router A would accept only routes announced from ISP A that belong to it and its customers.

The trick, in this case, is to effectively filter the routes out that do not belong to your provider or their customers. There are two ways to achieve the same result: the easy way and the not-so-easy way.

- **The Easy Way**—Ask your providers only to advertise to you their routes and their customer's routes. Any provider will be glad to comply.

  A variation involves asking your provider to set a community on their routes and their customer's routes. All you have to do is filter out all the routes that do not have the agreed upon community marking.

  Your choice, along with the use of local preference, will guarantee the shortest path to the destinations received.

- **The Not-So-Easy Way**—Set up a filter to accept only routes with an AS_PATH length of 1 or 2. The value of 1 will identify your provider's routes, whereas the value of 2 will identify their customer's routes. This might work out well enough, but you will leave out any prefix on which the AS_PATH is prepended.

Being a Transit AS

So far, the issues revolving around load sharing inbound and outbound traffic across the two service provider links have been covered. Consider the situation where you are running iBGP between routers within your AS, as illustrated in Figure 8-11.

Assuming that Company A is accepting at least a partial routing table from the ISPs that it is connected to, there is some danger of either ISP selecting the path through Company A as its best path to reach networks in other ASs. In fact, AS100 could become a transit network for traffic between its two providers' networks. This situation is not desirable mainly because of the burden that AS100 would have to carry due to the potential high traffic load.

There are a few ways to prevent this from happening; the first is, simply, to use a default route and not accept any BGP advertisements from the two ISPs. Although this solves the problem, it directly undermines any work aimed at providing some sort of outbound load balancing.

The easiest way to accept advertisements and prevent transit traffic is by configuring an AS path filter so that you only advertise routes originating in the local AS. For Routers C and D in this network, this would look like the following configuration:

```
Router C:
router bgp 100
 neighbor <A> remote-as 200
 neighbor <A> filter-list 1 out
ip as-path access-list 1 permit ^$
Router D:

 neighbor <C> remote-as 300
 neighbor <C> filter-list 1 out
ip as-path access-list 1 permit ^$
```

Figure 8-11   *Transit AS*

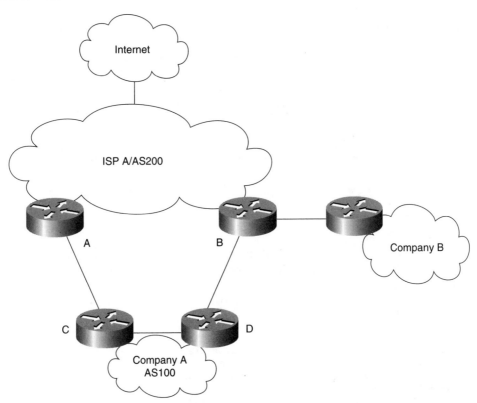

This configuration would allow only routes originating in the local AS to be advertised to the eBGP peers. One thing that looks odd about this configuration is the **as-path access-list** — why is the AS_PATH empty?

The AS_PATH attribute is changed only as a route is advertised to an eBGP neighbor. In Cisco's implementation, this occurs after any corresponding filters have been applied. (After all, why would you go through the chore of prepending information on routes that might be filtered out?)

Case Study: Route Dampening

One thing that causes major problems in truly large-scale networks is a destination that flaps regularly, or goes up and down several times in succession within a short period of time. BGP allows a network administrator to stop accepting a route from an external neighbor for a certain period of time through dampening. Note that dampening works for eBGP routes only.

The configuration for this capability is very simple—it's just a single extra configuration command (see Figure 8-12).

Figure 8-12   *Simple Dampening Example*

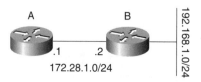

172.28.1.0/24

For example, if you wanted to dampen the routes from Router B in Figure 8-12, you would configure:

```
router bgp 100
 bgp dampening
```

Now, assume the link 192.168.1.0/24 flaps several times in a row. Router A will add a penalty to the route each time it flaps, which will eventually dampen the route. On Router A, this looks like the following:

```
A#show ip bgp flap
BGP table version is 7, local router ID is 10.1.1.1
Status codes: s suppressed, d damped, h history, * valid, > best, i - internal
Origin codes: i - IGP, e - EGP, ? - incomplete
   Network         From           Flaps Duration Reuse    Path
 h 192.168.1.0     172.28.1.2       3    00:02:10          100
A#show ip bgp
BGP table version is 7, local router ID is 10.1.1.1
Status codes: s suppressed, d damped, h history, * valid, > best, i - internal
Origin codes: i - IGP, e - EGP, ? - incomplete
   Network         Next Hop          Metric LocPrf Weight Path
 h 192.168.1.0     172.28.1.2             0          0 100 I
```

Note the **h** beside the route in both displays—the route is being marked as a route that is flapping. Once dampened, how does a route come out of this state? The penalty against the route is halved until the route's penalty has fallen below the reuse limit once every 15 minutes (by default). Once the penalty against the route has fallen below the reuse limit, the route will be advertised to BGP neighbors again. There are five attributes of a route when dampening is configured that you need to be concerned with:

- **Penalty**—The penalty that is applied to the route each time it flaps; the default is 1000.

- **Suppress limit**—Once the penalty reaches this mark, the route will be dampened; the default is 2000.

- **Half-life**—Each time the half-life passes, the penalty that is currently assessed against the route is halved; the default is 15 minutes.

- **Reuse limit**—The penalty must drop below this number for the route to be advertised again; the default is 750.
- **Maximum suppress limit**—The maximum number of half-lives a route can be suppressed; the default is 4 half-lives.

These can be configured as part of the **bgp dampen** command. To give an example of how this works, look at the penalty that occurs over time for a given route as shown in Figure 8-13.

Figure 8-13   *Route Dampening Affects*

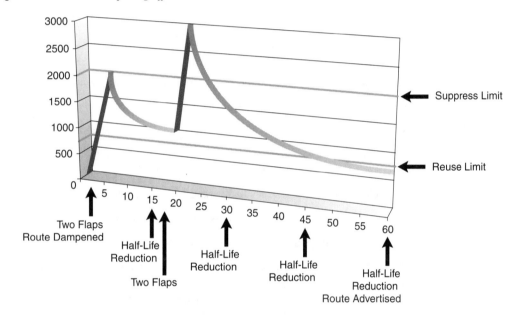

Here, a given route is withdrawn and re-advertised by an eBGP router twice in 5 minutes; each time the route flaps, a penalty of 1000 is applied for a total of 2000. When the second flap occurs, the route is dampened.

After 15 minutes, the penalty in force against the route will have decayed exponentially to 1000. Immediately after this, the route flaps twice more, raising the total penalty to 3000. 15 minutes later, at the 30-minute mark, the penalty has now decayed to 1500.

At the 45-minute mark, the penalty will have decayed half of its value to 750, and the route can be reused again.

Review

1   What is an EGP?

2   What prevents iBGP from being an effective IGP?

3   Where will routes learned from an eBGP peer be propagated?

4   Why shouldn't you redistribute BGP routes into an IGP?

5   What protocol do all BGP packets ride on top of?

6   If a neighbor relationship between two BGP peers constantly cycles through the Idle, Active, and Connect states, what action should you take?

7   Explain the significance of the next hop in BGP.

8   What possible solutions are there for load sharing outbound traffic to multiple ISPs?

9   All attributes being the same, what will break a tie in the BGP decision process?

10   What two things can be done to reduce the number of updates generated and sent by a router?

11   What is the default half-life of a dampened route?

12   How does a route reflector advertise routes learned from an iBGP peer?

13   What does a confederation of routers appear as outside the confederation area?

14   What is an example of an application of conditional advertisement?

15   Treating the network shown in Figure 4-10 in Chapter 4, "Applying the Principles of Network Design," as a service provider network (with the access layer connecting to external networks), configure the network to run BGP throughout. What changes would you make to the network? Would you use route reflectors or confederations anywhere?

CHAPTER 9

Other Large Scale Cores

Scalability of full mesh, Layer 3 designs is a major issue when building very large networks. Chapter 3, "Redundancy," discussed problems with Layer 2, full mesh designs. Layer 3, full mesh designs have many of the same problems.

At some point, the number of possible neighbors and paths becomes overwhelming, and you need to reduce the amount of work that needs to be done by the core routers.

Two possible solutions to this problem are Next Hop Resolution Protocol (NHRP) and Multiprotocol Label Switching (MPLS).

NHRP

One possible solution to the Layer 3 meshing problem is the Next Hop Resolution Protocol (NHRP). NHRP is technically a routing protocol rather than a new Layer 2/3 switching mechanism. Figure 9-1 provides an example network for discussion.

Figure 9-1   *Full Mesh Neighbors*

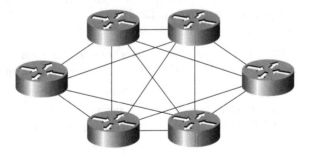

Now, as you know from Chapter 3, the full mesh design in Figure 9-1 results in 6(6–1)=30 paths through the network. Suppose that you want to reduce the paths through the network by making it a hub and spoke design. It could look like the one illustrated in Figure 9-2.

Figure 9-2   *Hub and Spoke Network Design*

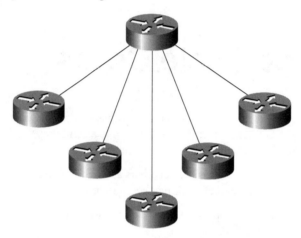

The real difficulty with this design (other than the single point of failure) is the amount of traffic that must pass through the hub router. If all of these links are 2.4 Gbps, the hub router needs to switch traffic at 12 Gbps or faster. There must be some way to spread this work out a bit.

If you are using a lower layer media that supports switched virtual circuits (SVCs), such as ATM (or Frame Relay SVCs), you should be able to take advantage of them to make direct connections between the spoke routers when needed.

The problem with this is routing. How does the router know that a given destination is reachable through some other means than the hub router? How does it know which SVC to use (what number to dial, so to speak) to reach this destination?

This is where NHRP comes in. In NHRP, a number of routers are configured as route servers. Each router advertises its reachable destinations to this route server along with a SVC to use to reach them.

When a router wants to reach a given destination, it queries the route server to find out if there is a direct path through the cloud. If there is, it will bring up a SVC to the next hop and pass the traffic along.

This effectively provides the advantages of a full mesh topology while also providing the scalability of a partial mesh topology.

Case Study: NHRP in an ATM Network

In the network shown in Figure 9-3, traffic sourced from 172.16.2.0/24 destined to 172.16.1.0/24 normally flows through Router A, which is at the hub of the switched ATM network. Instead of having all the traffic pass through one router, it makes more sense to have Routers B and C set up SVCs to one another when they are needed.

Figure 9-3   *NHRP in an ATM Network*

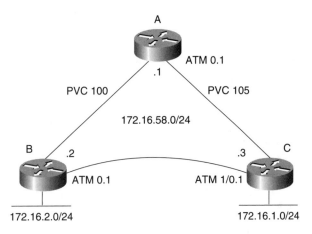

To accomplish this goal, you can run NHRP over the ATM cloud. Then, the configuration on Router A is as follows:

```
interface ATM0
 no ip address
 atm pvc 5 0 5 qssal
 atm pvc 16 0 16 ilmi
!
interface ATM0.1 multipoint
 ip address 172.16.58.1 255.255.255.0
 ip nhrp network-id 1
 ip nhrp interest 101
 ip ospf network point-to-multipoint
 atm esi-address 852852852852.01
 atm pvc 100 0 40 aal5snap inarp 5
 atm pvc 105 0 90 aal5snap inarp 5
```

continues

```
!
router ospf 1
 network 0.0.0.0 0.0.0.0 area 0
!
access-list 101 deny ip any any
On router B, we have:
interface Ethernet0
 ip address 172.16.2.1 255.255.255.0
!
interface ATM0
 no ip address
 atm pvc 5 0 5 qsaal
 atm pvc 16 0 16 ilmi
!
interface ATM0.1 multipoint
 ip address 172.16.58.2 255.255.255.0
 ip nhrp network-id 1
 ip nhrp interest 101
 ip route-cache same-interface
 ip ospf network point-to-multipoint
 atm esi-address 145145145145.01
 atm pvc 100 0 40 aal5snap inarp 5
!
router ospf 1
 network 0.0.0.0 0.0.0.0 area 0
!
access-list 101 permit ip any any
```

Router C is identical to Router B except for IP addresses and ATM information. To understand how this works, look at this Telnet session that is from a host on the 172.16.2.0/24 network to a host on the 172.16.2.0/24 network:

1 Router C sends its traffic for the 172.16.2.0/24 network toward Router A because it has a route for that network in that direction through OSPF.

2 Router A notices this destination is reachable through an interface on Router C, which is in the same NHP group Router B is in.

3 Router A sends Router C's connect information (its ATM address) to Router B, and it also sends Router B's ATM address to Router C.

4 Router B and Router C open a SVC to each other and traffic between the 172.16.1.0/24 and the 172.16.2.0/24 networks flows along this path.

On Router B, before the Telnet session between the hosts takes place, you'll see the following in the ARP cache:

```
B#show arp
Protocol  Address      Age(min)  Hardware Addr    Type  Interface
....
Internet 172.16.58.1 3           VCD#0100         ATM   ATM0.1
```

After the Telnet session, Router B has built an ARP cache entry for this destination over the newly established SVC between Router B and Router C:

```
B#show arp
Protocol  Address      Age(min)  Hardware Addr    Type  Interface
....
Internet 172.16.58.1 71          VCD#0100         ATM   ATM0.1
Internet 172.16.2.1  1           VCD#0060         ATM   ATM0.1
```

MPLS

MPLS resolves the same problem as NHRP but in a different way. MPLS is a new concept (as of this writing), and not all of the standards and mechanisms are fully worked out. This chapter covers an overview of the theory.

Normal Packet Switching

Switching an IP packet normally involves the following procedure:

1 Looking up the destination IP address in a table that might contain several overlapping matches

2 Choosing the matching destination network with the longest prefix length

3 Finding the MAC header for the next hop and copying it onto the front of the packet

The deployment of ATM and Frame Relay brought a new idea to the forefront in switching packets: switching based on a short label that can be swapped hop by hop as a packet moves toward its destination. Figure 9-4 provides a network illustration for demonstrative purposes.

Figure 9-4   *Simple Network Illustrating Switching by Tags*

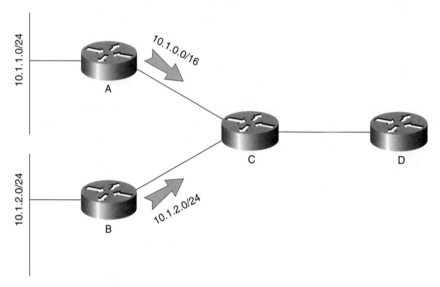

Because Router A is advertising a summary, and Router B is a component within that summary, Router C has two entries in its routing table:

```
10.1.0.0/16 via A
10.1.2.0/24 via B
```

These two entries are passed to Router D so that it will also have two entries in its table:

```
10.1.0.0/16 via C
10.1.2.0/24 via C
```

If Router D receives a packet destined to 10.1.2.1, it first finds that there are two matches for this destination, and it must compare the prefix length of these two matches to determine the best path.

Instead of using the IP address to switch the packet, these routers could assign labels to represent each hop along the path, and then switch based on these labels.

For instance, assume that the following conditions are true:

- Router A assigns the label 100 to the destination 10.1.0.0/16, which it is advertising to Router C.

- Router B assigns the label 200 to the destination 10.1.1.0/24, which it is advertising to Router C.

- Router C assigns the label 300 to 10.1.0.0/16 and advertises this upstream to Router D.
- Router C assigns the label 400 to 10.2.0.0/16 and advertises this along to Router D.

Now, when Router D receives a packet destined to 10.1.2.1, it notes that this route corresponds to 10.1.0.0/16, which is labeled 400. So, Router D marks the packet with the label 400 and forwards it to Router C. Instead of looking at the destination address and choosing the next hop based on the longest prefix match from the IP routing table, Router C simply looks up the label, 400, and sees that this belongs 10.1.0.0/16, which is labeled 100. Router C swaps the labels and passes the packet along.

When Router B receives the packet, it sees from the label (200) that this packet is destined to a directly attached subnet. Then, it strips the label off the packet and forwards it as usual.

The preceding example doesn't provide much network savings. You've saved only one router the expense of looking up a longest prefix match. If that one router was really a cloud, however, and the cloud contained numerous routers, the savings could be significant.

When a Label Switching Router (LSR) removes a label from the packet, this is called a *pop*; when it adds a new label on the packet, this is called a *push*.

Streams and Label Merging

MPLS doesn't restrict itself to one label for each destination. It uses a label to designate a stream, or a flow, of traffic instead—a Forwarding Equivalence Class (FEC). Abstracting individual packets into an FEC allows MPLS routers (LSRs) to merge a large number of streams that require the same handling (Class of Service, next hop, and so on) into one FEC and use the same label to identify all of them.

To understand this better, look at the example in Figure 9-5.

If you were using normal IP routing, you couldn't summarize the two routes advertised by Router D—10.1.1.0/24 and 172.16.1.0/24. Assume Router D is advertising label 100 for 10.1.1.0/24 and label 200 for 172.16.1.0/24 toward Router C. If Router C is capable of merging these FECs advertised by Router D, it can advertise a single label toward Routers A and B for both streams, which effectively summarizes them into one FEC, one label, and one advertisement.

This capability to merge streams, regardless of the destination addresses, greatly improves the scalability of MPLS by cutting down on the amount of routing information the LSRs must store and work with.

Figure 9-5   *Merging Streams*

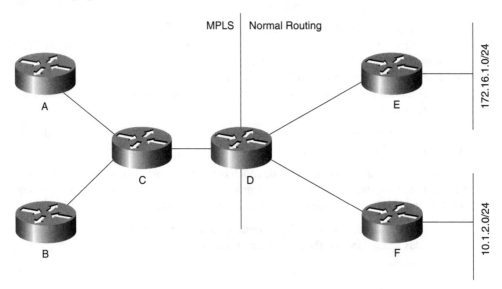

Label Granularity

Until now, you've worked only with labels that are bound to a destination network. (Unless they are merged; in which case, a single label can represent a number of destination networks.) In reality, labels can bound at different granularities to a flow of traffic. The following are a few common label assignment possibilities:

- **Host pair**—Each source and destination address pair is assigned a label; all packets from 10.1.1.1 to 172.16.1.1 are placed in one FEC.

- **Port quadruple**—Each source address:port to destination address:port pair is assigned a label; all packets from 10.1.2.1:1024 to 172.16.1.1:23 are placed in one FEC.

- **Port quadruple with Type of Service (ToS)**—Each source address:port to destination address:port pair with a given ToS is assigned a label; all packets from 10.1.2.1:1024 to 172.16.1.1:23 ToS 3 are placed in one FEC.

- **Network pair**—Each source/destination network pair is assigned a label; all packets from 10.1.2.0/24 to 172.16.1.0/24 are placed in one FEC.

- **Network pairs with ToS**—Each source/destination network pair within a given ToS is assigned a label; all packets from 10.1.2.0/24 to 172.16.1.0/24 marked for ToS 3 are placed in one FEC.

- **Destination network**—All packets travelling to a given destination network are assigned a label (which is what you've seen in the examples so far).

- **Egress router**—All packets exiting the MPLS cloud at a given egress LSR are assigned the same label.

- **Next hop BGP autonomous system (AS)**—Each source AS is assigned a label, and that label is used to reach any destination within, or through, that AS.
- **Destination BGP AS**—This is similar to assigning labels based on the next hop AS mentioned in the preceding item, but only destinations sourced within a given AS use a label associated with that AS.
- **Multicast source/group pair**—For multicast, a given source/group pair can be assigned a label through the multicast distribution tree.
- **Multicast */group pair (any source for this group)**—Rather than assigning a label per source, this scheme assigns only a label per multicast group.

Assigning Labels

How are labels assigned to streams or flows of traffic? There are two aspects of this question that MPLS must answer:

- What device assigns them?
- What drives label assignment? (What causes a label to be assigned?)

The *control component* is the device that assigns a label to a new flow presented while arriving at the edge of the MPLS cloud. This will most likely be an MPLS-capable router (an LSR) running BGP with the other edge routers connected to this cloud. The egress router assigns labels based on requests from upstream neighbors.

There are two ways to determine if a label needs to be assigned:

- When the first packet in a new flow reaches an edge router on the MPLS cloud, the edge router can cause the label assignment process to begin.
- As edge routers receive updates to their routing tables, they can drive the assignment of labels through the cloud based on the information in the routing table.

The first way of driving label assignment is data driven; the labels are assigned in response to data traffic. The second is control driven; the labels are assigned in response to control traffic.

Source Routing

Because a single label pushed onto the packet at the ingress to the MPLS cloud defines the entire path through the cloud, MPLS can be considered a type of source routing. It is more scalable than traditional source routing, though, because the current hop information needs to be carried only in the packet—not the entire path.

Strict source routing provides many capabilities over traditional hop-by-hop routing (which are currently implemented by IP). For example, traffic engineering is easier because the entire path of a given stream of data is known. It's easier to size links and determine what capacity is needed where when the path of any given stream can be known (and in fact, administratively chosen, when the packet enters the network).

Tunneling and Label Stacks

Packets aren't limited to one label; labels can be stacked on top of one another with the current LSR acting on the "top" label of the stack. Figure 9-6 demonstrates how this can be used for tunneling.

Figure 9-6   *Tunneling and Label Stacks*

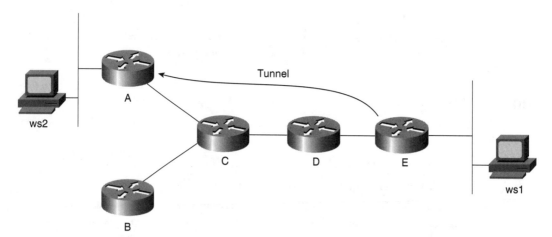

If ws1 wants to communicate with ws2 without users (or hackers) attached to LSR C or LSR D being able to see the traffic, then the edge Router E can negotiate a label with LSR A to represent this traffic and push this label onto the stack. (LSR A is also called the ingress LSR because it is where the traffic enters the MPLS network.)

Router E can also look in its routing table and find the label for traffic going to LSR A. Then, it can push this label onto the stack ahead of the first label.

Following is an example:

- Routers A and E negotiate the label 900 for the tunneled (hidden) traffic.
- The label for traffic destined to LSR A through LSR D is 100.
- The label for traffic destined to LSR A through LSR C is 200.

LSR E will first push 900 onto the label stack, followed by 100, and pass the packet onto LSR D. When LSR D receives this packet, it will act on the label on the top of the stack, which indicates the traffic is destined to egress at LSR A. It pops the top label, which is 100, and replaces it with the label for the next hop in the path, which is 200.

Now, LSR C receives the packet and sees that the label indicates this traffic is destined for LSR A. Seeing the next hop is the egress LSR (the edge of the MPLS network where the traffic will be leaving), LSR C simply pops the label and passes the traffic to LSR A.

When LSR A receives the packet, there will be only one label (900), which indicates that this traffic is for ws2. LSR A will pop the final label and forward the packet. Figure 9-7 shows this series of label pushes and pops.

Figure 9-7   *A Label Stack through a Short Tunnel*

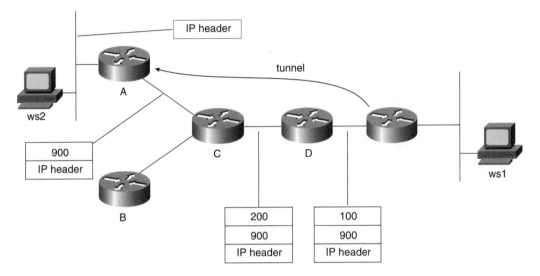

The preceding example shows that LSR C would pop the label before the packet actually leaves the tunnel (which terminates at LSR A). The next to the last LSR along a path (either through a tunnel or through an MPLS cloud), also known as the *penultimate LSR*, should pop the label before passing it on to the egress node.

Time to Live

The way IP guarantees that a packet will not be passed back and forth between two routers in a routing loop is the Time To Live (TTL) field in the packet header. Each router that the packet passes through will subtract one from the TTL until it reaches zero; when the TTL reaches zero, the packet will be discarded.

Because MPLS allows LSRs to switch packets based only on the label, the IP header is never touched. Therefore, the TTL on IP packets passing through an MPLS cloud may never be decreased.

For this reason, MPLS suggests that the ingress router on an MPLS cloud decrease the TTL in the IP header by the number of hops the packet will travel through the cloud. If the packet's TTL is low enough that it will reach zero before reaching the egress LSR, then the packet should be discarded before entering the MPLS network.

Other MPLS References

This short overview doesn't cover many details of how MPLS works; refer to the draft and standards documents of the IETF for a complete explanation of the mechanisms used to prevent loops, distribute labels, and encapsulate traffic through MPLS networks.

Review

1 Is NHRP a routing protocol, or is it a protocol that helps routing protocols do their job?

2 How many paths exist through a network with 30 nodes? 40?

3 What task does a route server in NHRP perform?

4 When a router on an NHRP network wants to find the SVC to use for a given destination, what does it do?

5 What three steps are normally involved in routing a packet?

6 What type of switching paradigm do ATM and Frame Relay use?

7 What type of switching paradigm does MPLS use?

8 What is a push? A pop?

9 What is a FEC?

10 Why do you merge FECs?

11 Explain each type of label assignment:

— Host pair

— Port quadruple

— Port quadruple with ToS

— Network pair

— Destination network

— Egress router

— Destination AS

12 Which device assigns labels in an MPLS network?

13 Do downstream devices or upstream devices assign labels?

14 What are the two ways of driving label assignment?

15 How is tunneling performed in an MPLS network?

PART IV

Appendixes

OSPF Fundamentals

Open Shortest Path First (OSPF) is a protocol standardized in RFC 2328 by the Internet Engineering Task Force (IETF). OSPF is a *link-state* protocol that has many advantages, including low traffic levels during normal operation and rapid convergence.

This appendix will give you a general overview of the protocol rather than a complete understanding of every aspect of OSPF's operation. You should also look at the relevant RFCs published by the IETF and *OSPF Network Design Solutions* by Thomas M. Thomas II, which is published by Cisco Press.

How OSPF Works

In a typical distance vector protocol (such as IGRP), each router advertises its table of reachable destinations *(vectors)* and the distances to them *(distance)* on each of its interfaces on a regular basis *(periodic updates)*. OSPF routers advertise the state of their directly connected links to all routers on the network (through *flooding*). Although OSPF uses periodic updates to the entire network, there are long periods of time between them, reducing network traffic to a minimum. Each router receives these *link-state advertisements (LSAs)* from its neighbors and floods them out each of its other interfaces, making certain that all routers on the network receive all LSAs.

Once all routers have received all advertisements, they perform the *shortest path first* calculation to find the best path to each destination on the network. OSPF uses *neighbor relationships* to reliably flood LSAs and enforces hierarchy in a network through *areas*.

Router IDs

Each router running OSPF on a network must have a unique identifier—the *router ID*. This router ID is used in combination with an LSA sequence number to detect duplicate LSAs and to prevent a router from accepting an LSA.

The router ID is chosen from among the interfaces configured for IP on a Cisco router; it is either the highest IP address from any operational interface (interface and line protocol both up), or it is the address of the loopback interface. The recommendation is to use loopback interfaces to set the router ID because this provides more stability in the network and makes the router ID more predictable.

In newer versions of IOS, there will be a command to set the router ID independently.

LSA Types

LSAs are classified by type. Each type serves a different purpose and is described in the following list:

- **Router LSAs (type 1)**—Contain information about a router and the links it has in an area; they are flooded within an area only. The router indicates if it can compute paths based on Quality of Service (QoS), if it is an area border router, if it is one end of a virtual link, or if it is an autonomous system boundary router (ASBR) within this LSA. Type 1 LSAs are also used to advertise *stub networks*, which have only one router attached.

- **Network LSAs (type 2)**—Used for transit networks within an area; they are not flooded outside of an area. A transit network has at least two routers connected.

- **Summary LSAs for ABRs (type 3)**—Advertise internal networks to routers in other areas *(interarea routes)*. Type 3 LSAs may represent a single network or a set of networks summarized into one advertisement. Summaries are generated only by area border routers (ABR).

- **Summary LSAs for ASBRs (type 4)**—Used to advertise the location of an autonomous system boundary router. Routers that are trying to reach an external network use these advertisements to determine the best path to the next hop. Autonomous system border routers (ASBR) generate these.

- **Autonomous System External LSAs (type 5)**—Used to redistribute routes from other autonomous systems, generally using a different routing protocol, into OSPF.

Reliable Flooding of LSAs

Each LSA flooded to the network has an age parameter *(LSAge)*, which is set by the originating router to 0. When a router receives an LSA from a neighbor, it begins aging it out by adding 1 to the LSAge for each second it holds the LSA in its database. Once the LSAge equals *MaxAge*, the router will set the cost to unreachable, flood the LSA, and then remove the LSA from its database. This has the effect of clearing any LSA from the network that has not been refreshed within the MaxAge timeframe.

Due to this aging out mechanism, OSPF routers must reflood their LSAs periodically to prevent them from being timed out. How often a router floods its LSAs is called the *LSRefreshTime*. The MaxAge is set to 1 hour, and the LSRefreshTime is set to 30 minutes.

When a router receives an LSA (or the status of one of its directly connected links changes), it marks the database entry and builds a list of neighbors to which this entry needs to be flooded. As the router builds a packet to send (which can contain more than one LSA), it will do the following:

- Choose database entries that have been marked for sending and places them in the packet
- Note in the database the neighbors to which the LSA has been advertised

As acknowledgments are received, neighbors are removed from the "waiting for acknowledgment" list associated with the LSA. Every so often the router will check this list of outstanding acknowledgments to see if some neighbor hasn't responded; it will resend the LSA to those that haven't responded. This interval is configurable on a per interface basis using the **ip ospf retransmit-interval** command on a Cisco router.

Building Adjacencies

Because adjacencies are vital to the reliable flooding of these link-state advertisements, you should examine how an adjacency is built and learn from some special cases. Figure A-1 begins with an illustration of two routers connected to the same network.

Figure A-1   *Building Adjacencies*

When Routers A and B are first attached to the serial link between them, they will begin sending *hello packets* on this network. Next, the routers begin receiving each other's hello packets, as shown in Figure A-2.

When Routers A and B receive each other's hellos, they will place their new neighbors in *init state*.

Figure A-2   *Router Exchange of Hello Packets*

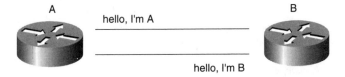

After placing a new neighbor in init state, a router begins including the router ID of that neighbor in its hellos, as shown in Figure A-3. Once a router has received a hello from a neighbor with its router ID enclosed, it places the neighbor in *two-way state*. This "two-way" step ensures there is two-way communication between the routers before they begin exchanging database information. Routers will not enter the two-way state if the link type, hello time, wait time, or dead time do not match.

Figure A-3 *Two-Way State*

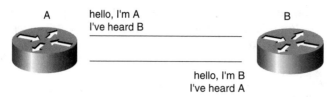

After determining that an adjacency should be built (routers will remain in two-way state under some circumstances—see the section, "Adjacencies on Multi-Access Networks," later in this appendix), the routers will begin to negotiate the exchange of their OSPF databases. If a new router on the network were to wait until normal flooding occurred to obtain a complete database, it could take a half an hour to do so—during which time the router would not be able to reach all areas in the network and could cause routing loops.

This stage is called *exstart*; a master and slave will be chosen to synchronize the database exchange. The master controls the exchange of the database descriptors (DBDs) between the routers. Figure A-4 shows how the exstart stage operates.

Figure A-4 *Exstart*

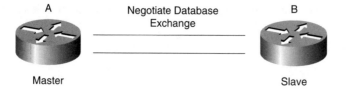

Once the routers have negotiated which one will control the DBD exchange, they begin exchanging their databases as shown in Figure A-5. With this process finished, the routers will be in *full state*, meaning that they have synchronized their databases.

Figure A-5 *Router Database Exchange*

Adjacencies on Multi-Access Networks

It isn't efficient for every router on a multi-access (broadcast or NBMA) network to build full adjacencies with every other router on that network. So, OSPF uses the concepts of designated routers (DRs) and backup designated routers (BDR) to reduce the number of adjacencies that must be built (and reduce the number of LSAs flooded throughout the area for the common network). Each router on the network will build a full adjacency with the DR and the BDR and leave all other neighbors on that network in the two-way state. The DR is responsible for advertising a link to the network and for flooding LSAs to other routers on the link.

The DR and BDR are elected based on the router priority (configured on a per interface basis on a Cisco router with **ip ospf priority**) and the router ID.

Assuming Routers B, C, and D in Figure A-6 attempted to connect to the same network link at the same time (this is unlikely, but possible), each would see each other's hellos, progress to the two-way state, and then begin electing a BDR and a DR for this link.

Figure A-6   *A Multi-Access Network*

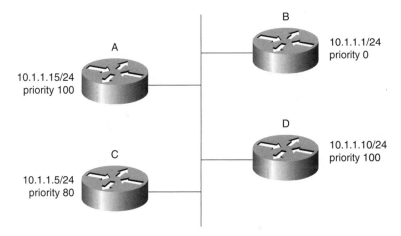

Take a look at this process from Router A's perspective. Router A receives three hellos, one each from Router B, Router C, and Router D. Because Router B's priority is set to 0, which means B cannot become the DR or the BDR, Router A keeps its neighbor state with Router B at the two-way state. The hello from Router C indicates that it has a router priority of 80 and an ID of 10.1.1.5, and the hello from Router D indicates that it has a router priority of 100 and an ID of 10.1.1.10.

Router A first compares the priorities with its own; Router D's matches, but Router C's is lower. Because Router C has a lower priority, it is removed from the possibilities. Because Router D's matches, the router ID is used to determine the BDR. (The BDR is always elected first.) Router A's router ID is higher than Router D's, so Router A is chosen as the BDR.

Now, Router A determines that there is no DR on the link. So, it promotes the BDR to the position of DR and then elects a new BDR. Router A promotes itself to DR and examines each of its other neighbors in two-way state to see which one should become the BDR. Once again, Router B is not considered because its priority is 0. Router A compares the hellos from the remaining two neighbors, and it discovers that Router C has a lower priority than Router D. So, the new BDR is Router D.

The order in which this occurs is of some importance because the process must be repeatable when the DR is lost—the BDR is promoted, and a new BDR is elected.

Because you probably can't get all of these routers to connect to the link at the same moment, you need to examine how an OSPF router deals with a new link when there are already DRs and BDRs in place. Assume that Routers B, C, and D are all three attached to this Ethernet and have been running for some time. What happens when Router A is attached?

Without Router A, Router D would be the DR, and Router C would be the BDR. When Router A is first attached, it sees Router D's hellos asserting that it is the DR and does not attempt to re-elect a new one (even though Router A would be chosen if a new election were to occur). This prevents unnecessary DR election and usually results in the router that is up the longest being the DR.

OSPF and Nonbroadcast Multi-Access Networks

Nonbroadcast multi-access (NBMA) networks, such as the one depicted in Figure A-7, pose a special problem for OSPF and DR election. On a Cisco router, these networks can be configured to act as a single broadcast interface with multiple connections.

Figure A-7   *An NBMA Network as a Point-to-Multipoint Network*

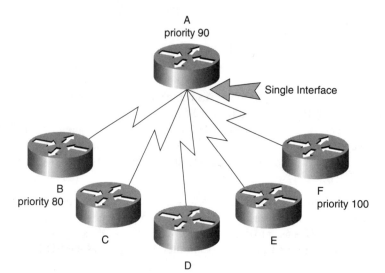

Because Router A is using a single *multipoint* interface (a Frame Relay interface using inverse ARP or **frame-map** configurations to separate the traffic between the permanent virtual circuits [PVCs]) when Router A broadcasts a packet, all the other routers receive it. But when Routers B or F broadcast a packet, the only router that receives the packet is Router A.

Because all the routers connected to this multi-access network assume it is a single broadcast domain, they will attempt, unsuccessfully, to elect a BDR and DR. Assuming that all routers are connected to the link at the same time, the following scenario will occur:

- Routers A and B will elect Router A as the DR and Router B as the BDR.
- Routers A and F will elect Router F as the DR and Router A as the BDR.
- Router B will not receive Router F's hellos.
- Router F will not receive Router B's hellos.

Essentially, this is broken; there is no way to determine what the final outcome will be. It may actually work for some time until a link flaps or one of the routers on the network goes down.

There are three possible solutions to this problem:

- Set all remote sites to OSPF priority 0, and the hub or core router to anything else.
- Use point-to-point subinterfaces (on Cisco routers).
- Configure the network as a point-to-point network type.

The first solution—configuring the OSPF router priorities—was the only solution for some time (before the availability of point-to-point subinterfaces or network type point-to-multipoint). Some network administrators, however, configure the remote routers with a low priority rather than a priority of 0, which works but can still cause problems because the BDR status will be in question. It is best to simply configure the remote routers to be ineligible to become DR or BDR.

The second solution—using point-to-point subinterfaces—has been available for some time now and has many advantages. It has one disadvantage that many administrators don't like, though: A separate network address must be used for each serial link. If a network has a lot of remote sites connected to distribution or access layer routers in this fashion, this can become a major administrative nightmare.

The final solution—network type point-to-multipoint—is a recent development. Instead of the hub router treating the NBMA network as a broadcast domain, it treats each PVC as a point-to-point link, building full adjacencies with each router. This technique is effective, but it results in the creation of host routes for each remote router on the NBMA network.

When considering which of these three solutions to use, you need to consider the advantages and disadvantages of each and decide which best suits your network.

Areas

OSPF provides for (and enforces) hierarchical network design through *areas*. There are four types of areas provided for in OSPF:

- **Core area, which is area 0 (or 0.0.0.0)** — All traffic transits through the core area, and all other areas must touch the core area in at least one place.

- **Stubby** — External routes are not advertised into stub areas, nor can they be generated from stub areas; routers in these areas rely on the default route to reach all externals.

- **Not-so-stubby areas (NSSAs)** — External routes are not advertised into NSSAs (unless they originate within the area), but they can be generated within the area.

- **Totally stubby** — Neither external nor internal routes are advertised into a totally stubby area; all routers rely on a default route to reach any destination outside the area.

All areas can be identified with a single integer (area 1) or with a four-octet number similar to an IP address (area 1.1.1.1). All traffic between areas (interarea traffic) passes through the core; links between areas that do not pass through the core area will not be used. The core area must be contiguous — there cannot be two core areas within the network.

Routers that border or touch two areas — the core and some other area — are *area border routers* (ABRs). ABRs are where summarization is performed in an OSPF network — both into area 0 and into the other areas they connect to (see Figure A-8).

Figure A-8 *ABRs and ASBRs*

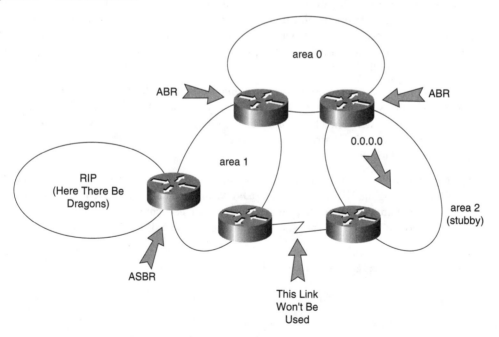

In a totally stubby area, the ABR generates only a default route, which reduces the amount of routing information that must be flooded to routers within the stubby area. Each router in the stubby area must be configured with the **area** *area id* **stub** command. The core area may not be defined as a stubby area, and external routes may not be injected into stubby areas. The primary difference between stubby and not-so-stubby areas is the capability of stubby areas to propagate external routes that originate within the area toward the core.

External Route Injection

External routes — routes from other autonomous systems or protocols — are injected into OSPF by *autonomous system boundary routers* (ASBRs). External routes are flooded throughout the OSPF autonomous system (throughout all areas) without change. (This means no summarization.) External routes within OSPF also have a *Forward Address field*, which allows an OSPF router to act as a route server.

In Figure A-9, Router B is an ASBR for the OSPF cloud and is also learning routes from Router A and Router C through the Border Gateway Protocol (BGP). Router D is not learning these BGP routes, but it is advertising an internal OSPF link to the Ethernet. When Router B advertises these routes it has learned from BGP, it will put the Ethernet addresses for Router A and Router C in the Forward Address field so that other routers in the OSPF cloud can forward traffic to them directly, rather than through Router B specifically. This means other routers could choose the route to Router D to get to Routers A or C, even though Router D is not advertising these routes. Router B is acting as a route server in this case for the externally derived BGP routes.

If the Forward Address field is set to 0.0.0.0, the router advertising the external route is where the traffic should be forwarded. If a router wanted to forward traffic to the external network advertised, it would look for an ASBR link-state to determine how to reach the ASBR that is advertising the external route.

Figure A-9   *External Route Injection*

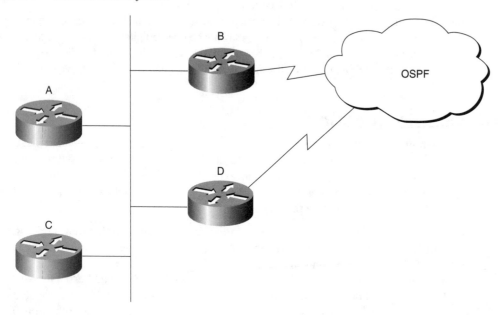

Virtual Links

There are times when the core area becomes divided, or an area loses contact with the core — generally, when there is some network outage. For these situations, the designers of OSPF provided the *virtual link*. The virtual link acts as a tunnel, allowing traffic that needs to traverse to and from the core area to pass through another area.

Router A in Figure A-10 has gone down for some reason, effectively partitioning area 1 from the rest of the network (making it unreachable). The network administrator could, by configuring a virtual link between Router C and Router B across the backup link, make area 1 accessible until Router A could be repaired and restored to service.

NOTE   One of the most confusing aspects of configuring virtual links is the mysterious area number included in the command. This is not the area you are trying to reach or repair, but rather the area through which the virtual link passes.

Virtual links are typically a sign of poor network design; rather than using them, you should evaluate your network design and attempt to eliminate them where you can.

Figure A-10   *Virtual Links*

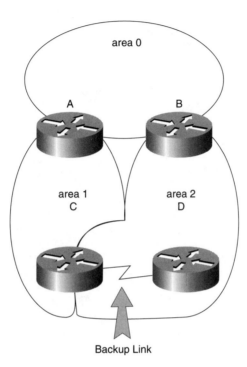

Backup Link

On-Demand Routing

On-demand routing (ODR) is a way to provide for on-demand circuits (such as dial-on-demand ISDN circuits) within an OSPF autonomous system. Because OSPF generally uses hello packets and periodic reflooding of LSAs to maintain network state, it would normally be impossible to run this protocol over a dial-on-demand circuit because the circuit would need to remain up at all times.

To resolve this, OSPF allows a special bit to be set within the advertisement, which indicates this LSA should never be aged out. This allows two routers connected over an on-demand circuit to exchange databases when the circuit is up and not lose information about destinations across the link when it is down.

ODR is relatively simple to configure—the one caveat is that all routers in the area must support ODR (even if they don't have it configured) so that they will understand the special bit settings in the LSA. Routers that aren't ODR capable will simply time the routes out as usual, and the network will periodically lose connectivity to any destinations beyond the dial-on-demand link.

IS-IS Fundamentals

IS-IS (Intermediate System-to-Intermediate System) is a protocol standardized by the International Organization for Standardization (ISO) for use with Connectionless Network Service (CLNS) and other ISO routed protocols. The Internet Engineering Task Force (IETF) has integrated IP routing with IS-IS through a series of RFCs.

This appendix will give you a general overview of the IS-IS protocol. For more information, you should refer to the relevant ISO documents and RFCs.

How IS-IS Works

IS-IS is a link-state protocol that runs the shortest path first (SPF or Dijsktra) algorithm to calculate the best path through a network. IS-IS provides two levels of routing for hierarchy—level 1 (L1) routing areas are interconnected using level 2 (L2) routing. The L2 routing domain is sometimes called the core.

IS-IS uses hierarchical addressing to break an autonomous system up into L1 routing areas and to distinguish between L1 and L2 routes. All nodes within a given area use L1 routing to reach each other, whereas nodes in different areas must use L2 routing to reach one another.

As a link-state protocol, IS-IS relies on routers flooding the state of their links to all other routers within their area (L1 or L2) to propagate topology information. Each router runs the SPF algorithm over the information it has received in link-state packets (LSPs) from other routers to find the shortest path to each destination in the network.

Because routers in link-state protocols rely on all the routers within a given routing area that have information in their databases to preclude routing loops, IS-IS doesn't generally permit filtering of routing information.

End Systems and Intermediate Systems

In IS-IS, two different hello-type protocols are used to build adjacencies and exchange information—ES-IS and IS-IS. The End System-to-Intermediate System (ES-IS) protocol is used by routers to discover hosts (and hosts to discover routers) and for exchanging configuration information and redirecting packets to a better path.

The IS-IS protocol builds and maintains adjacencies between routers (intermediate systems). This is similar in function to the Hello protocol used in OSPF to discover and maintain neighbor adjacencies.

CLNS Addressing

To understand the way IS-IS allows hierarchy, you first need to understand a little about CLNS addressing. CLNS identifies nodes on a network (hosts or routers) by using network service access points (NSAPs).

The following list identifies the fields typically found in an NSAP:

- **NSAP Selector (NSEL)**—Identifies the user or service on a particular host (much like a TCP or UDP port number).
- **System ID**—Identifies an individual system or host.
- **Area Address**—Identifies the L1 area that this host resides in.
- **Initial Domain Identifier (IDI)**—A variable-length field identifying the routing domain that this system is in.
- **Authority Format Identifier (AFI)**—A one-byte field that identifies both the authority that assigned this address and the format the address is in.

NSAPs are divided into two major parts—the Initial Domain Part (IDP) and the Domain Specific Part (DSP)—and can be a maximum of 20 bytes in length. The NSEL, system ID, and area address are considered part of the DSP, whereas the IDI and AFI are part of the IDP.

For 47.0012.00C0.A94B.51C1.00, the fields are defined as follows:

- **47.00**—AFI and domain.
- **12**—area.
- **00C0.A94B.51C1**—System ID; this is always 6 bytes.
- **00**—NSAP; this is always 1 byte.

You will often see an NSAP of 00, which means *this system* rather than some upper-level entity on this system. Note that the AFI and IDI are often treated as one piece rather than as two separate pieces. This addressing example continues:

- Anything sent from this host and destined to 47.0012.xxxx.xxxx.xxxx.xx is L1 routed.
- Anything sent from this host to 47.00xx.xxxx.xxxx.xxxx.xx is L2 routed.
- Anything else needs to be routed between domains (interdomain routed).

Whereas IP addresses are assigned to a wire or link, NSAPs are assigned to a host. Therefore, a system (such as a router) with connections to multiple networks will have multiple IP addresses (one for each network it attaches to) but only one NSAP.

Routing in an IS-IS Network

When a group of end systems (hosts) and intermediate systems (routers) with the same area IDs in their NSAPs are connected together, they begin forming adjacencies using ES-IS and IS-IS.

Hosts rely on the nearest L1 router within their area to forward all traffic for them unless they are redirected. A router may use ES-IS either to tell a host to send its packets for a given destination to another L1 router, or to tell a host to send its packets directly to the receiving ES (if they are on the same physical link).

Hosts send any traffic with a destination outside the area to the nearest L2 router, which examines its database to find a path to another L2 router within that area and forwards the traffic.

L1 routers that receive traffic for a destination outside of their area automatically forward this traffic to the nearest L2 router.

All L2 routers must be contiguous; L1 areas cannot break up the core of the network.

Metrics & External Routes in IS-IS Networks

The metrics for internal routes range from 0 to 63; interfaces generally have a default metric of 10.

NOTE   A *metric* is the method by which a routing algorithm determines that one route is better than another route. This information is stored in routing tables. Metrics include bandwidth, communication cost, delay, hop count, load, MTU, path cost, and reliability.

Routes from other protocols can be injected into IS-IS as external LSPs. Externals are injected as L1 and/or L2 routes and can have either internal or external metric types.

The two metric types in IS-IS are similar to type 1 and type 2 externals within OSPF. IS-IS supports externals with internal metrics (which implies that they are in the local domain) and externals with external metrics. External routes with internal metrics are always preferred over external routes with external metrics.

Building Adjacencies

When an IS-IS router is connected to a broadcast (or multi-access) network, it immediately begins sending out IS-IS hellos. When connected to a point-to-point link, a router waits until it builds an ES-IS adjacency with the device on the other end before it determines to transmit IS-IS hellos.

These hellos are always padded to the maximum transmission unit (MTU) size of the link. This way, two routers will not build an adjacency over a link with different MTUs configured on either end.

When two IS-IS neighbors first begin bringing up an adjacency, they exchange Complete Sequence Number Packets (CNSPs) to synchronize their databases. Once a pair of routers are adjacent, Partial Sequence Number Packets (PSNPs) are used to request and send information about a subset of the link-state's database.

To reduce the problems associated with building a full mesh of adjacencies on multi-access links, such as Ethernet or Token Ring, IS-IS builds pseudonodes. One of the ISs is specified as the Designated Intermediate System (DIS); this router becomes the pseudonode on the network.

All routers attached to the multi-access network build an adjacency with this DIS rather than with one another. The DIS is selected by router priority; when there is a tie, the tie is broken by the router with the highest subnetwork point of attachment (SNPA).

DIS status is pre-emptive, unlike designated router (DR) status in OSPF. This means that if a new router with a higher priority is connected to a multi-access link, it will take over the role of DIS.

The DIS is responsible for generating pseudonode LSPs for all adjacent routers on the multi-access network. These packets are for reporting the link status of other routers to the multi-access network. The DIS also broadcasts a packet containing information on every (configurable) LSP in its database every 10 seconds onto the link it is the pseudonode for; this packet is a Complete Sequence Number PDU, or CSNP.

Other routers on the multi-access network will examine these CSNPs to determine if their database is complete. If the database isn't complete, the other routers on the multi-access network will request particular LSPs from the DIS.

One interesting point to note is the possibility for different L1 and L2 DISs to co-exist on the same multi-access network. There is a separate election process for each level of routing, and the same router may or may not be both the L1 and L2 DIS for a given multi-access link.

LSP Flooding and SPF Recalculation Timers

IS-IS, like OSPF, uses a complex, recursive algorithm for calculating the best path to a particular destination and ages out LSPs every so often. The intervals where these events normally occur are configurable on Cisco routers. Chapter 6, "IS-IS Network Design," has some information on the importance of adjusting these timers in large IS-IS networks.

To adjust the interval at which IS-IS does a SPF run, use the **spf-interval** command. The default interval is 5 seconds. IS-IS will automatically run SPF each time a change in the network occurs, regardless of whether this interval of time has passed.

Each LSP advertised also contains a Remaining Lifetime field (also known as the **max-lsp-lifetime** or Maxage) that determines how long the LSP should be kept in memory before it is timed out. As a router times out LSPs in its database, it will flood to all other routers that this destination is no longer reachable. Aging out occurs when the Remaining Lifetime field reaches 0.

The router that originates an LSP will time the LSP out of its database slightly faster than normal. Therefore, it should flood a new copy of the LSP before any other router on the network times it out and marks it as unreachable.

The default Remaining Lifetime is 20 minutes; the router that originates the LSP times it out in 15 minutes. The Remaining Lifetime that a router places in LSP can be adjusted using the **max-lsp-lifetime** command; the rate at which the originating router will time out its own LSPs can be adjusted using **lsp-refresh-interval**.

Neighbor Loss and LSP Regeneration

Look at what happens when Router B in Figure B-1 reboots for some unknown reason.

Figure B-1   *An IS-IS Adjacency*

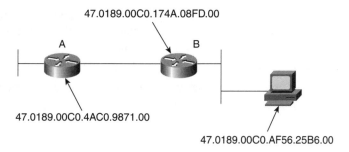

Router A will not immediately flush the LSPs that Router B has advertised as you might expect. Instead, Router A waits until the Remaining Lifetime field of these LSPs reaches 0 (they time out). Then, it floods to the rest of the network that the LSPs are unreachable. Finally, Router A flushes the LSPs from its database.

Therefore, Router A will not flush the LSP advertised by Router B for NSAP 47.0189.00C0.AF56.25B6.00 until its Maxage timer reaches 0. When Router B finishes rebooting and rebuilds its adjacency with Router A, it sends this LSP to Router A with a sequence number of 1.

When Router A receives this LSP, it examines its database and finds that it has an existing LSP for this destination with a higher sequence number. Then, Router A replies to Router B with a copy of this later LSP.

Router B, on receiving this later LSP, sets its LSP sequence number for this destination so that it is higher than the copy that Router A replied with.

IP Integration into IS-IS

IP routing is integrated into IS-IS via carrying IP reachability information in LSPs. All IP networks are considered externals, and they always end up as leaf nodes in the shortest path tree when IS-IS does a SPF run.

This means that changes in IP reachability alone result only in a partial SPF run (Partial Route Calculation, or PRC); the routers in the tree need to calculate only the parts of the tree in which the leaf node for that destination network resides.

Only L2 routers can summarize IP destinations to shorter masks.

Multiple net Statements

Sometimes, you will see a Cisco router configured with multiple **net** statements under router IS-IS. This is a useful technique for merging two domains or transitioning from one addressing scheme to another, but it's not generally recommended.

When you configure two **net** statements, the router simply combines, or merges, the databases into one database. This means that routing occurring between what may normally be considered domains ends up appearing as simple L2 routing.

EIGRP Fundamentals

Enhanced Interior Gateway Routing Protocol (EIGRP) is an advanced distance vector protocol with many advantages:

- **Minimal use of network resources in normal operation**—EIGRP transmits only small hello packets during normal operation to maintain neighbor relationships; there are no periodic routing updates (flooding of the routing table to neighbors).

- **Restricted use of network resources when reacting to network topology changes**—EIGRP transmits only information about what has changed and also restricts (paces) the rate at which it sends packets so that it will not overwhelm a link.

- **Rapid convergence**—EIGRP converges very quickly during topology changes.

- **Scalability**—Because there are no periodic updates, and there is minimal use of network resources during convergence, EIGRP can scale into very large networks.

A major revision of the protocol occurred in IOS revisions 10.3(11), 11.0(8), and 11.1(3). Running software that implements the later revision of EIGRP is recommended to promote stability and interoperability. The primary addition to EIGRP in the newer revision is the pacing of packets so that EIGRP won't use more than 50 percent of the available bandwidth; although there are others, this is the most important change. EIGRP is based on the Diffusing Update Algorithm (DUAL) to find the best loop-free paths through a network.

This appendix will give you a general overview of the protocol rather than a complete understanding of every aspect of EIGRP's operation.

DUAL Operation

Typical distance vector protocols, such as RIP, use the distance (metric—in most cases, the hop count) to a destination network to determine the best path and save the vector (next hop) for only the best path. If the best path becomes unusable, the router waits until the next set of updates from each of its neighbors to find a new path (or rediscover an old path that was previously discarded).

Waiting for periodic updates to discover alternate paths to a destination slows convergence time dramatically.

For example, if the network in Figure C-1 is running RIP, Router B will choose the path to 10.1.4.0/24 by examining the hop count through each available path. Because the path through Router C is three hops, and the path through Router A is two hops, Router B will choose the path through Router A and discard the alternate path it learned through Router C.

Figure C-1 *Choosing the Best Route in an RIP Network*

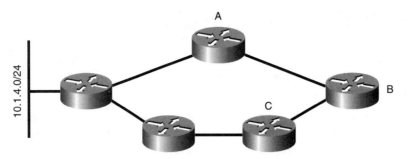

If Router A's path to 10.1.4.0/24 fails, Router B will continue believing that the best route to this destination is through Router A until it hasn't heard about 10.1.4.0/24 from Router A for three update periods (90 seconds in RIP). Once Router B has timed out the router through Router A, it must wait for Router C to re-advertise the route (which occurs every 30 seconds in RIP). Not including any hold-down time, it could take between 90 and 120 seconds for Router B to switch from the path through Router A to the path through Router C to reach 10.1.4.0/24.

Rather than discarding information about alternate paths, EIGRP builds a *topology table* from each of its neighbor's advertisements and converges by either looking for an alternate route in the topology table, or querying its neighbors if it knows of no other route.

Then, EIGRP must provide:

- Some means of building and maintaining neighbor relationships. Because EIGRP doesn't periodically re-advertise routes, it relies on neighbor relationships to determine if the routes through a given neighbor are still usable.

- A way of determining if a given path advertised by a neighbor contains a loop. EIGRP must be able to determine if a route is a loop so that a list of valid alternate routes is available.

- A method of querying neighbors to find previously unknown paths. Split-horizon and other circumstances can cause a router not to advertise all the destinations it can reach. Because EIGRP doesn't rely on periodic updates, routers must be able to query neighbors to find alternate routes that may be hidden.

Establishing Neighbor Relationships in an EIGRP Network

EIGRP conserves network bandwidth by using nonperiodic, incremental updates, which means changes to the network topology are transmitted between routers as needed. There are no full routing updates once a neighbor relationship has been established, and there are no periodic updates.

The basic problem with nonperiodic updates is knowing when a path through a neighboring router is no longer available. There are no periodic updates to age routes and time them out.

Instead, EIGRP relies on neighbor relationships; if the neighbor router has learned that a path through is reachable, the path is assumed to be valid. Because neighbor relationships are so important to the operation of the protocol, it is important to look at them closely. Refer back to Figure C-1 and examine the neighbor relationship between Routers A and B.

Assume Router B is powered up and running; when Router A is powered on, it will begin sending hello packets out to the multicast address 224.0.0.10 on each of its interfaces. When Router B receives Router A's first hello (only one simple situation will be examined here), it will send a hello packet with the *initialization bit* set. Router A will receive this hello packet with the initialization bit set and begin transmitting its full routing table to Router B.

Once Routers A and B have finished exchanging their routing tables, they will maintain this neighbor relationship with periodic hello packets. This raises the question of how often to transmit hello packets.

Determining how often to send hello packets is a matter of balancing between fast convergence and minimal network utilization. On higher speed and point-to-point links it's generally safe to transmit hello packets rather frequently, whereas on lower bandwidth, multipoint links conservation of bandwidth becomes more important.

Specifically, hellos are sent every 5 seconds on:

- Broadcast media, such as Ethernet, Token Ring, and FDDI
- Point-to-point serial links, such as PPP or HDLC leased circuits, Frame Relay point-to-point subinterfaces, and ATM point-to-point subinterfaces
- High bandwidth, multipoint circuits, such as ISDN, PRI, and Frame Relay multipoint circuits greater than T1 (as configured using the **interface bandwidth** command)

Hellos are sent every 60 seconds on multipoint circuits of T1 bandwidth or slower, such as Frame Relay multipoint interfaces, ATM multipoint interfaces, ATM switched virtual circuits, and ISDN BRIs.

The rate at which hello packets are sent is called the *hello interval* and can be adjusted per interface using the **ip eigrp hello-interval** command. The amount of time that a router will consider a neighbor up without receiving a hello (or some other EIGRP packet) is called the *hold time*, and is typically three times the hello interval; so, the hold times are 15 seconds for a

5 second hello interval and 180 seconds for a 60 second hello interval by default. The hold time can be adjusted with the **ip eigrp hold-time** interface command.

Note that if you change the hello interval, the hold time is not automatically adjusted to account for this change. You must manually adjust the hold time to reflect the configured hello interval.

It is possible for two routers to become EIGRP neighbors even though the hello and hold timers do not match because the hold time is included in hello packets. A router will keep a neighbor up as long as it receives hello packets from that neighbor within the hold time advertised in the neighbor's hello packet.

Although there is no direct way to determine the hello and hold intervals, executing **show ip eigrp neighbor** several times in a row can give you a good idea of what the hello interval and hold timers are for a *neighboring* router. (**show ip eigrp neighbor** cannot be used to determine the hello and hold timers on *this* router.) For example:

```
router#show ip eigrp neighbor
IP-EIGRP neighbors for process 1
H   Address      Interface   Hold Uptime    SRTT   RTO   Q Seq
                                            (sec)  (ms) Cnt Num
1   10.1.1.2     Et1             13 12:00:53   12   300   0  620
0   10.1.2.2     S0             174 12:00:56   17   200   0  645
router#show ip eigrp neighbor
IP-EIGRP neighbors for process 1
H   Address      Interface   Hold Uptime    SRTT   RTO   Q Seq
                                            (sec)  (ms) Cnt Num
1   10.1.1.2     Et1             12 12:00:55   12   300   0  620
0   10.1.2.2     S0             173 12:00:57   17   200   0  645
router#show ip eigrp neighbor
IP-EIGRP neighbors for process 1
H   Address      Interface   Hold Uptime    SRTT   RTO   Q Seq
                                            (sec)  (ms) Cnt Num
1   10.1.1.2     Et1             11 12:00:56   12   300   0  620
0   10.1.2.2     S0             172 12:00:58   17   200   0  645
```

The **Hold** column will never get above the hold time and should never get below the hold time minus the hello interval (unless, of course, you are losing hello packets). If the **Hold** column usually ranges between 10 and 15 seconds, the hello interval is 5 seconds and the hold time is 15 seconds. If the **Hold** column usually has a wider range—between 120 and 180 seconds—

the hello interval is 60 seconds and the hold time is 180 seconds. If the numbers do not seem to fit one of the default timer settings, check the interfaces on this router and the neighbor because the timers have probably been configured manually.

It's possible for a link that can pass traffic in only one direction to result in a "half relationship" between two neighbors. Both routers will report *retransmission limit exceeded* errors at the console, and one router will have high *Q Counts* and an *SRTT* of zero in **show ip eigrp neighbor**.

Metrics in an EIGRP Network

Before discussing the way EIGRP implements DUAL, you need to have some understanding of the metrics used. EIGRP uses the minimum bandwidth and the total delay to compute metrics. Other metrics can be used by adjusting the "k" values, but it's not recommended. (The "k" values change the way EIGRP uses the metric to determine the best path. I'm not certain why they are called "k" values. The reason is probably buried deep in the history of the original EIGRP design.) *Adjusting the "k" values is very complex; it's possible to create routing loops when trying to use these other metrics.*

Following is the formula that EIGRP uses for computing the metric from the minimum bandwidth and the total delay (or the sum of the delays on the path):

$$\left[\left(\frac{10^7}{min(bandwidth)}\right) + \Sigma(delays)\right] \times 256$$

$\Sigma(delays)$ *represents the sum of the delays on the path.*

Use Figure C-2 to see how the metrics are calculated in a simple network.

Figure C-2   *EIGRP Metrics*

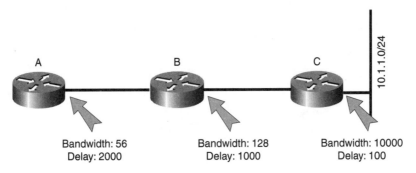

When Router C advertises 10.1.1.0/24, it sets the bandwidth to 10000 and the delay to 100. When Router B receives the advertisement, it compares the bandwidth in the advertisement (10000) with the bandwidth of the interface that it received the advertisement on (128) and uses the lower of the two (in this case, 128). Then, Router B adds the delay configured on that interface to the delay in the advertisement so that the total delay will be 1100. When Router A receives the advertisement from Router B, it performs the same procedure, reducing the minimum bandwidth to 56 and adding 200 to the delay for a total delay of 3100.

In Router B, the total metric to 10.1.1.0/24 would be

$$(\frac{10^7}{128} + 1100) \times 256 = 20281600$$

In Router A, the total metric to 10.1.1.0/24 would be

$$(\frac{10^7}{56} + 3100) \times 256 = 46507776$$

In case you're wondering, the infinity is 4,294,967,296, which is 2^{32}. You'll probably get a different answer on some of these if you use a calculator to check them. This is because routers don't do floating-point math, so they truncate the decimal places at each division.

Loop Free Routes in EIGRP Networks

To understand how EIGRP determines if a path is valid (loop free), take a look at Figure C-3, which is a simple geometric figure. Each line here is assigned a length of 1 for simplicity. (Figure C-4 applies the same mechanics using real metrics.)

Figure C-3   *Model for Valid Route Discovery*

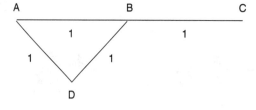

Because the length of each of these line segments is 1, the following total distances would be true:

- B to C=1
- A to B to C=2
- D to B to C=2
- A to D to B to C=3
- D to A to B to C=3
- B to A to D to B to C=4
- B to D to A to B to C=4

If A advertises to B that it has a path to C through D, the total distance it advertises is 3. This is greater than B's best path to C, which is 1. In fact, it's mathematically impossible for A to *ever* advertise a better route to C than B's best path because it always includes the distance between B and C.

Given this, it's relatively simple for B to determine if the path to C that A is advertising has already passed through B (and if it is looped, or invalid)—simply compare the total distance A is advertising with the best path currently known. If the path A is advertising is longer (has a higher total distance) than the best path currently known, it's possible that the advertised path is a loop and shouldn't be used.

With this in mind, look at the example in Figure C-4 and see how this works with real metrics.

Figure C-4   *EIGRP Loop Detection*

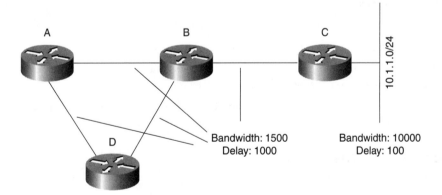

Router B will receive three advertisements for 10.1.1.0/24 as follows:

* Through Router A with a metric of 2500096
* Through Router C with a metric of 281600
* Through Router D with a metric of 2500096

Normally, Router B receives only one of these advertisements—through Router C—because of split-horizon. Split-horizon is turned off in this example to explain how EIGRP finds invalid routes based only on the metrics.

Router B adds the metric through the interface that it receives the advertisements on, and now it has these paths:

* Through Router A with a metric of 2756096
* Through Router C with a metric of 1988096
* Through Router D with a metric of 2756096

Now, Router B chooses the best path (lowest metric) to 10.1.1.0/24, which is through Router C, and uses this as a "measuring stick." Because the distances advertised by Routers A and D (before Router B adds the metrics in through its interfaces) are both higher than the best path (after Router B adds in its interface metrics), neither of these paths are valid.

Remember from the previous example in Figure C-3 that it's mathematically impossible for the metric through A or D to be lower than the total distance to the destination if the path contains a loop (passes through B more than once).

To put this in EIGRP terms:

* The distance to the destination advertised by the neighbor is the *reported distance*.
* The best metric available to the network is the *feasible distance*.
* The neighbor with the best metric to a destination is the *successor*.
* Any neighbors whose reported distances are less than the feasible distance are *feasible successors*. (They are advertising a loop free route.)

This model is conservative. Sometimes, a route is determined to be a possible loop when it isn't.

Split-Horizon in EIGRP

Split-horizon in EIGRP network can be a bit confusing. Following is a short example. Going back to basics, split-horizon is a loop prevention rule, which states that a router should not advertise a route through the interface it learned the route on. Take a look at Figure C-5 for an example.

Figure C-5   *Split-Horizon in EIGRP*

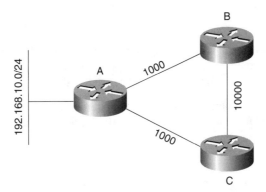

In this figure, Router A is advertising the 192.168.10.0/24 network to Routers B and C. The numbers indicated on the links between the routers represent the bandwidth configured on the links rather than the total metric or some other measurement.

If you examine the EIGRP topology table for each of these three routers, you will find that Router A has only one path to 192.168.10.0/24 (as you would expect) because it has a directly connected route. Router B has two routes—one through Router A, and the other through Router C—and it is choosing the path through Router C (the minimum bandwidth through Router C is 10,000 rather than 1,000).

However, Router C is showing only one path—through Router A. Why isn't it showing the path through Router B? Because Router B is "split-horizoning" the advertisement of this destination to Router C. Why? Because Router B chose the route through Router C as its best path to 192.168.10.0/24.

What about Router C? Because it could be learning about this network through Router B, shouldn't it be split-horizoning its advertisement to Router B as well? No, the split-horizon rule for EIGRP is slightly different than it is for other distance-vector protocols.

EIGRP split-horizons, or doesn't advertise a route, out of a given interface only when the router is using that interface to forward packets toward the destination in question. In this example, Router C isn't using the link between itself and Router B to reach 192.168.10.0/24—it's using the link toward Router A. So, Router C advertises this destination out toward Router B, regardless of what alternate paths it might be learning from Router B.

Clearing the Topology Table and Querying Neighbors in EIGRP Networks

Once EIGRP has built a topology table and decided which paths are not looped, it needs some way to adjust to changes in that topology table. Because EIGRP uses nonperiodic updates, it does not time routes out of its table; the route must either be removed by new information from a neighbor, or through tearing down a neighbor relationship.

When a router loses its connection to a destination, it will examine its topology table first to determine if it has a feasible successor for that destination. If a feasible successor exists, the router will do the following:

1 Remove the old route.

2 Replace the old successor with the new one.

3 Re-compute the topology table for that destination. (Changing the feasible distance may produce a new set of feasible successors.)

4 Update any neighbors on the change in its path.

If, however, a router loses its route to a destination, and it has no other loop free routes to that destination, the router will query each of its neighbors to see if any of them has another path. At first glance, this may seem unnecessary, but it serves three purposes:

- To re-evaluate paths that may have been rejected as looped.

- To learn of paths that may not have been originally advertised due to split-horizon rules.

- To inform all neighbors that this router no longer has a path to this network; if they are relying on this path to reach this destination, they need to find a new path because this one is no longer available.

In Figure C-6, if Router D's interface on 10.1.1.0/24 goes down (later, you discover the cable dangling out of the router, of course), Router D would immediately mark this destination as unreachable and query each of its neighbors—Routers B and C in this case—for a new path to this destination (arrow 1 in Figure C-6).

Routers B and C are both using Router D as their successor to this network and, therefore, mark the destination as unreachable and query each of their neighbors (arrows 2 and 3). Because the link between Routers A and C is faster than the link between Routers A and B, Router A uses Router C as its successor to this network, and the query from Router C arrives first (in theory anyway—there are many other sequences in which these events could occur, but the end result will be the same).

Figure C-6   *Query Path through a Network*

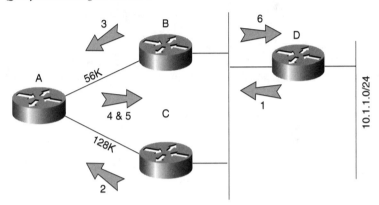

When Router A receives the query from Router C, it examines its topology table, notes that it has a feasible successor for this destination through Router B, and queues a response for Router C. Assume the query from Router B arrives before that response is sent; Router A notes that it has no other feasible successors and marks the route as unreachable. Then, Router A adjusts its response to Router C to make the replied metric unreachable and also sends a packet to Router B, notifying it that this path is unreachable (arrows 4 & 5).

When these replies arrive at Routers B and C, these routers remove the destination from their topology tables and send responses back to Router D that this path is unreachable (arrow 6). Once Router D receives all the answers, or replies, to its queries, it sends updates to Routers B and C to notify them that 10.1.1.0/24 is no longer reachable. Routers B and C, in turn, propagate this information to Router A.

Stuck-in-Active Routes

When a router queries its neighbors about a route, the route is placed in *active* mode. (The router is actively seeking a path to this destination.) A route that has remained active for three minutes is called *stuck-in-active*. When a route is stuck-in-active, the neighbor that has not answered is reinitialized, effectively clearing the stuck-in-active state.

There are many reasons a route could be in the stuck-in-active state; the reason that is most likely is a poorly performing link (or a series of borderline links) in the query path. Other possibilities include either a router that cannot immediately answer the query (being out of memory or having high CPU utilization are common problems), or the network is simply so large that the queries cannot travel through the network in under three minutes.

Bounding Queries in EIGRP Networks

The stability of a large-scale EIGRP network is often dependent on the range of a query through the network. If a query must travel from one end of a large network to the other, the odds are high that stuck-in-actives will be common. Essentially, the greater the number of routers and links a query must travel, the greater the likelihood of encountering a poor link or a router that cannot answer immediately. Therefore, the likelihood is greater that a route will become stuck-in-active.

There are two primary ways to bound the range of a query:

- Summarization, which is covered in the next section.
- Distribution lists, which are covered in Chapter 7, "EIGRP Network Design."

EIGRP Summarization

EIGRP routes, external and internal, can be summarized manually or automatically. (This is called *autosummarization*.) Manual summarization can be configured at any bit boundary using an interface level command such as the following:

```
ip summary-address eigrp autonomous system summary address mask
```

With this configured, EIGRP will do the following:

1   Build a routing table entry for this summarized network to the interface null0.

2   Advertise the summary out of the interface it is configured on.

3   Advertise the components of this summary as unreachable out of the interface it is configured on.

The route will be marked as a summary in both the routing table and the topology table on the router where the summarization takes place (the router generating the summary).

Autosummarization occurs when a router is on the boundary of two different major networks. A router running EIGRP will automatically create a summary for each of the major networks to advertise toward its neighbors in the other major network.

In Figure C-7, Router B would build a route for 10.0.0.0/8 to **null0** and advertise it to Router C; it would also build a route for 172.16.0.0/16 to **null0** and advertise it to Router A. This behavior can be modified by configuring **no auto-summary** under the router EIGRP process on B, in which case it would advertise the subnets rather than the major network summaries.

Figure C-7   *Autosummarization in EIGRP*

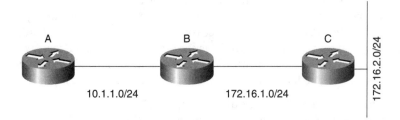

There is a caveat concerning autosummarization and external routes in EIGRP: external routes will not be autosummarized unless there is some internal component of the same major network. In the network in Figure C-7, if Routers A and B are running EIGRP and Routers B and C are running RIP (or some other protocol), Router B advertises the 172.16.1.0/24 rather than 172.16.0.0/16 to Router A. If, however, Router C is running RIP toward its Ethernet link and EIGRP toward its serial link (with both Routers A and B running EIGRP), then Router B will autosummarize because the 172.16.1.0/24 network is an internal route, and it is in the same major network as the external from RIP.

This has some implications for designs that use multiple EIGRP autonomous systems. If the autonomous system borders are on major network boundaries, designs of this type will do more harm than good because autosummarization will be defeated.

Changing Metrics in EIGRP for Reliable Transport

Whenever you are trying to change the path EIGRP chooses between two routers, it is best to change the *delay* metrics along the path rather than the *bandwidth* metrics. The primary reason for this is that the bandwidth configured on the interface affects the operation of EIGRP's reliable transport mechanism.

Using the bandwidth statements to influence routing decisions can have unintended consequences because the installation of a new link can unexpectedly override your bandwidth configuration. The delay metrics are cumulative; so, their effect is more predictable and manageable in the long run.

Load Balancing in EIGRP Networks

Like all other protocols on a Cisco router, if EIGRP discovers up to six equal cost paths to a given destination, it installs all six routes in the routing table (assuming **max-paths 6** is configured), and the router will load balance (or traffic share) over them. EIGRP, however, has the capability to install unequal cost routes in the routing table, and the router will share traffic over them in proportion to their metrics. Use the **variance** command in router configuration mode to allow EIGRP to load balance over paths with unequal metrics.

The *variance* is a divider; if a route's distance, divided by the variance configured, is less than or equal to the best metric, the route will be installed in the routing table. For example, if you had the paths with metrics of 100, 200, 300, and 400 in the topology table, and the variance is set to the default value of 1, only the path with a metric of 100 will be used.

If you set the variance to 2, both the best path (with a metric of 100) and the path with a metric of 200 will be installed in the routing table. Setting the variance to 3 includes the route with a metric of 300, and so on. The router will load balance over these multiple paths in proportion to their metrics.

BGP Fundamentals

The Border Gateway Protocol version 4 (BGP4, or just BGP) is an exterior gateway routing protocol used between routing domains (or autonomous systems). BGP is the protocol used between all Internet service providers (ISPs) and in the cores of other very large networks.

BGP provides extremely stable routing between autonomous systems (ASs)—even with huge routing tables—and provides network administrators with a great deal of control and flexibility over routing policy.

This appendix provides an overview of the BGP protocol, not a detailed explanation of every aspect of BGP's operation. For further detail, see *Internet Routing Architectures* by Bassam Halabi (Cisco Press), *CCIE Professional Development: Routing TCP/IP*, Volume I by Jeff Doyle (Cisco Press), and the relevant RFCs published by the IETF.

Mechanics of a Path Vector Protocol

BGP is unique among all the currently used routing protocols because it relies on information about the vector (direction) to a destination and the path to a destination to prevent routing loops. All other commonly used routing protocols, such as OSPF, IS-IS, and EIGRP, rely on metrics or costs combined with some level of topology information to prevent routing loops.

Look at Figure D-1 for an example of the operation of a path vector protocol.

Suppose that Router A originates a route to 10.1.1.0/24 toward Router B. In the information on how to reach this destination, Router A notes that it is the first router in the path. Router B receives this route, adds itself to the path, and advertises the destination to Router C. Router C adds itself to the path and advertises it to Router D.

When Router D receives the route to this destination, it sees that the path is through Routers C, B, and A. It, likewise, adds itself to the path and advertises it back to Router A. When Router A receives this advertisement, it sees that it is already in the path to this destination and rejects the route.

This is essentially how BGP works—except that instead of individual routers marking the route with some information, each AS in the path marks the route. Any router that receives the route can see if the path to this destination is a loop by checking if the AS they are listed in is one of the ASs listed in the path.

For a concrete example, see Figure D-2.

Figure D-1   *A Path Vector Example*

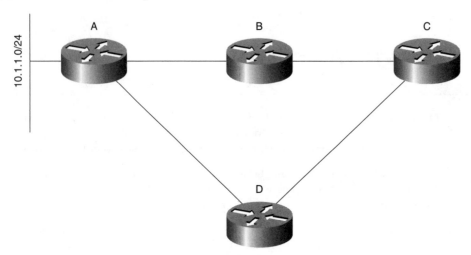

Figure D-2   *An AS-Based Path Vector Example*

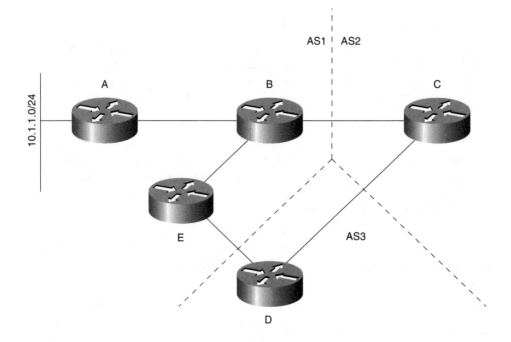

In this case, Router A originates a route for 10.1.1.0/24 toward Router B, which in turn forwards it to Router C. When Router C receives this route, it recognizes that the route originated from a router in another AS and adds that AS to the path to this destination (the AS path).

Router C forwards the route to Router D, which also recognizes that this route originated in an AS other than its own, and Router C adds that AS, AS2, to the AS path. Router D then forwards the route to Router E.

When Router E receives this route, it examines the AS path and sees that the AS it is in, AS1, is already in the AS path. Because of this, Router E will assume this advertisement represents a loop (it does from an AS-level view) and discards the advertisement.

Path Decision

Because BGP doesn't rely on any type of metric to determine if a path is looped, the metrics it does use are more policy-based—that is, they can be used by network administrators to set policies for routers to use when selecting a path.

BGP only advertises the best route to each of its neighbors (unless BGP multipath is configured—this is covered in Chapter 8, "BGP Cores and Network Scalability"). Listed in order of importance, these metrics are as follows:

- Administrative weight
- Local preference
- Locally originated routes
- Shortest AS path
- Lowest origin
- Multiple Exit Discriminator (MED)
- Prefer externals
- Path through nearest neighbor if synchronization is on
- Path through neighbor with the lowest router ID

The sections that follow discuss some of these metrics individually.

Local Preference

A route map generally sets local preference when a destination network (prefix) is advertised or received from a BGP peer. The local preference is advertised with the prefix throughout the AS.

The local preference is used to set a preferred exit point for this destination from this AS.

AS Path Length

The path with the shortest AS path length is preferred if all factors with more weight than path length are equal.

MED

The MED, or metric, is generally set using a route map when a prefix is advertised to a neighboring AS. The MED is not carried when a prefix is advertised from one AS to another. It is *non-transitive*.

The MED is considered to be a hint about which entry point into an AS the administrator would like traffic for that destination to use. It is generally checked only if the AS paths on two routes are equal in length and identical. In other words, the MEDs of two prefixes learned from different neighboring ASs are not considered. On a Cisco router, **bgp always-compare-med** will compare MEDs from different ASs. This is not the default.

Lowest Router ID

If all metrics previously listed are equal, BGP selects the path through the neighbor with the lowest router ID. This final metric can become an issue in places where an AS has two connections to another AS. (See "Case Study: Dual-Homed Connections to the Internet" in Chapter 8, "BGP Cores and Network Scalability.")

Community Strings

A community string is a string of numbers (and you thought it was characters) that can be used to tag a prefix. This tag can then be used for things like:

- **Entry point control**—Because the MED, in many cases, isn't used in path determination (because the AS path of two routes must be the same for the MED to be compared), there is a system where a router receiving a prefix with a given community string set will set its local preference.

- **Propagating Quality of Service (QoS) information**—An arrangement could be made between two BGP peers so that tagging a prefix with a given community string results in the packets destined to that subnet being treated differently.

Community strings are set and checked using route maps. (See the section, "Filtering with Route Maps," later in this appendix for more on this topic.)

Neighbor Relationships

Most advanced routing protocols have some system of neighbor discovery, generally a hello protocol, so that a router can discover neighbors and trade routing information reliably. BGP is an exception because it requires the manual configuration of neighbor relationships; it does not discover neighbors automatically.

Like other advanced routing protocols, though, BGP requires a reliable transport system to guarantee that packets don't get lost between peers. BGP uses TCP for reliable transport.

When a router running BGP (a BGP speaker) is configured to build a neighbor relationship with another BGP speaker, it first builds a TCP connection to transport information. (Port 179 is the well-known port for BGP.) This means that IP connectivity between BGP speakers must exist before a BGP session can be set up between the two routers.

Once a neighbor relationship is set up between two routers, they trade full routing information (as allowed by any filters that are applied—more on filters in the section "Route Filtering in BGP"). After this, BGP speakers send only incremental updates to neighbors advertising or withdrawing prefixes as necessary.

Exterior BGP

BGP peers in two different ASs will automatically form an Exterior BGP (eBGP) neighbor relationship. Refer to Figure D-3 for an overview of how eBGP works.

Figure D-3   *eBGP Peers*

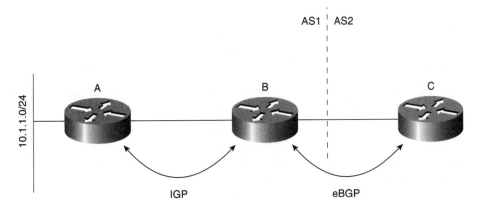

Router A advertises the 10.1.1.0/24 prefix through an Interior Gateway Protocol (IGP) to
Router B, which has an eBGP neighbor relationship with Router C. There are several ways this
route can be injected into BGP by Router B:

- **Redistribution**—Router B can redistribute routes from the IGP used between Router A
  and Router B into BGP. This results in the origin code for the redistributed routes to be
  marked as "unknown."

- **network Statement**—Router B can have a **network** statement configured under **router
  bgp**, which matches 10.1.1.0/24. Note that unlike many other routing protocols, the
  network statement in BGP does not indicate which interfaces to run the protocol on, but
  rather it indicates the prefixes to advertise. If a router has an exact match (including prefix
  length) in its routing table for a **network** statement under **router bgp**, it advertises this
  prefix.

- **aggregate-address Statement**—Router A can summarize the 10.1.1.0/24 network into a
  larger block of IP addresses through an **aggregate-address** statement configured under
  router bgp.

Once Router B determines that it should advertise this prefix to Router C, it sends an update.
The AS path field in this update is blank because the destination originates within Router B's
AS. The next hop for this route is Router B's IP address.

When Router C receives this update, it notes that the update came from an eBGP peer, adds that
peer's AS to the beginning of the AS path, and places the prefix in the BGP table. Router C may
or may not install this prefix in its routing table, depending on other routes available to this
prefix, and so forth.

Interior BGP

When a BGP speaker is configured with a neighbor in the same AS, these routers become iBGP
peers. To understand iBGP better, refer to Figure D-4 for the discussion that follows.

As Figure D-4 demonstrates, Router A is advertising the 10.1.1.0/24 destination as an eBGP
route to Router B; Router B is in turn advertising this route through iBGP to Router C.

When this prefix is passed to Router C, the next hop isn't changed (it remains Router A's IP
address) unless **next-hop-self** is configured, and the AS path isn't changed (because the prefix
wasn't advertised across an AS boundary). The AS path not changing explains one of the most
severe restrictions of iBGP—iBGP peers cannot advertise a route learned via iBGP to another
iBGP neighbor. Figure D-5 adds a couple of routers to provide a better idea of why iBGP peers
must be full mesh.

Figure D-4   *iBGP Peers*

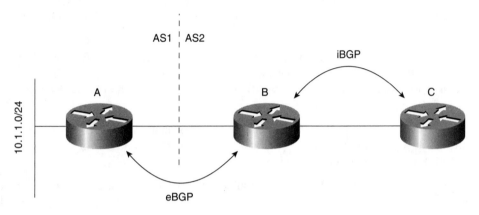

Figure D-5   *iBGP Peers*

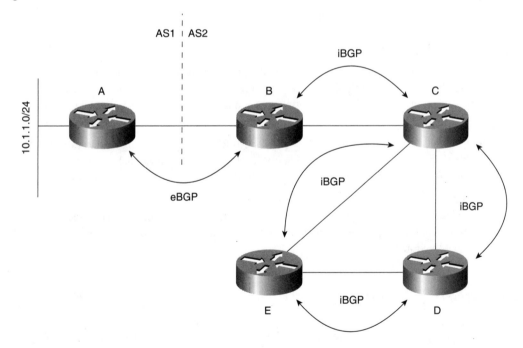

Using the iBGP peering shown in Figure D-5, follow the chain of events that occur if 10.1.1.0/24 is advertised from Router A to Router B. Note that this normally does not occur—iBGP doesn't allow routes to be advertised in this manner. This discussion is only to illustrate why iBGP doesn't allow this.

Router B advertises this prefix to Router C, which in turn advertises it to Router D. Router D advertises this prefix to each of its peers, including Router E, which advertises it to Router C. At this point, Router C has received two iBGP advertisements for the 10.1.1.0/24 prefix—one through Router B and one through Router E.

Which path does Router C choose? Because the next hop and AS path aren't changed when a prefix is advertised from one iBGP peer to another, Router C has no way of knowing the path that it's learning from Router E is a loop!

To prevent this sort of problem, iBGP peers are not allowed to advertise a route learned through iBGP to another iBGP neighbor. The practical application of this rule results in another rule: iBGP peers must be fully-meshed.

There are ways around the full mesh rule in iBGP, but they are covered in Chapter 8 rather than here.

The Next Hop Attribute

The previous section briefly mentioned that the next hop attribute in the advertised prefix is not changed between iBGP neighbors. The next hop may also be set to a router other than the advertising router when eBGP is running across a multi-access network. For an example, see Figure D-6.

Router C is advertising the 10.1.1.0/24 network to Router B via an IGP, and, in turn, Router B is advertising this prefix to Router A via eBGP. Because it doesn't make any sense in this situation for the traffic to flow from Router A to Router B (then, over the same Ethernet to Router C), Router B will advertise the next hop as Router C.

The **neighbor** {*ip-address*|*peer-group-name*} **next-hop-self** command can be used to alter this behavior. Configuring this on Router B causes all traffic to flow through Router B if this is the desired behavior.

Route Filtering in BGP

Because BGP focuses on administrative control of routing, it's only natural that it should have vast filtering capabilities—and it *does* have *vast* filtering capabilities! This is, in fact, one the most confusing areas of configuring BGP. The following sections discuss the filtering capabilities of BGP via route maps, **set** and **match** statements, prefix lists, and distribution lists.

Figure D-6   *Next Hop on a Multi-Access Network*

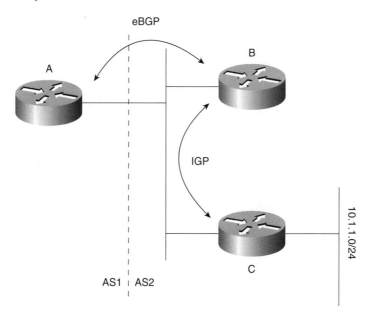

Filtering with Route Maps

Filtering in BGP on Cisco routers is typically done using route maps, which are constructed as a set of matches and sets within a sequence. The matches, for filtering, specify the condition that a prefix must match in order to be considered. The **set** statement determines what is to be done to the prefix once it's determined that the prefix matches.

The sequences represent the order in which **route-map** statements are checked, much like BASIC line numbers represented program execution order (if you've ever used the original BASIC). A typical route map is constructed something like the following:

```
route-map filter permit 10
 match something
 set something
route-map filter permit 20
 match something
 set something
```

In the route map named *filter*, the permit sequence 10 will be evaluated before the permit sequence 20.

Filtering with Sets and Matches

To give you a better idea of the type of filtering that can be done with a route map, here is a short list of possible matches that can be configured as options of the **match** command:

- *ip address* — Matches either the IP address listed or the IP addresses permitted by the listed access list.
- *as-path* — Matches the path listed in an *as-path* list.
- *community-list* — Matches a given community string from within a community list.
- *metric* — Matches a given MED value.

If the prefix advertised is permitted by the condition in the **match** statement, then a **set** may be applied. Some possible **set** statements used to alter the prefix are

- **set community** — Sets the community string associated with the prefix.
- **set metric** — Sets the MED associated with the prefix.
- **set local-preference** — Sets the local preference associated with this prefix.
- **set weight** — Sets the administrative weight associated with the prefix.
- **set origin** — Sets the BGP origin code.
- **set as-path-prepend** — Prepends extra hops onto the AS path.

These various combinations allow to you filter (or classify) prefixes advertised by a neighbor and then set various aspects of that prefix. The administrator has very fine control over what path is chosen through the network.

Filtering with Prefix Lists

BGP also supports the use of prefix lists for filtering the destinations received from or advertised to a peer. A prefix list can be configured either in a way similar to a route map (with sequence numbers within the given prefix list being used to determine the order of evaluation) or in a way similar to access lists (with the order of operation being determined by the order of configuration). For example, to filter all of the private address space out of advertisements to a peer, you could use:

```
ip prefix-list noprivates deny 10.0.0.0/8
ip prefix-list noprivates deny 172.16.0.0/19
ip prefix-list noprovates deny 192.168.0.0/16
ip prefix-list noprivates permit any
!
router bgp 100
  distribute-list prefix noprovates out
```

Filtering with Distribution Lists

Prefixes accepted from or advertised to a neighbor can also be controlled using distribution lists. Standard access lists used as distribution lists operate as expected, blocking those prefixes denied and allowing those prefixes permitted.

Extended access lists, however, can be used to filter based on the subnet mask as well as the destination network. The standard form of the extended access list is

access-list *number* {**permit|deny**} *protocol source wildcard destination wildcard*

There are further options dealing with protocol types and/or port numbers not listed here, as well as some keywords. When using an extended access list as a BGP distribution list, however, the syntax becomes

access-list *number* {**permit|deny**} **ip** *network wildcard subnet mask wildcard*

This allows you to configure a distribution list that filters out all destinations in the 10.0.0.0 network with a prefix length of greater than 24 bits, for example:

access-list 101 **permit ip** 10.0.0.0 0.255.255.255 0.0.0.0 255.255.255.0

iBGP Synchronization

iBGP synchronization is probably one of the least understood concepts in BGP. To understand why synchronization between the IGP and BGP routing tables is important when deciding if a route should be advertised to an eBGP peer, refer to Figure D-7 and the discussion that follows.

Figure D-7   *iBGP Synchronization*

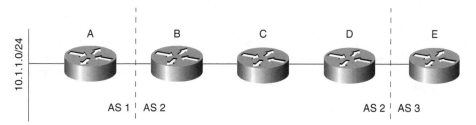

AS 2, as pictured here, is a transit AS, which means it passes traffic between two other ASs; in other words, hosts connected to Router E should be able to send traffic across AS 2 to destinations in 10.1.1.0/24.

Assume that Routers A and B are eBGP peers, Routers B and D are iBGP peers, and Routers D and E are eBGP peers. Router C, in the middle of AS 2, is only running some IGP to Routers B and D.

Router E transmits a packet along its path to 10.1.1.0/24 toward Router D. Router D, in turn, forwards this packet to Router C. When Router C receives this packet, it must have a route to

10.1.1.0/24 to forward it correctly. Because Router C is running only an IGP, the eBGP routes learned from AS 1 need to be redistributed into this IGP for Router C to know how to reach 10.1.1.0/24.

One solution in this situation is to have Router C run iBGP with both Routers B and D rather than redistributing the routes into the IGP.

However, it's not uncommon to find situations like this where the AS in the middle (in this case, AS 2) is not expected to transit traffic between the two ASs on the outside but rather, is just trying to gain connectivity to destinations in both of these networks. In this case, it's valid for Router C not to know about any of the routes in these other ASs. (It may lead to suboptimal routing if it doesn't, but it is valid.)

If AS 2 isn't a transit AS, synchronization isn't important and can be turned off.

BGP Summarization

BGP can summarize routes advertised to peers using the **aggregate-address** command. As an example, assume you have multiple subnets of the 172.30.0.0/16 network and you want to advertise this summary if any of these subnets exist:

```
router bgp 1
 neighbor 10.1.1.1 remote-as 2
 network 172.30.1.0 mask 255.255.255.0
 network 172.30.8.0 mask 255.255.255.0
 network 172.30.14.0 mask 255.255.255.0
 network 172.30.25.0 mask 255.255.255.0
 network 172.30.42.0 mask 255.255.255.0
 aggregate-address 172.30.0.0 255.255.0.0
```

The preceding configuration will advertise the 172.30.0.0/16 prefix and all of the subnets for which there are network statements and matching routes in the routing table. To advertise the summary address only, you can use the **summary-only** keyword on the **aggregate-address** command:

```
aggregate-address 172.30.0.0 255.255.0.0 summary-only
```

When a BGP speaker originates a summary, it usually places only its AS number in the AS path. This can lead to loops if the prefixes being summarized are from several eBGP peers rather than originating within the router's AS.

To prevent these loops from occurring, use the **as-set** keyword in the **aggregate-address** command.

```
aggregate-address 172.30.0.0 255.255.0.0 as-set
```

This tells the router to place all the ASs in the AS paths from each component in an **as-set** and advertise them with the route.

Answers to the Review Questions

The questions that appear in the Review Sections in Chapters 1–9 are restated here for your reference along with the correct answers.

Answers to Chapter 1 Review Questions

1 Why is the topology of the network so important? Are the topology and the logical layout of a network the same thing?

The topology directly affects the stability of the network. No.

2 Why are hierarchical networks built in "layers"?

To break the problem domain into smaller, more manageable pieces. The concept of hierarchical design is similar to the OSI model, which breaks the process of communication between computers into layers, each having different design goals and criteria.

3 Note the layer of the network in which each of these functions/services should be performed and why:

a Summarize a set of destination networks so that other routers have less information to process.

Distribution layer, because this reduces the area through which information about topology changes must pass.

b Tag packets for quality of service processing.

Access layer, because devices in the access layer should be concerned with feeding traffic to the network and controlling the types and amount of traffic admitted. This should not generally be done in other layers, because it can complicate configurations and maintenance, and it can also reduce switching speeds.

c Reduce overhead so that packets are switched as rapidly as possible.

Core, because the core of the network is where switching speeds are the most critical.

d Meter traffic.

Access layer, because devices in the access layer should be controlling the traffic admitted into the network. Allowing traffic into the network at the edge, and then metering it out, or dropping it for traffic engineering purposes, at some other place in the network is an inefficient use of bandwidth.

e Use a default route to reach internal destinations.

Access and distribution layers, because within the core of the network, all routers should know how to reach all internal destinations.

f Control the traffic that is admitted into the network through packet level filtering.

Access layer, because access layer devices should control traffic being admitted into the network. Allowing packets into the networks only to be filtered at some other point is a waste of resources, and filtering can slow down some operations.

g Aggregate a number of smaller links into a single larger link.

Distribution layer, because the access layer is focused on feeding traffic into the network, and the core is focused on the switching of traffic. Traffic aggregation should occur before any traffic reaches the network core and cannot occur as the traffic enters the network.

h Terminate a tunnel.

Access layer, because tunnel processing can consume a good deal of processor time, which is most likely not acceptable in a device in the core of the network. Access layer devices should be the main point for traffic to enter the network, and tunnels usually represent a point where traffic enters the network.

4 What two factors is speed of convergence reliant on?

The number of routers participating in convergence, and the amount of information they must process.

5 What types of controls should you typically place on an access layer router to block attacks from within the network?

No address spoofing, no broadcast sources, and no directed broadcast.

6 What are the positive and negative aspects of a single router collapsed core?

Pros: It's only a single router. So, it's easy to manage.

Cons: It's only a single router.

  — It won't scale.

  — It's easy to overwhelm.

  — It is a single point of failure.

7 What aspects of policy-based routing are different than the routing a router normally performs?

Normal routing occurs based on destination address lookup in the routing/forwarding table, whereas policy routing packets are routed based on policy configured.

8 Should you normally allow directed broadcasts to be transmitted onto a segment?

No—this is a security hazard because an attacker can tie up a great deal of network resources and discover a great deal about what hosts exist on various segments by sending packets to the directed broadcast addresses.

9 What determines the number of routers participating in convergence?

Convergence depends on the area through which the topology change must propagate. The number of routers can be reduced via the use of a well-planned addressing scheme leveraging summarization.

10 Should a failing destination network in the access layer cause the routers in the core to re-compute their routing tables?

No. Topology changes within each layer shouldn't cause routers in other layers to recalculate their routing tables. The convergence area should be bound by the distribution layer.

11 What is the primary goal of the network core? What are the strategies used to reach that goal?

The primary goal of the network core is switching packets. Anything that takes processing power from core devices or increases packet switching latencies should be seriously discouraged. The strategies employed to meet this goal are full reachability, no policy implementations, and no access control.

12 Why is optimum routing so important in the core?

You don't want packets taking extra hops across the core because the core's job is to get the packet switched and back out to the destination as quickly as possible.

13 What are the primary goals of the distribution layer?

Topology change isolation, route summarization, and traffic aggregation.

14 What strategies are used in the distribution layer to achieve its goals?

Route summarization and minimizing connections to the network core.

15 What are the primary goals of the access layer?

To feed traffic into the network and implement network policy.

Answers to Chapter 2 Review Questions

1 Why is it difficult to change IP addresses after they've been assigned?

Each host on the network must be renumbered.

2 Why is address allocation so closely tied to network stability?

Because address allocation directly impacts summarization, and summarization directly affects stability.

3 What are the goals you should keep in mind when allocating addresses?

Controlling the size of the routing table, and controlling the distance information about topology changes that must travel through the network.

4 What does it mean to say that summarization hides topology details?

Devices beyond the summarization point don't know about every subnetwork or link that has been summarized into a single destination.

5 How does hiding topology details improve stability?

Devices beyond the summarization don't learn about topology changes they don't need to know about, and they can also work with less information, reducing processing effort.

6 Where should summarization take place?

The general rule of thumb is to "only provide full topology information where it's needed." In a hierarchical network, the distribution layer is the most natural summarization point, although summarization can occur anywhere in the network design.

7 What is the one case where access layer devices should be passed more than a default route? Why?

Dual-homed remotes—to reduce suboptimal routing.

8 An IP address can be divided into two parts; what are they?

Network and Host.

9 What is the prefix length of a network?

The number of bits set in the subnet mask.

10 Find the longest prefix summary for these addresses.

 — Set A: 172.16.1.1/30, 172.16.1.5/30, 172.16.1.9/30, 172.16.1.14/30

 — Set B: 10.100.40.14/24, 10.100.34.56/24, 10.100.59.81/24

 — Set C: 172.18.10.10/23, 172.31.40.8/24, 172.24.8.1/22, 172.30.200.1/24

 — Set D: 192.168.8.10/27, 192.168.60.14/27, 192.168.74.90/27, 192.168.101.48/27

For Set A, the longest prefix summary is 172.16.1.0/28.

For Set B, the longest prefix summary is 10.100.32.0/19.

For Set C, the longest prefix summary is 172.16.0.0/20.

For Set D, the longest prefix summary is 192.168.0.0/16.

11 Explain the effects of pointing a default route to a broadcast network interface.

The router will ARP for each destination address that it receives a packet for, which means possibly overrunning the ARP cache. So, use next-hop address not the broadcast interface.

12 What does a pair of colons with no numbers in between signify in an IPv6 address? How many times can you use this symbol in an address?

Every bit between the colons is 0. This can be used only once in an IPv6 address.

13 Explain the difference between Network Address Translation (NAT) and Port Address Translation (PAT).

In NAT, each inside host is assigned a single outside (outside global) address. In PAT, each session is assigned a port number from an outside global address.

14 Address the network depicted in Figure 2-19 by:

 — **Organization** — Addressing by organization places Leningrad Sales, NY Sales, and Paris Sales in one set of IP addresses, Tokyo Manufacturing in another set of IP addresses, Tokyo Finance in a third set of IP addresses, and the New York Headquarters in a fourth set of IP addresses. This leaves you with no possible summarization.

 — **Geographical location** — Addressing by geographical location places each location (Leningrad, New York, Paris, and Tokyo) in their own address space. Again, because of the design of this network, there is no place to summarize any addresses.

 — **Topology** — Addressing by topology places each location attached to a given router an IP address within a range. This allows summarization at each of these routers toward the other routers in the network.

Figure 2-19 *Exercise Network*

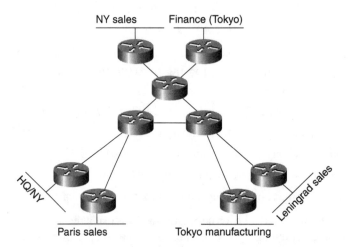

NY sales   Finance (Tokyo)

HQ/NY

Paris sales   Tokyo manufacturing

Leningrad sales

15 Which addressing scheme is the best? Is there any way to combine two different addressing schemes to provide administrative ease?

Topological addressing is the best. It is possible to address by topology and organization if the addresses are spread far enough apart. For example, the following addresses combine the two schemes:

— New York Sales: 10.1.1.0/24

— New York Headquarters: 10.1.2.0/24

— Paris Sales: 10.2.1.0/24

— Tokyo Manufacturing: 10.3.3.0/24

— Leningrad Sales: 10.4.1.0/24

— Tokyo Finance: 10.5.4.0/24

Answers to Chapter 3 Review Questions

1 Why is it important to consider link capacities when designing redundancy?

The backup link should be able to handle the full traffic load normally placed on the primary link.

2 Why is designing redundancy in the core easier than at other layers?

Suboptimal routing should be easier to deal with because the devices in the network core should have full routing information.

3 If all the core routers are in one building, what is a natural way to provide redundancy?

Connect them with multiple high speed LANs.

4 How many links on a ring core can fail before at least one section of the core is isolated?

Two.

5 Do ring designs provide consistent hop count through the core network when a link fails?

No—the hop count can increase dramatically when a single link fails.

6 What ring technologies provide redundancy at Layer 2?

FDDI and SONET.

7 Do redundant ring technologies provide redundancy against failed devices?

No.

8 Given a full mesh core with 25 routers, how many paths would there be through the network?

300

9 What method does a Cisco router use to differentiate between routes from two different routing protocols?

Administrative distance.

10 What is the first, and most important factor, used in deciding which route to use for a particular destination?

Prefix length. The longest specific match is used.

11 What mechanism in OSPF needs to be considered when it is being configured on a partial mesh network?

Designated router election.

12 What are the possible techniques you can use in OSPF partial mesh network designs to get around this problem?

Using point-to-point subinterfaces, using the router priority to predetermine that only the hub router becomes DR, using OSPF network type point-to-multipoint, or configuring the network as a non-broadcast OSPF network type and manually configuring the neighbors.

13 When dual homing a distribution layer or access layer router, what major problem should you be careful of?

Transiting traffic across the router that should be passed through the next higher layer in the network and increasing the size of the routing table in the next higher layer of the network.

14 When interconnecting the distribution or access layer router to provide redundancy, what issues should you be careful of?

Transiting traffic across the router that should be passed through the next higher layer in the network, increasing the size of the routing table in the next higher layer of the network, and that the path between the routers could be preferred over the normal (correct) path through the next higher layer.

15 What are the two main goals you must be careful to address when building redundancy into a network?

Redundant paths should only be used when the main path is down, unless they are engineered specifically for load sharing.

Traffic shouldn't be allowed, under any network conditions, to pass through links that aren't designed to handle the full load of the primary link.

Answers to Chapter 4 Review Questions

1 What does hierarchy provide in a well-designed network?

The foundation, or the skeleton on which everything else hangs.

2 What is the primary tool used to bound the area affected by network changes?

Summarization.

3 How can it be determined which links can be removed from a full mesh core network to decrease the number of links?

By looking at the normal traffic patterns and determining which points the majority of the traffic will flow between.

4 What provides ways around failure points in the network?

Redundancy.

5 What two things are most desirable in a routing protocol?

Low overhead and fast convergence.

6 What can a routing protocol do to decrease its burden to hosts that are not running routing on a network?

Use multicast or unicast routing updates, reduce the frequency of updates, and reduce the number of packets required to transmit the required information.

7 List the addressing problems that are caused by having multiple links to external networks.

— Addressing conflicts with partners

— Injecting multiple routes from external networks into your network

8 Given the network in Figure 4-10, how many routes do you think a core router will have in its table if no summarization is done?

At least 179, not counting redundancy.

48 dial-ins, 95 remote sites, 8 links between the access and distribution layers, 6 common services networks, 9 HQ VLANs, 2 default routes, 3 routes to partner networks, 10 links from the core to other parts of the network, and 7 core network links. The total would be at least 179, not counting redundancy.

9 Given the network in Figure 4-10, how many routes do you think a core router will have in its table if all possible summarization is done?

9 summaries from routers outside the core, 10 links from the core to other parts of the network, and 7 core network links. The total would be around 26.

Answers to Chapter 5 Review Questions

1 What parameters must be matched for OSPF routers to become adjacent?

Hello interval, Dead interval, Wait interval, and the link type.

2 Is it ever normal for two OSPF routers to reach only a two-way state? When?

Yes; when neither one of them are DR or BDR on a multi-access network.

3 What is a good way to test for MTU mismatches?

Extended **ping** using various packet sizes.

4 Explain why having a router dial backup beyond the point of summarization is bad.

The only way to make it work is to inject more specific routes into the routing table of all the other routers in the network, which can cause problems. (It won't scale.)

5 What options do you have with a remote dual-homed into two different areas?

Place the remote link in one of the two areas, which results in suboptimum routing and loss of connectivity if the router loses its connection to that area. Place the remote link in a third area and build virtual links to area 0; create statics and redistribute them into the two areas.

6 Explain how you can end up throwing packets away if you summarize on Routers A and B in Figure 5-17 to 172.27.0.0/16?

If Router A or Router B lose their connection to one of the Ethernet links, but they are still advertising the 172.27.0.0/16 summary, they will throw away packets that are destined to the network to which they are no longer connected.

Figure 5-17 *Diagram for Review Question 6*

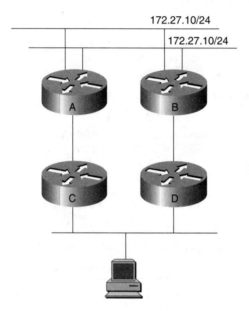

7 Can you have multiple areas with the same area number?

Yes. When routes are advertised into area 0 (the core area), all information about the area that they originated from is removed.

8 What one issue must you design around when dealing with dial-in links?

Host routes injected by the terminal service whenever a client connects.

9 Where are external LSAs flooded?

Through all areas except for stubby areas.

10 What type of SPF run is required when the state of external links change?

Partial. (Note that this doesn't mean all routers implement partial SPFs; it means only that a partial is all that is required.)

11 How do you inject default routes into OSPF?

With the **default-information originate** command.

12 What does the **always** keyword do on the end of the **default-information originate** command?

always originates a default route, regardless of the existence of a default in the routing table.

13 What is the Forward Address in the OSPF database used for?

To allow an OSPF router to forward packets directly to the next hop toward an external destination rather than through the ASBR.

14 What is the difference between a totally stubby area and a stubby area?

Totally stubby areas do not receive information on internal or external OSPF routes outside of the area; stubby areas receive internal, but not external, routing information. Neither can contain an ASBR.

Answers to Chapter 6 Review Questions

1 What protocol was IS-IS originally designed to provide routing information for?

Connectionless Network Service (CLNS).

2 Where can summarization take place in IS-IS?

On any L2 router.

3 How many levels of routing are there in an IS-IS network?

Two. L1 and L2.

4 How many pseudonodes are allowed in an IS-IS area?

255.

5 Is it possible to overflow the LSP database on a router? What are the indications this is occurring?

Yes. The overflow bit will set in LSAs advertised by the router with the database that has overflowed.

6 What is the range of internal metrics in IS-IS? Are they external? Why is this a problem in a large-scale network?

Internals 0–63, Externals 64–127. With this small of a range of metrics, you may not be able to configure the costs of each interface so that the most optimum route is always taken through the network.

7 Why isn't it good to have a dial backup dial into a router behind a summarization point for the networks behind the dial backup router?

Because when the dial backup is connected due to a link failure, the routes through the dial backup link cannot be summarized. This produces a lot of possible confusion and effort in the core and distribution layers of the network.

8 Will routers in different areas form L1 neighbor adjacencies?

No, they will form L2 adjacencies only.

9 Should you just let all the routers in your network run both L1 and L2 routing?

No, this incurs unnecessary overhead.

10 Will IS-IS automatically repair a partitioned L2 routing domain?

Although the mechanisms have been defined for doing so, most implementations do not support this.

11 Will routers running integrated IS-IS, which are in the same area but different IP subnets, form an adjacency? What could you look at, and what would you see to determine this is happening?

No. When you look at a router's CLNS neighbors, you would see the following:

```
A#show clns neighbor
System Id       Interface   SNPA            State  Holdtime  Type Protocol
00C0.1465.A460 Se0          *HDLC*          Up     297       IS   ES-IS
```

Note that the protocol is ES-IS rather than IS-IS; you would expect an IS-IS adjacency between these two neighbors. Because they are ES-IS neighbors, they will not exchange routing tables.

12 Must all L2 routers form one contiguous group of routers?

Yes. By definition, all L2 routers must form a contiguous core. In other words, two L2 routers cannot be separated by an L1 router someplace in the middle. It is important to leave enough redundancy between the L2 routers so that a single link failure will not cause the core to be partitioned.

13 How often does IS-IS flood link-state packets? Is this adjustable?

20 minutes. Yes, the rate at which LSPs are flooded can be set using the **lsp-refresh-interval** command.

14 How do you advertise a default route in IS-IS?

Use the **default-information originate** command under router IS-IS.

15 How do you configure a router so that a default route is advertised only under some conditions?

You can attach a route map to the default information originate command to conditionally advertise a default route.

16 What is the effect of an LSP that is corrupted at the data link layer, but the error correction codes are correct?

A possible LSP update storm.

Answers to Chapter 7 Review Questions

1 What are the two basic tools you can use to summarize routes (or hide destination details) in EIGRP?

Summarization and distribution lists.

2 How can you tell that a route is a summary when you look at the routing table?

It's marked as a summary, and the next hop interface is null0.

3 What is the default administrative distance for a summary route? What is the problem with this?

The default administrative distance is five. Using the default administrative distance for a summary route can displace valid routes learned from other routers and can cause a router to throw packets away unintentionally.

4 What bounds a query?

Distribution lists and summarization because they limit knowledge of specific destinations.

5 How far beyond one of the possible query bounds will a query travel?

One hop, generally, or until a router that doesn't have any information about that specific destination receives the query.

6 What is the primary advantage to summarizing between core routers rather than between the distribution layer and core?

The core routers will have enough information to make optimal routing decisions.

7 How is it possible to "black hole" packets when summarizing destinations behind dual-homed remotes into the core?

Even if one of the distribution routers loses connectivity with one of the remotes, it will still advertise a summary covering the destinations available at the disconnected host.

8 Why should summarization be configured outbound from the distribution layer routers toward access layer routers at remote sites?

To reduce the amount of traffic on the distribution layer to the remote router link and to bound queries at the remote router.

9 What is the most common problem with dual-homed remotes? What options are available to resolve it?

The remote routers appear to be transit paths to EIGRP. To resolve this, you should summarize routes outbound from the distribution layer toward the access layer routers.

10 What methods can be used to break a redistribution routing loop?

Distribute lists, route maps, prefix lists, setting the administrative distance on routes that are likely to produce loops, and using administrative tags in external routes to make the routes and block their redistribution.

11 Under what conditions is the administrative distance ignored between EIGRP and IGRP?

This happens when an IGRP route and an EIGRP route in the same AS compete for inclusion in the routing table.

12 What options do you have for generating a default route in EIGRP?

Either configuring a default network, or redistributing a 0.0.0.0/0 default route.

13 How can you prevent multiple parallel links within a network from all being used as transit paths?

By not running EIGRP on some of them; this is accomplished by using the **passive-interface** command.

14 What does EIGRP use to pace its packets on a link?

The bandwidth configured on the interface.

Answers to Chapter 8 Review Questions

1 What is an EGP?

An EGP is an Exterior Gateway Protocol, which is a protocol designed to carry routing information between ASs. BGP is an EGP.

2 What prevents iBGP from being an effective IGP?

iBGP cannot determine if a path within an AS is a loop because the AS path remains the same within the AS.

3 Where will routes learned from an eBGP peer be propagated?

To all peers, iBGP and eBGP.

4 Why shouldn't you redistribute iBGP routes into an IGP?

Because BGP isn't an effective IGP, and redistributing iBGP routes into an IGP can cause routing loops.

5 What protocol do all BGP packets ride on top of?

TCP.

6 If a neighbor relationship between two BGP peers constantly cycles through the Idle, Active, and Connect states, what action should you take?

Check to make certain IP connectivity is good between them.

7 Explain the significance of the next hop in BGP.

The route will be inserted and removed from the routing table. It will also be advertised and withdrawn constantly from any BGP peers. The overall effect is high CPU utilization and a possible router crash.

8 What possible solutions are there for load sharing outbound traffic to multiple ISPs?

Using only default routes out, accepting the full Internet routing table, using local preference or MEDs to prefer one path to another for certain external destinations, and accepting only a partial routing table.

9 All attributes being the same, what will break a tie in the BGP decision process?

The router ID of the advertising router.

10 What two things can be done to reduce the number of updates generated and sent by a router?

Either reducing the number of neighbors or reducing the number of updates that is required to send the entire routing table using peer groups.

11 What is the default half-life of a dampened route?

The rate at which the penalty will be divided in half.

12 How does a route reflector advertise routes learned from an iBGP peer?

When using route reflectors (RR), the RR will reflect routes that are learned by iBGP to other clients (IBGP peers) of the RR.

13 What does a confederation of routers appear as outside the confederation area?

A single AS.

14 Give an example of an application of conditional advertisement.

To advertise destinations that are normally sent to one provider through another provider if the connection through the normal provider fails.

Answers to Chapter 9 Review Questions

1 Is NHRP a routing protocol, or is it a protocol that helps routing protocols do their job?

A routing protocol.

2 How many paths exist through a network with 30 nodes? 40?

30 nodes has 870 paths; 40 nodes has 1560 paths.

3 What task does a route server in NHRP perform?

Collects and stores routing information from the routers on the NHRP network.

4 When a router on an NHRP network wants to find the SVC to use for a given destination, what does it do?

It queries the route server.

5 What three steps are normally involved in routing a packet?

1 Look up the destination in the routing table.

2 Perform a longest prefix match to find the correct destination.

3 Rewrite the MAC header on the packet.

6 What type of switching paradigm do ATM and Frame Relay use?

Label swapping.

7 What type of switching paradigm does MPLS use?

Label swapping.

8 What is a push? A pop?

A push is when a label is pushed onto the top of the label stack; a pop is when a label is removed from the top of the label stack.

9 What is a FEC?

A forwarding equivalence class; a stream or flow of packets between a given set of sources and a given destination.

10 Why do you merge FECs?

FECs, or streams, are merged for scalability. Once several FECs have been merged, downstream LSRs need only to deal with a single label and a single path for multiple source/destination pairs.

11 Explain each type of label assignment:

— **Host pair**—A label is assigned for each source/destination address.

— **Port quadruple**—A label is assigned for each source address and port/destination address and port.

— **Port quadruple with ToS**—A label is assigned for each source address and port/destination address and port with a given ToS, or class of service.

— **Network pair**—A label is assigned for each source/destination network.

— **Destination network**—A label is assigned for each destination network.

— **Egress router**—A label is assigned for each egress router.

— **Destination AS**—A label is assigned for each destination BGP AS.

12 Which device assigns labels in an MPLS network?

The control component.

13 Do downstream devices or upstream devices assign labels?

Downstream devices.

14 What are the two ways of driving label assignment?

— Data driven, where a label is assigned when the first data packet arrives in the network.

— Control driven, where a label is assigned when the routing information changes.

15 How is tunneling performed in an MPLS network?

By stacking labels. An extra label is pushed onto the stack by the LSR at the tunnel entrance and is popped at the egress of the tunnel. (Actually, it could be popped one hop before the tunnel exit.)

A

ABR. area border router. A router that connects to areas in an OSPF network.

access layer. The area or layer of the network that is responsible for controlling the traffic admitted to the network and for providing end user attachments to the network.

active. An EIGRP route state that indicates the router is actively searching for alternative paths to the destination in question by querying its neighbors.

address resolution protocol. See ARP.

administrative distance. A system of weights or distances assigned to routing protocols by Cisco routers; it is used for determining which path to take to a destination network when several routing protocols have routes to it.

area border router. See ABR.

ARP. Address Resolution Protocol. A method for binding network (Internet protocol) addresses to a physical layer address; it is described in IETF RFCs.

AS. autonomous system. A group of routers under the same administrative control.

AS path. The set of autonomous systems a route has passed through in BGP; it is used to determine if a given path is a routing loop.

ASBR. autonomous system border router. An OSPF router that connects two routing domains and redistributes routes from another routing protocol into OSPF.

autonomous system. See AS.

autonomous system border router. See ASBR.

autosummarization. Automatically summarizes routes to their major net mask (natural mask) when a boundary between two major networks is passed.

B

backup designated router. See BDR.

BDR. An OSPF router that acts as the backup for the designated router on a broadcast network.

branch. A section of the network that is relatively independent of the rest of the network; for example, a group of distribution and access layer routers that could logically split off as a separate network.

broadcast. A packet that is addressed so that every device on a segment will listen to it.

C

CIDR. classless interdomain routing. Forwarding packets based on their prefix length and destination, ignoring the major network in which they reside.

CIDR block. Grouping or summarization of major networks. Given that 200.200.200.0/24 is a Class C address, 200.200.0.0/16 is a CIDR block. The address 10.1.0.0/16 is not a CIDR block; it is a subnet of the 10.x.x.x network. With a CIDR block, the prefix is shortened from the "natural" mask for that network; with subnetting, the prefix is lengthened.

classless interdomain routing. See CIDR.

CLNS. Connectionless Network Service. A routed (data carrying) protocol; routing information for CLNS is provided by IS-IS.

collapsed core. A single router (or switch) acting as the core of a network.

common services. Services internal to an organization that are used by all or most of the end users of the network.

conditional advertisement. The capability of a routing protocol to advertise a given destination under only certain conditions, such as the existence of another path to that destination.

confederation. A group of BGP autonomous systems that appear as one AS outside of the confederation.

control component. A device that assigns labels in an MPLS network.

control-driven label assignment. Assigning labels based on control traffic, such as routing updates.

convergence. The process of all the routers in a network determining the best path to reach the destinations available; when the network has converged, all the routers in the network have decided on the best path to each destination.

core. The area of the network that concentrates on switching traffic.

D

data-driven label assignment. Assigning labels based on data traffic.

data link layer. A layer in the OSI model that is responsible for determining the way physical media will be accessed and the way data is formatted.

default network. A network that is designated as the default; a router will send all packets to destinations for which it has no specific route to the default network; used only in EIGRP and IGRP.

default route. A route that matches all IP addresses (0.0.0.0) but has a short prefix length (0); this is the route that the router will use when it has no more specific information on how to reach a given destination.

DeMilitarized Zone. See DMZ.

designated router. See DR.

directed broadcast. A packet that is destined to the broadcast address of another segment; for example, 10.1.1.255 is the directed broadcast address of the 10.1.1.0/24 segment.

discontiguous network. A network address that is used in several different areas of a network, which are not connected; generally, this refers to a major network, but it could refer to virtually any unit of addressing.

distance vector. A routing protocol in which each router advertises all reachable destinations known to directly connected neighbors; EIGRP is an advanced distance vector protocol. Other distance vector protocols are IGRP and RIP.

distribution. The area or layer of the network that is responsible for traffic aggregation and route summarization.

distribution list. Used to block the advertisement of given destinations by a routing protocol.

DMZ. DeMilitarized Zone. A buffer between a dirty, or untrusted, network and the clean, or trusted, area of the network.

DR. designated router. An OSPF router that is responsible for flooding routing information onto a broadcast link and advertising reachability to the link.

dual-homed. Attaching one device to two places in the next layer of the network.

E

eBGP. Exterior BGP. Two routers in two different ASs running BGP.

eBGP multihop. The capability to place eBGP neighbors several hops away from each other.

edge services. Services, such as filtering, policy routing, or packet marking for QoS, that occur either on the edge or at the entrance point of the network.

EGP. Exterior Gateway Protocol. A protocol designed to pass large amounts of routing information between ASs; EGP, BGP, and IDRP are examples of EGPs.

End System-to-Intermediate System. See ES-IS.

ES-IS. End System-to-Intermediate System. A protocol that CLNS uses for buildings passing information between end systems and routers.

exchange. A state in the OSPF router adjacency process that occurs when the routers are actually exchanging information about their databases.

exstart. A state in the OSPF router adjacency process when the routers are arranging to exchange routing information.

Exterior BGP. See eBGP.

Exterior Gateway Protocol. See EGP.

F

FDDI. Fiber Distributed Data Interface. A dual ring (redundant) network media standardized by the IEEE.

feasible successor. An EIGRP neighbor that is advertising a loop-free route to a given destination.

FEC. Forwarding Equivalence Class. A set of forwarding parameters, such as destination, egress router, class of service, and so forth, that can be used to group streams.

Fiber Distributed Data Interface. See FDDI.

floating static. A static route configured with a high administrative distance so that it is used only when all other paths to the destination are lost.

Forwarding Equivalence Class. See FEC.

full mesh. Topology in which every device has a direct connection to every other device.

full reachability. A default route is not needed to reach any destination.

G–H

hierarchy. The principle of building a network in layers or sections, giving each layer specific tasks and goals.

hold timer. In EIGRP, the amount of time a neighbor will remain up and active without receiving any traffic.

host route. A route with a 32-bit mask; a route that specifies the path to one host rather than to a link or network.

Hot Standby Router Protocol. See HSRP.

HSRP. Hot Standby Router Protocol. A Cisco protocol that provides a virtual IP address that is shared between two routers; if one router fails, the other takes over by accepting traffic for this virtual IP address.

I–J

iBGP. Interior BGP. BGP running between two routers in the same AS.

init. A state in the OSPF neighbor adjacency process where the neighbors have seen each other's Hellos but have not established that two-way communication is possible between them.

Integrated IS-IS. IS-IS that is providing routing information for IP destinations.

Interior BGP. See iBGP.

Intermediate System-to-Intermediate System. See IS-IS.

Internet Protocol version 6. See IPv6.

IPv6. Internet Protocol version 6. A revision of the Internet Protocol that provides more security, provisions for label switching, and a much larger address space.

IS-IS. Intermediate System-to-Intermediate System. IS-IS is an Interior Gateway Protocol (IGP) that uses link-state packets (link-state advertisements) flooded to all devices in the network to advertise destination reachability. Originally, IS-IS was designed for routing CLNS traffic, but it has been adapted to provide reachability information for IP.

K–L

k values. Values used to determine the effect that the bandwidth, delay, load, and reliability will have on the total metric EIGRP used to reach a destination.

label. A short, fixed-length header that may be used instead of an IP address to determine how to switch a packet.

label stack. A stack of labels; an LSR evaluates the top label to switch the packet, and as labels are popped, the stack becomes shorter, exposing other switching information. Label stacks are a way of tunneling packets through an MPLS network.

Label Switching Router. See LSR.

link-state. A routing protocol in which each router advertises the state of its links to all other routers on the network through a flooding mechanism; each router then calculates a shortest path tree to each destination. IS-IS and OSPF are two examples.

link-state advertisement. See LSA.

link-state packet. See LSP.

local preference. A metric used by BGP to determine which path should be chosen when leaving this AS.

Logical AND. To AND the bits from two binary digits together; for each bit, if both numbers have a 1 in a given digit, the result is 1; otherwise, it is a 0.

LSA. link-state advertisement. A packet used by OSPF to transport routing information through the network.

LSP. link-state packet. A packet used by IS-IS to transport link state information between routers.

LSR. Label Switching Router. An MPLS-capable router or switch.

M

mask. A set of four octets that separates the network portion of the IP address from the host portion of the IP address.

MED. Multiple Exit Discriminator. Used in BGP to provide a hint about which path an external router should take to reach a destination in this AS.

MPLS. Multiprotocol Label Switching. A method of switching packets based on swapping short, fixed-length labels.

multicast. Single packets copied by the network and sent to a specific subset of network addresses. These addresses are specified in the Destination Address field.

Multiple Exit Discriminator. See MED.

Multiprotocol Label Switching. See MPLS.

N

NAT. Network Address Translation. Translating source and destination addresses; commonly used to permit private addresses in a network to appear as registered addresses on the Internet.

NBMA. nonbroadcast multi-access. A network media that allows multiple devices to attach, but devices cannot send packets directly to all other devices; for example, Frame Relay configured as a multipoint interface.

network. The most significant digits in the IP address; defined by setting bits in the subnet mask.

Network Address Translation. See NAT.

network layer. The layer of the OSI model that is responsible for providing globally unique addressing and the means to find destinations within the network.

network service access point. See NSAP.

Next Hop Resolution Protocol. See NHRP.

NHRP. Next Hop Resolution Protocol. A routing protocol used over SVC-capable networks to gain the advantages of full mesh topologies without some of the problems.

nonbroadcast multi-access. See NBMA.

not-so-stubby area. See NSSA.

NSAP. network service access point. An identifier used to identify a host and service in CLNS.

NSSA. not-so-stubby area. An OSPF area into which external routes (type 5 LSAs) are not advertised but in which external routes can originate.

null0. A virtual interface; packets sent to this interface are thrown away.

O–P

octet. A group of eight binary digits; an octet can represent the numbers 0 to 255 in decimal.

OSI model. The seven-layer model for designing network protocols.

partial mesh. A network where each router has only one connection to a subset of all the other routers in the network.

passive. The state of a route in EIGRP when the router has a successor through which to forward packets.

passive interface. An interface on which the protocol is not running, although the link itself is advertised as reachable by the routing protocol.

PAT. Port Address Translation. Translating source and destination address at the port level, which allows multiplexing many sessions from different hosts onto a single address. Commonly used to permit privately addressed hosts to access servers on the Internet using registered addresses.

peer group. A group of BGP neighbors that are treated the same; a BGP router only builds one update per peer group if they are configured, rather than one update per neighbor.

permanent virtual circuit. See PVC.

physical layer. The physical plant, cables, and modulation methods used to transmit data in a network.

policy routing. Routing packets based on some criteria other than the destination address; choosing different paths for QoS purposes isn't generally considered policy routing.

pop. The act of removing a label from the top of the MPLS label stack.

Port Address Translation. See PAT.

prefix length. The number of bits in the subnet mask; for instance, the subnet mask 255.255.255.0 has 24 bits set to 1 and is, therefore, a 24-bit subnet mask. The prefix length is often expressed with "/x" after the IP address.

presentation layer. The layer in the OSI network model that is responsible for presenting data in an appropriate format to the devices that are communicating.

private address. Address or range of addresses defined by the IETF as unusable (unroutable) on the Internet.

pseudonode. A mechanism used in IS-IS to reduce the full mesh adjacency normally required on broadcast networks.

push. The act of putting a new label on the top of an MPLS label stack.

PVC. permanent virtual circuit. A permanent virtual (or multiplexed) point-to-point link; common in Frame Relay, X.25, and ATM networks.

Q–R

QoS. Quality of Service. Specifying different levels of service and possibly different paths through the network based on a given level of service required by a packet or a flow of packets.

Quality of Service. See QoS.

query. Used by EIGRP to find alternate paths that have not been advertised due to split horizon or other network conditions.

redundancy. Alternate (extra) equipment and links placed in a network to ensure that a single failure in the network doesn't isolate the entire network.

registered address. Address that is registered for a particular organization's use on the Internet.

reply. An EIGRP router uses a reply to answer a query about a given destination.

ring. A network design that uses a ring of routers connected by point-to-point links; also, a physical/data link layer network that uses a ring media.

Round Trip Timeout. See RTO.

route dampening. The capability of a routing protocol to refuse to advertise or use a route if it has changed state a number of times over a short period of time.

router reflector. A BGP router that either advertises routes learned from iBGP neighbors to other iBGP neighbors or reflects them to other iBGP neighbors.

RTO. Round Trip Timeout. The amount of time EIGRP will wait before deciding to take further action when a packet isn't acknowledged.

S

shortest path first. See SPF.

SIA. stuck-in-active. A route in EIGRP that has been active for 3 minutes.

single point of failure. Any point in a network where losing a single link or device can make some destinations (servers or end devices) unreachable.

Smooth Round Trip Time. See SRTT.

SONET. Synchronous Optical Network. A redundant ring network media standardized by the CCITT.

source routing. When the ingress device in a network (possibly a router, LSR, or the originating host) determines the best path through the network and uses labels or other fields to direct the packet along that path.

SPF. shortest path first. An algorithm used by IS-IS and OSPF to calculate the shortest path tree to each reachable destination in the network.

spoofing. Changing the source address of a packet so that it appears to be originating from a trusted host or so that the source of an attack cannot be traced.

SRTT. Smooth Round Trip Time. A weighted average of the amount of time it takes for a packet to be acknowledged; used by EIGRP in determining how long to wait for an acknowledgement before taking further action.

stream. A flow of packets between two devices.

stream merge. Combining two or more streams into one FEC.

stub site. A site through which no traffic should flow; only traffic to and from the stub site should flow along links to and from the site.

stubby area. An OSPF area into which no external routes (type 5 LSAs) are advertised.

stuck-in-active. See SIA.

subnet. In the original meaning, a part of a major network; currently, this term is used interchangeably with network.

subnet mask. See mask.

suboptimal routing. Occurs when a router chooses a path through the network, which incurs extra hops or slower links than the best path.

successor. The EIGRP neighbor this router is using to forward packets to a given destination.

summarize. To combine multiple destinations, advertisements, or prefixes into one destination by shortening the subnet mask.

summary-address. A command used to configure address summaries on interfaces in IOS.

SVC. switched virtual circuit. A switched point-to-point link, common on ATM networks but also supported on other media, such as Frame Relay and X.25.

switched virtual circuit. See SVC.

Synchronous Optical Network. See SONET.

T

Time To Live. See TTL.

topology. Physical layout of a network.

topology table. A database of reachable destinations used by EIGRP for inserting destinations into the routing table and determining what alternate routes are available.

totally stubby area. An OSPF area into which no summary routes (type 3 LSAs) or external routes (type 5 LSAs) are advertised.

transit path. A link in the network over which traffic passes to other areas of the network; transit traffic is not destined to a network attached directly to either end of the path.

transport layer. The layer in the OSI model that is responsible for end-to-end transport of data from its source to its destination.

TTL. Time To Live. The amount of time or number of hops a packet is allowed to exist in a network; it prevents packets that are looping from doing so forever.

tunneling. Encapsulating a packet into multiple layers of headers so that the outer header has no bearing on the final destination of the packet; the contents of the packet, including the inner (encapsulated) headers are sometimes encrypted.

two-way. A state in the process of building neighbor adjacencies in OSPF; the neighbors have established that two-way communication is possible between the routers at this stage.

U–Z

unicast. A packet that is addressed to only one device.

Variable-Length Subnet Masking. See VLSM.

virtual LAN. See VLAN.

virtual link. A link between some other area and area 0 (the core) in an OSPF network; the link effectively extends area 0 so that it reaches isolated areas of the network.

VLAN. virtual LAN. A term used for networks attached to switched links, which are divided into separate broadcast domains or subnets using ISL.

VLSM. Variable-Length Subnet Masking. When several subnets of a major net are subnetted with differing lengths; for example, 10.1.1.0/24 and 10.1.2.0/25 are VLSM subnets. 10.1.1.0/24 and 11.1.2.0/25 are not because they are not in the same major network.

INDEX

F–G

H

L

M

N

R

CCIE Professional Development

Cisco LAN Switching

Kennedy Clark, CCIE; Kevin Hamilton, CCIE

1-57870-094-9 • AVAILABLE NOW

This volume provides an in-depth analysis of Cisco LAN switching technologies, architectures, and deployments, including unique coverage of Catalyst network design essentials. Network designs and configuration examples are incorporated throughout to demonstrate the principles and enable easy translation of the material into practice in production networks.

Advanced IP Network Design

Alvaro Retana, CCIE; Don Slice, CCIE; and Russ White, CCIE

1-57870-097-3 • AVAILABLE NOW

Network engineers and managers can use these case studies, which highlight various network design goals, to explore issues including protocol choice, network stability, and growth. This book also includes theoretical discussion on advanced design topics.

Large-Scale IP Network Solutions

Khalid Raza, CCIE; and Mark Turner

1-57870-084-1 • AVAILABLE NOW

Network engineers can find solutions as their IP networks grow in size and complexity. Examine all the major IP protocols in-depth and learn about scalability, migration planning, network management, and security for large-scale networks.

Routing TCP/IP, Volume I

Jeff Doyle, CCIE

1-57870-041-8 • AVAILABLE NOW

This book takes the reader from a basic understanding of routers and routing protocols through a detailed examination of each of the IP interior routing protocols. Learn techniques for designing networks that maximize the efficiency of the protocol being used. Exercises and review questions provide core study for the CCIE Routing and Switching exam.

Cisco Press

www.ciscopress.com

Cisco Press Solutions

Enhanced IP Services for Cisco Networks
Donald C. Lee, CCIE

1-57870-106-6 • AVAILABLE NOW

This is a guide to improving your network's capabilities by understanding the new enabling and advanced Cisco IOS services that build more scalable, intelligent, and secure networks. Learn the technical details necessary to deploy Quality of Service, VPN technologies, IPsec, the IOS firewall and IOS Intrusion Detection. These services will allow you to extend the network to new frontiers securely, protect your network from attacks, and increase the sophistication of network services.

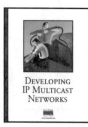

Developing IP Multicast Networks, Volume I
Beau Williamson, CCIE

1-57870-077-9 • AVAILABLE NOW

This book provides a solid foundation of IP multicast concepts and explains how to design and deploy the networks that will support appplications such as audio and video conferencing, distance-learning, and data replication. Includes an in-depth discussion of the PIM protocol used in Cisco routers and detailed coverage of the rules that control the creation and maintenance of Cisco mroute state entries.

Designing Network Security
Merike Kaeo

1-57870-043-4 • AVAILABLE NOW

Designing Network Security is a practical guide designed to help you understand the fundamentals of securing your corporate infrastructure. This book takes a comprehensive look at underlying security technologies, the process of creating a security policy, and the practical requirements necessary to implement a corporate security policy.

Cisco Press   **www.ciscopress.com**

Cisco Press Solutions

EIGRP Network Design Solutions
Ivan Pepelnjak, CCIE

1-57870-165-1 • AVAILABLE NOW

EIGRP Network Design Solutions uses case studies and real-world configuration examples to help you gain an in-depth understanding of the issues involved in designing, deploying, and managing EIGRP-based networks. This book details proper designs that can be used to build large and scalable EIGRP-based networks and documents possible ways each EIGRP feature can be used in network design, implmentation, troubleshooting, and monitoring.

Top-Down Network Design
Priscilla Oppenheimer

1-57870-069-8 • AVAILABLE NOW

Building reliable, secure, and manageable networks is every network professional's goal. This practical guide teaches you a systematic method for network design that can be applied to campus LANs, remote-access networks, WAN links, and large-scale internetworks. Learn how to analyze business and technical requirements, examine traffic flow and Quality of Service requirements, and select protocols and technologies based on performance goals.

Cisco IOS Releases: The Complete Reference
Mack M. Coulibaly

1-57870-179-1 • AVAILABLE NOW

Cisco IOS Releases: The Complete Reference is the first comprehensive guide to the more than three dozen types of Cisco IOS releases being used today on enterprise and service provider networks. It details the release process and its numbering and naming conventions, as well as when, where, and how to use the various releases. A complete map of Cisco IOS software releases and their relationships to one another, in addition to insights into decoding information contained within the software, make this book an indispensable resource for any network professional.

Cisco Press   **www.ciscopress.com**

Cisco Press Solutions

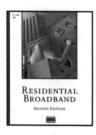

Residential Broadband, Second Edition
George Abe
1-57870-177-5 • AVAILABLE NOW

This book will answer basic questions of residential broadband networks such as: Why do we need high speed networks at home? How will high speed residential services be delivered to the home? How do regulatory or commercial factors affect this technology? Explore such networking topics as xDSL, cable, and wireless.

Internetworking Technologies Handbook, Second Edition
Kevin Downes, CCIE, Merilee Ford, H. Kim Lew, Steve Spanier, Tim Stevenson
1-57870-102-3 • AVAILABLE NOW

This comprehensive reference provides a foundation for understanding and implementing contemporary internetworking technologies, providing you with the necessary information needed to make rational networking decisions. Master terms, concepts, technologies, and devices that are used in the internetworking industry today. You also learn how to incorporate networking technologies into a LAN/WAN environment, as well as how to apply the OSI reference model to categorize protocols, technologies, and devices.

OpenCable Architecture
Michael Adams
1-57870-135-X • AVAILABLE NOW

Whether you're a television, data communications, or telecommunications professional, or simply an interested business person, this book will help you understand the technical and business issues surrounding interactive television services. It will also provide you with an inside look at the combined efforts of the cable, data, and consumer electronics industries' efforts to develop those new services.

Performance and Fault Management
Paul Della Maggiora, Christopher Elliott, Robert Pavone, Kent Phelps, James Thompson
1-57870-180-5 • AVAILABLE NOW

This book is a comprehensive guide to designing and implementing effective strategies for monitoring performance levels and correctng problems in Cisco networks. It provides an overview of router and LAN switch operations to help you understand how to manage such devices, as well as guidance on the essential MIBs, traps, syslog messages, and show commands for managing Cisco routers and switches.

Cisco Press   **www.ciscopress.com**

Cisco Press Fundamentals

IP Routing Primer

Robert Wright, CCIE

1-57870-108-2 • **AVAILABLE NOW**

Learn how IP routing behaves in a Cisco router environment. In addition to teaching the core fundamentals, this book enhances your ability to troubleshoot IP routing problems yourself, often eliminating the need to call for additional technical support. The information is presented in an approachable, workbook-type format with dozens of detailed illustrations and real-life scenarios integrated throughout.

Cisco Router Configuration

Allan Leinwand, Bruce Pinsky, Mark Culpepper

1-57870-022-1 • **AVAILABLE NOW**

An example-oriented and chronological approach helps you implement and administer your internetworking devices. Starting with the configuration devices "out of the box;" this book moves to configuring Cisco IOS for the three most popular networking protocols today: TCP/IP, AppleTalk, and Novell Interwork Packet Exchange (IPX). You also learn basic administrative and management configuration, including access control with TACACS+ and RADIUS, network management with SNMP, logging of messages, and time control with NTP.

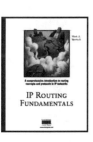

IP Routing Fundamentals

Mark A. Sportack

1-57870-071-x • **AVAILABLE NOW**

This comprehensive guide provides essential background information on routing in IP networks for network professionals who are deploying and maintaining LANs and WANs daily. Explore the mechanics of routers, routing protocols, network interfaces, and operating systems.

Cisco Press

www.ciscopress.com

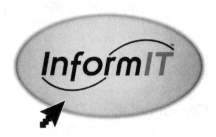